Christianity in Britain, 300 - 700

Christianity in Britain, 300 - 700

Papers presented to the Conference on Christianity in Roman and Sub-Roman Britain
held at the University of Nottingham
17-20 April 1967

Edited by
M. W. Barley and R. P. C. Hanson

Leicester University Press 1968

Printed in Great Britain
by John Waddington of Kirkstall Ltd.
for Leicester University Press

Distributed in North America
by Humanities Press, Inc., New York

SBN 7185 1077 1

Contents

Contents (*continued*)

Note : the numbers in square brackets at the head of a page indicate the page on which the appropriate notes will be found.

Illustrations

PAGE

The Archaeological Background on the Continent

Eccles in English Place-Names

The Evidence from North Britain

Illustrations (*continued*)

Pagan Motifs and Practices in Christian Art and Ritual in Roman Britain

Plates

Acknowledgements

The editors and contributors are greatly indebted to the Council for British Archaeology, which undertook the detailed organisation of the Conference. Without this collaboration, the Conference could scarcely have taken place, and this volume would not have appeared. They are also greatly indebted to the University of Nottingham, which has made a grant towards the cost of publishing this volume.

Acknowledgement is here made to those individuals and institutions who have allowed illustrations, as listed above, to be reproduced. The editors are grateful to Mrs. M. Todd for preparing the index.

Abbreviations

AA	*Archaeologia Aeliana*
Anal Boll	*Analecta Bollandiana*
Ant J	*Antiquaries Journal*
Arch Ael	*Archaeologia Aeliana*
Arch Camb	*Archaeologia Cambrensis*
Arch Cant	*Archaeologia Cantiana*
Arch J	*Archaeological Journal*
BBCS	*Bulletin of the Board of Celtic Studies*
BDA	Ordnance Survey Map, *Britain in the Dark Ages* (1966)
Bonn Jahrb	*Jahrbüch der Altertumsfreunde in Rheinland*
Bowen (1954)	Bowen, E. G., *The Settlements of the Celtic Saints in Wales* (Cardiff, 1954)
CBA	Thomas, A. C. (ed), *Rural Settlement in Roman Britain*, Council for British Archaeology Research Report 7 (London, 1966)
CE	Foster, I. Ll. and Alcock, L. (ed), *Culture and Environment* (London, 1963)
CEB	Williams, H., *Christianity in Early Britain* (Oxford, 1912)
CIIC	Macalister, R. A. S., *Corpus Inscriptionum Insularum Celticarum*, Vol. I (Dublin, 1954)
CIL	*Corpus Inscriptionum Latinarum*
Cod Theod	*Theodosian Code*
CSEL	*Corpus Scriptorum Ecclesiasticorum Latinorum*
DEB	Gildas, *De Excidio Britanniae;* the chapter, page and line in all references given are those of the edition of Mommsen, T., in *MGH* Auct. Ant. XIII, vol. III (Berlin, 1898)
DP	Alcock, L. *Dinas Powys, An Iron Age, Dark Age and Early Mediaeval Settlement in Glamorgan* (Cardiff, 1963)
EA	Davies, J. C., *Episcopal Acts Relating to the Welsh Dioceses* (Hist. Soc. of the Church in Wales, 1946–8)
ECMW	Nash-Williams, V. E., *The Early Christian Monuments of Wales* (Cardiff, 1950)
EHR	*English Historical Review*
HF	Jenkinson, F. J. H. (ed), *Hisperica Famina* (Cambridge, 1908)
HE	Bede, *Historia Ecclesiastica*
HW	Lloyd, J., *History of Wales* (London, 1939)
IANB	Rivet, A. L. F. (ed), *The Iron Age in Northern Britain* (Edinburgh, 1966)
Insc Lat Sel	*Inscriptiones Latinae Selectae*
JBAA	*Journal of the British Archaeological Association*
JRS	*Journal of Roman Studies*
JTS	*Journal of Theological Studies*
LAASR & P	*Lincolnshire Architectural & Archaeological Society Reports & Papers*

Lewis (1960*a*) — Lewis, C., *Agweddau ar Hanes Cynnar yr Eglwys yng Nghymru* (Aspects of Early Welsh History), Part I, Llen Cymru, VI (1960), 46–62.
Lewis (1963) — Part II of above
Lewis (1960*b*) — Ibid, *The Liber Landavensis and the Diocese of Llandaff*, Morgannwg, IV (1960), 50–65
LHEB — Jackson, K., *Language and History in Early Britain* (Edinburgh, 1953)
LHSz Lat Gr II — Leumann–Hofmann–Szantyr, *Lateinische Grammatik*, Band II Syntax und Stilistik (Munich, 1964)
LRE — Jones, A. H. M., *The Later Roman Empire* (3 vols. Oxford, 1964)
Mansi — Mansi, J. D., *Sacrorum Conciliorum Nova et Amplissima Collectio*
Med Arch — *Medieval Archaeology*
MGH — *Monumenta Germaniae Historica*
MGH Conc. — *do. Legum Sectio III, Concilia*
MGH Ep. — *do. Epistulae*
MGH Lang. — *do. Scriptores Rerum Langobandicarum et Italicarum*
MGH Merov. — *do. Scriptores Rerum Merovingicarum*
PEW — Foster, I. Ll., & Daniel, G. (ed), *Prehistoric and Early Wales* (London, 1965)
PG — Migne, J. P., *Patrologia Graeca*
PL — Migne, J. P., *Patrologia Latina*
PPS — *Proceedings of the Prehistoric Society*
Problem — Wainwright, F. T. (ed), *The Problem of the Picts* (London, 1955)
PRIA — *Proceedings of the Royal Irish Academy*
PSAS — *Proceedings of the Society of Antiquaries of Scotland*
RCAM — *Royal Commission on Ancient Monuments in Wales and Monmouthshire*
RIB — Collingwood, R. G., & Wright, R. P. (ed), *The Roman Inscriptions of Britain* (Oxford, 1965)
RNNB — Richmond, I. A. (ed), *Roman and Native in North Britain* (London, 1958)
Scot Hist Rev — *Scottish Historical Review*
SEBC — Chadwick, Mrs. N. K. (ed), *Studies in the Early British Church* (Cambridge, 1958)
SEBH — Chadwick, N. K. (ed), *Studies in Early British History* (Cambridge, 1954)
TCWAAS — *Transactions of the Cumberland and Westmorland Antiquarian and Archaeological Society* (2nd Series)
TDGNHAS — *Transactions of the Dumfriesshire and Galloway Natural History and Archaeological Society*
Thiel — Thiel, A., *Epistulae Romanorum Pontificum*
THSC — *Transactions of the Honourable Society of Cymmrodorion*
Toynbee 1953 — Toynbee, Jocelyn, 'Christianity in Roman Britain' (*JBAA* 16 (1953), 1–24)
Wall 1965 — Wall, J., 'Christian Evidences in the Roman Period; the Northern Counties' (Part I, *Arch Ael* 43 (1965), 201–25)
Wall 1966 — Wall, J., 'Christian Evidences in the Roman Period; the Northern Counties' (Part II, *Arch Ael* 44 (1966), 147–64)
Watson 1926 — Watson, W. J., *The History of the Celtic Place-Names of Scotland* (Edinburgh, 1926)
WHR — *Welsh History Review*

Introduction

J. N. L. Myres

This volume contains the principal papers presented to the Conference on Christianity in Roman and Sub-Roman Britain held at the University of Nottingham under the auspices of the Council for British Archaeology from 17 to 20 April 1967. The idea of such a conference arose in the first instance from discussions between Professor R. P. C. Hanson, D.D., Head of the Department of Theology at Nottingham University, and Mr M. W. Barley, F.S.A., Reader in Archaeology in the Department of Classics, and at the time President of the Council for British Archaeology. It was on their joint initiative that the programme was planned, the speakers were invited, and all the arrangements were made. It was apparent even before the conference was held that the subject was one that would arouse widespread interest alike among historians, theologians and archaeologists, and that, in addition to those present, many people who were unable to attend, or to take a personal part in the gathering, would welcome the issue of some permanent record of its main proceedings. This volume is published in response to that demand.

The importance of the various related issues which the conference was called to explore and to discuss needs no emphasis. To theologians the period on which it was focused, roughly from the late third to the seventh century, is that of the triumph of Christianity over all its rivals in the pagan religions and mythologies of the classical and barbarian worlds: to historians it is the age of the collapse of Roman Imperial authority in the west and of the formation of those regional succession-states which set the political pattern for medieval and modern Europe: to archaeologists it illustrates not only the contact and ultimate fusion of Rome's Mediterranean culture with those of the Celtic west and the Germanic north, but also the passage, in Britain at least, from the long ages in which the bulk of our evidence for human activity comes from material artefacts to one, which still continues, in which knowledge rests more and more upon the written word. In all these and many other ways it is a period in which fundamental changes took place in man's outlook on his environment, in his awareness of the natural and supernatural forces surrounding his life, and in his conscious or unconscious reactions to them.

In no part of the western world are the nature, the extent and the course of these complex changes so difficult to trace and so hard to comprehend as they are in the British Isles. There are several reasons for this. Britain was always marginal to the political and cultural affairs of Rome. Little interest was taken by Roman writers in a land whose situation and climate did nothing to attract their sympathy. The failure to effect its complete conquest, an objective which had, according to Tacitus, certainly been the ambition of its most farsighted first-century governor, Agricola, meant that only the southern and central parts of what afterwards became England experienced fully the beneficent force of Roman material civilization. Wales, the north of England and the lowlands of Scotland remained frontier areas where to the native mind Rome never stood for cultural enlightenment or economic progress, but only for military repression and the dominance of ruthless power. The rest of Scotland knew Rome simply as the distant and incomprehensible source of occasional, and mainly ineffective, diplomatic or punitive interventions, while Ireland had no direct experience of her might at all.

As Roman authority declined, the power vacuum so generated inevitably increased the tensions arising from these divergencies of development in the different regions of the British Isles. While Ireland and the highlands of Scotland were not directly affected and in the main continued undisturbed the natural evolution of their Iron Age cultures, their more enterprising spirits were inevitably tempted by prospects of loot and adventure to engage in marauding expeditions and even some substantial settlement on the western and northern frontiers of Roman Britain. To meet such attacks semi-Romanized tribal princes, already involved by imperial diplomacy in the defence of the weakened borders, used their nominal obligations to Rome to justify the creation of succession-states for themselves. This is no doubt the situation that lies behind St Patrick's letter of reproach to the chieftain Coroticus whose followers had slaughtered some of the saint's Irish converts in struggles of this kind: Patrick's jibe that the conduct of his opponents belied their claim to be 'fellow citizens of the holy Romans' acquires its point precisely in such a context.

Further south and east, the lowland areas of Roman Britain, the upper crust of whose population had eagerly and successfully adopted the veneer of culture provided by their masters, and had greatly profited from the cessation of tribal conflicts under the *Pax Romana*, were to face far more traumatic experiences from the collapse of Roman power. Their efforts to protect themselves by the time-honoured expedients of employing friendly barbarians as a shield against the onslaughts of the less friendly broke down about the middle of the fifth century in an orgy of blood and flames, in which all that was left of the Romano-British civilization of the last three centuries was destroyed. A blanket of illiterate Germanic heathenism temporarily smothered the *lux aeterna* of Rome in all that part of Britain where it had shone most brightly. Broken for a century or more were the direct cultural contacts that had for so long linked the whole of southern and central Britain to Gaul and the Mediterranean world through the Channel ports. Only by the western seaways were those contacts precariously maintained, and for a while the paradoxical situation persisted in which what had been the least Romanized parts of Britain were alone in touch with southern Europe; such things as Mediterranean pottery, a glass of wine, or a silk dress were now more likely to be found at a chieftain's stronghold in Cornwall or Strathclyde than in the ruins of London or of York.

Eventually, of course, this situation was reversed. The Germanic kingdoms that took shape in southern Britain during the sixth century not only established some degree of settled life and internal order, but began themselves to take an admiring interest in the continental scene. The marriage of Æthelbert of Kent with a Frankish princess from Paris, the arrival of the Augustinian mission in 597, and the renewal of continental trade, symbolized by the return of London in the course of the seventh century to its natural status as 'the mart of many nations resorting to it by sea and land,' all indicate the re-emergence of a more familiar relationship between the culture of Britain and that of western Europe, a realtionship never since so completely interrupted. But these developments lie beyond the main subject matter of this book. They serve in part as its political epilogue, but, more significantly in this context, they provide the setting from which springs so much of the information which can be used to illuminate the earlier centuries that are our primary concern. The age of Bede and Eddius, of Adamnan and Muirchu, knew far more than we can ever know about Christianity in Roman and sub-Roman Britain; and much of the little that we do know has come down to us through them.

Such then in very summary outline is the political background in these islands to the momentous spiritual and psychological changes which in a few brief centuries transformed the outlook of classical antiquity and of pre-literate barbarism alike into the ways of thought common to medieval man. It was the Christian faith which, in its various and continuously evolving forms, played by far the largest part in those changes and in the last resort determined their outcome. It is therefore of the greatest consequence to ascertain the source and nature of this all-pervading influence, to appreciate the varying extent and quality of its power in different regions and at different times, and to understand how it was able to adapt its organization so successfully to the changing needs of many diverse types of human society. The main papers read at the conference were intended to illuminate these basic problems. The political triumph of Christianity was, humanly speaking, the work of a succession of fourth-century Emperors. The process begins with Constantine and his sons, who, from the religion of a persecuted minority, made it the favoured and privileged faith of a highly successful dynasty, with all the official authority and influencc which such a position gave. It ends with Gratian and Theodosius, who not only disendowed its pagan rivals, but made a determined effort to suppress and indeed to exterminate them. The organization of the Church in the fifth century, as here described by Professor A. H. M. Jones, was the outcome of these momentous events. It was inevitably based on the city-state structure of the Mediterranean world, with its bishops as the leaders of the urban churches descended from the first Christian communities established, as the Acts of the Apostles already indicates, by missionary contacts passing from one town to another. Equally inevitably it was related to the provincial organization imposed by Rome on these civic centres, and the metropolitical structure of the church, already taking shape at this time, closely followed the hierarchical grouping of provinces into dioceses and prefectures that now characterized the administration of the Empire. This structure proved a great source of strength to the church, for, as civil authority increasingly broke down in the growing political weakness of the western Empire, it was easy and natural for the bishops to take over such administrative and judicial functions as their opposite numbers in local government could no longer exercise. Its weakness lay in the neglect of the country folk outside the immediate ambit of urban churches: a weakness well illustrated by the change of meaning which at this time turned the word *paganus*, a countryman, into a general term for those who had not accepted the Christian faith.

We know all too little about the application of these principles to the churches of Britain, whose origins are indeed almost wholly obscure. But what little is known suggests that Britain, which for most of the fourth century was administered as a diocese comprising four provinces in the Prefecture of the Gauls, followed the normal western pattern in its Christian organization. Each of the *civitas* capitals (a post-Roman list suggests that 28 places were thought to be so qualified[1]) is likely to have had its bishop, and it has been plausibly proposed that the three (from York, London, and probably Colchester), who attended the Council of Arles in 314, were the metropolitans from three of the four provincial capitals.[2]

Their attendance at such councils – there were three bishops from Britain also at the Council of Rimini in 359 – as well as their doubtless more frequent participation at ecclesiastical functions in Gaul, is of great significance. For, however simple and countrified they may have been, compared with the sophisticated prelates of the great Mediterranean cities, these journeys must have been a most rewarding experience not only for them but for their British congregations. They would have spread a knowledge of the great world and its current problems far and wide in a way that generations of contact with Roman officials in the provincial society of Britain itself could never have done. The bishops would bring back all kinds of souvenirs of their travels, pictures and guidebooks from the holy places, literature, both devotional and secular, that was novel in Britain, and perhaps above all a fund of travellers' tales which would not only provide welcome spice to their sermons but would give them a standing and authority among their growing flocks that was unobtainable in any other way. They were among the few Britons who had been places and seen sights. These travelling British bishops of the fourth century were indeed the pioneers in that long, often somewhat bizarre, procession of Celtic saints, who, in the darkest days of the sixth century, still kept open, however precariously, the seaways between western Britain and Gaul, and ensured, in so doing, that

Christianity in Britain never really lost contact with the Roman past. Above all, of course, these fourth-century travellers would become personally conscious of another unity beside that of secular Roman power, the spiritual ties which, in spite of heresy and schism, still made the church one and united them with their brethren throughout the *orbis terrarum*. It was the strength of those ties, forged in the days of the first Christian emperors, and expressed in the universal language of latin civilization, which made their successors long afterwards still think of Rome as eternal, and caused them to look back to the days *dum adhuc Romani Britanniam incolerent* as a sort of Golden Age made something more than life-size by the distorting mists of memory.

The extent to which the urban society of late Roman Britain was penetrated by Christianity before the political links with imperial authority were broken in the early years of the fifth century is disguised for us by the paucity of architectural and artistic remains that are of demonstrably Christian character. It was certainly much more influential and widespread than these scanty indications might suggest. For, as Dr Ralegh Radford here demonstrates, Christian churches, mostly springing from the clandestine house-chapels of the days of persecution, were very slow to develop distinctive architectural forms, and had indeed hardly done so on any great scale even in southern Europe by the time that Britain was lost to the Empire. Moreover, as Professor Jocelyn Toynbee here emphasizes, much crypto-Christian symbolism was in the fourth century read, by those inclined to read it, into the familiar pagan scenes and motifs that were the fashionable stock-in-trade of Roman interior decorators. Mosaics and wall-paintings of traditional pagan character could thus carry hidden meanings to their Christian owners, and even such standard emblematic figures as those of the Four Winds might indicate to the devout the four evangelists puffing good news from every quarter of the sky.

Rural paganism was no doubt far more widespread and deeprooted at the end of the fourth century in Britain than was its urban counterpart. Though both alike were by this time formally outlawed by Imperial rescripts of Theodosius and his sons, the archaeological evidence for the continued use of many conspicuous rural sanctuaries well into the fifth century is undeniable. But even in the countryside the forces working against pagan survival were increasing powerfully at this time. In Gaul the new notions of a bishop's duty popularized in the circle of S. Martin included the deliberate evangelization of rural folk, and men imbued with these notions, such as Victricius, Bishop of Rouen, who is known to have visited Britain in the 390s, are not likely to have neglected this aspect of his teaching. Moreover, a clear obligation was laid by Imperial rescripts on Christian landowners to secure the religious conformity of the slaves and *coloni* on their estates. There is no structural evidence for the provision by them of places of permanent religious worship for their tenants, and there is no likelihood that the peasantry would be welcome participants in the worship of such aristocratic house-chapels as that discovered in the Lullingstone *villa*. But many landowners would be ready to demonstrate both their piety and their patriotism by following the Imperial suggestion that more frequent floggings, *verberum crebrior ictus*, might be a useful method of securing the salvation of their reluctant dependents' souls.[3] The evidence here discussed by Professor Cameron in his study of the place-name element 'eccles' may well be relevant to the later phases of the Christianization of the Romano–British countryside, when permanent churches arose, perhaps based originally on the *martyria* of local saints, on the *monasteria* of early communities, or on *Eigenkirchen* provided by pious chieftains.

It was not however the persistence of paganism but rather the emergence of the Pelagian heresy which seems to have been the most significant feature in the religious life of early sub-Roman Britain. I have discussed elsewhere the interest of this phenomenon in relation to the circumstances in which the political dependence of Britain on the Roman government came to an end.[4] I have suggested also how the Pelagian controversy in Britain provides a clue to the mysterious conflicts between Vortigern and Germanus, and between Vortigern and other British chieftains, such as Ambrosius, which are mentioned briefly in later authorities as factors which fatally weakened the resistance of Britain to the Anglo-Saxon invaders.

There is no need to go over this ground again. But it may well be worth emphasizing some reasons which made Romano–British society peculiarly susceptible to Pelagian teaching. That teaching, with its insistence on a man's capacity to contribute significantly to his own salvation by leading a moral life whose merit would claim recognition at the Day of Judgment, was in effect an attempt to revitalise in a Christian form the old Roman virtues of simplicity, integrity and self-reliance extolled by Virgil and Cicero, to which men still attributed the ancient glories and triumphs of Rome. It was all too obvious that in the current decline of standards in public life, these *boni mores Romanorum*, as Augustine called them, were being stifled by bureaucratic corruption and the license permitted to men of influence to bribe and overawe the courts and to oppress the poor. A passionate reaction against the corruption and injustice of the times can be illustrated over and over again from the little group of tracts, recently studied by Dr John Morris, which have strangely survived from the first generation of Pelagian writings, and seem in several cases to be directly related to British affairs.[5]

Now Professor Kenneth Jackson has taught us that the spoken Latin in use in Roman Britain remained purer and more classical than the vulgar Latin of Gaul, and, though Professor Greene has here suggested that the contrast can be pressed too hard, the point retains a basic truth. The reason for it is clear. In Britain Latin never became, as it did in Gaul, a native tongue learnt naturally, and so subject to all those changes that there accompanied over the centuries its slow transformation into French. In Britain the common speech remained British, however much it may have incorporated Latin loan-words, and even

Latin tricks of syntax and grammar. A knowledge of Latin was, of course, essential for official, legal and ecclesiastical business, and so it was taught to upper-class children, much as classical Latin is taught now (only no doubt much better) by generations of conservative schoolmasters using Golden Age texts. Since, as we have seen, Pelagianism appealed especially to the taste of those aristocratic circles which retained a veneration for the golden past, it would be particularly attractive where, as in Britain, the teaching of the schools forced the old morality, enshrined in Virgil, Cicero, or Livy, on the attention of pupils in a language that had to be learnt. It would therefore be very natural for the Christian aristocracy of the British *civitates*, thus trained, to take a specially vigorous part in opposing official corruption and eventually in ejecting the incompetent and oppressive bureaucracy in 410 as Zosimus implies that they did.[6]

Moreover it would appear that in so doing they could hope to retain at least for a time the sympathetic support of the lower classes. For the latter had not only an obvious interest of their own in the purification of the courts from bribery and corruption, but, to the extent that they were being newly evangelized by missionary bishops, they would inevitably be attracted, as converts always are, by the Pelagian doctrine that merit brought its own reward. That something of this sort happened is suggested by the fact that on Germanus' first visit to combat Pelagianism in Britain in 429 his opponents were specifically described as rich men confident in a large measure of popular support: they were *conspicui divitiis, veste fulgentes, circumdati assentatione multorum*.[7] There is no suggestion here that Pelagianism had led the lower orders in Britain into revolutionary or subversive activities, such as the displaced bands of Bagaudae were adopting in Gaul or Armorica to the disastrous internal disruption of Roman society. Rather it would seem that in Britain for at least a generation Pelagianism may have acted almost as a sort of social cement, binding together classes whose interests in the long run were hardly reconcilable. It was doubtless partly for this reason that it appeared so menacing a movement both to orthodox opinion and to the *potentes* of the establishment in Gaul and Italy.

But this happy state of affairs, of which dim memories survived to find a place as 'the prosperity period' in Gildas' confused account of the days before the Saxon revolt,[8] did not last long. The persistent interventions of Germanus and the Gaulish Catholics in British affairs served so effectively to discredit the dominant Pelagian party as to leave it both incapable of military leadership against Anglo-Saxon incursions, and all too dependent on unreliable barbarian mercenaries in the face of the real threat of Roman conquest from Aetius in Gaul. But it was easier for the Catholic party to discredit the Pelagians than to provide an efficient barrier to the barbarians without Roman military assistance, and the overthrow of Aetius in 453 removed the possibility of effective help to their cause from that source. In these circumstances there was nothing to prevent the Anglo-Saxons, mercenaries and invaders alike, from exploiting

British disunity in a wholesale orgy of destruction which put an end to all forms of Romano–Christian culture in the ruins of the cities on which its life was based.

From this point the story of Christianity in sub-Roman Britain passes away from the lowland regions of the southeast, where Germanic heathenism now reigned supreme, to Scotland, Wales and Ireland which were not directly affected by these disastrous events. How Christianity had reached the less Romanized communities of the west and north, and how its episcopal and urban organization was adapted to suit the needs of different kinds of tribal society, is discussed here for the different regions and from different viewpoints by Professor Bieler, Professor Davies and Professor Charles Thomas, with a sidelight on the activities of British clergy in sixth-century Spain by Professor E. A. Thompson. Much of the obscurity that has always impeded a clear view of these matters comes from the difficulty of assessing the value and interpreting the language of the basic texts. It is in these fields that the contributions of Dr John Morris on the literary evidence as a whole, of Professor Bieler on the Patrician documents, of M. Francois Kerlouégan on the Latinity of Gildas and of Professor D. Greene on the study of language will be found most helpful. It has also proved possible to include three more of the numerous shorter communications on special topics, which formed a welcome and useful feature of the Conference. Two of these, by Messrs D. R. Wilson and P. A. Rahtz, describe the excavation of Christian cemeteries in the Roman or sub-Roman contexts of Lincolnshire and Somerset, and the third is Mr G. R. Watson's study of the evidence for Christianity in the Roman army.

Notes

1. Stevens, C. E. 'Gildas and the Civitates of Britain,' *EHR*, L (1937), 193–203
2. Mann, J. C. 'The Administration of Roman Britain,' *Antiquity*, XXXV (1961), 316–20. The fourth seems to have been represented by the priest and deacon in the party
3. *Cod. Theod.* XVI.5.52
4. *JRS*, L (1960), 21–36
5. *JTS*, XVI (1965), 26–60
6. *Hist. Nova*, VI.5
7. Constantius, *Vita Germani*, 14
8. *DEB*, 19 (35, 8–26)

The Western Church in the Fifth and Sixth Centuries

A. H. M. Jones

The Church early evolved its basic unit, the bishopric. The bishopric usually corresponded to the city, the civil unit of administration, which was also the natural social group. Administrative units which were not cities, such as independent villages, and *saltus*, *regiones* and *tractus* of imperial land, often had their own bishops, and so sometimes did centres of population within city territories – market towns, large villages and in particular military stations.[1] In the east the rule, one city, one bishop, was by the fifth century strictly observed. The emperor Zeno, by an imperial law, enacted that every city, with two named exceptions, must have a bishop; even after this there survived some cases where a bishop ruled a small group of cities, but very rarely.[2] In the west there was no special legislation, but the rule was generally accepted. We can test it precisely only in Gaul, where the exceptions are negligible,[3] but in Italy it seems to have been normal.[4] In Africa there were over 500 bishops; not only did practically every little *civitas* have its bishop, but so did many large estates, imperial and private.[5] Spain appears to have been exceptional. In the signatures of the numerous and well attended councils held under the Vizigothic kings, only some 70 or 80 sees can be traced,[6] but in the early principate Spain had 399 *civitates*.[7] They may have been somewhat reduced in number by the fifth century, but hardly to a fifth of the original figure. Pope Hilarus (461–8) speaks of a *municipium* which was a *diocesis* or parish.[8] We also have evidence that in 619 the old *civitas* of Regina was subject to the bishop of Corduba.[9] In Spain, then, it would seem that the bishops of the large towns ruled groups of minor cities. This may explain why *chorepiscopi* existed in Spain, who are otherwise almost unknown in the west.[10] We have no evidence for Britain, but as its political structure corresponded to that of northern Gaul, with large predominantly rural *civitates*, it is probable that like Gaul it had a bishop for each of its 28 *civitates*,[11] and perhaps a few more for populous military stations which were not *civitates*.

As early as the Council of Nicaea, and probably before that time, the bishops of a civil province normally formed a group under the presidency of the bishop of the metropolis or provincial capital. Here again, despite the Council of Nicaea, exceptions persisted. In Africa, the president of the provincial council was the senior bishop by date of consecration, except that Carthage was the permanent metropolis of the proconsular province.[12] In the west too, as in the east, rivalry between the official metropolis and another great city of the same province sometimes led to a civil province being split ecclesiastically; thus in Gaul Arles established its jurisdiction over the greater part of Viennensis.[13] There is no reason to think that in Britain the normal rule was not followed.

Even before Nicaea certain great churches had built up wider empires. The bishop of Alexandria consecrated all the bishops of Egypt and Libya and Pentapolis, and the bishop of Rome had the same right over the suburbicarian provinces of Italy and Sicily. In these cases there were no provincial metropolitans. Antioch had a looser supremacy over what was later to become the civil diocese of Oriens; the bishop of Antioch consecrated the metropolitans of the provinces. In the west Carthage had an undisputed but vague primacy over all the civil diocese of Africa; its bishop claimed no control over the consecration of bishops, but regularly convened councils for the whole area.[14] At the end of the fourth century Pope Siricius obtained indirect control over Illyricum (the dioceses of Macedonia and Dacia) by making the bishop of Thessalonica his vicar and authorizing him to consecrate all bishops in the area.[15] A similar attempt by Pope Zosimus (417–18) to create a papal vicariate of Arles over Viennensis and the two Narbonenses was a failure, and thereafter the Roman see abandoned such overt empire building.[16] Later popes occasionally appointed prominent Gallic or Spanish bishops on a personal basis as their vicars for Gaul or Spain or parts of the area, but these vicars were merely intermediaries between the Pope and the local hierarchy.[17]

This is not to deny that the popes enjoyed great authority in the west. Their doctrinal decisions were generally accepted by the churches, though quite a number resisted their condemnation of Pelagius and their subscription to the Edict of the Three Chapters. The churches were less willing to accept papal jurisdiction on appeal. The Africans successfully resisted Pope Zosimus' attempt to intervene in the Apiarius case, and proved that the alleged Nicene canons on which Zosimus relied did not exist (they were actually canons of Sardica).[18] Pope Leo had to invoke the aid of Valentinian III and the patrician Aetius to enforce his claims in Gaul.[19] On the other hand, metropolitans and provincial councils often solicited papal pronouncements on points of doctrine and discipline.

As early as the beginning of the fourth century there were at Alexandria besides the principal church of the bishop eight other churches served by priests,[20] and a little later we hear of rural churches with their priests in the villages of Mareotes, a district attached to Alexandria.[21] Rome similarly had a number of city churches served by priests by 341.[22] These churches fell into two classes, known in the west as *tituli* and as *parochiae* or *dioceses* respectively. The former were annexes of the bishop's church, financed out of his funds and staffed by his clergy. The latter were separate foundations with their own endowments and clergy. *Tituli* were normally urban or suburban, but many city churches were *parochiae*. Rural churches were nearly always *parochiae*, usually the foundations of the landlord.[23] Martin in the last quarter of the fourth century is depicted as journeying around the territory of Tours and visiting his *dioceses*,[24] and parish churches are quite frequently mentioned in the councils of Gaul and Spain in the fifth and sixth centuries.

The revenues of the churches, apart from a state subsidy first granted by Constantine and continued on a much reduced scale by his successors, were derived from two sources, offerings (*oblationes*), and the rents of land or house-property given or bequeathed to the churches by pious benefactors. The offerings were sometimes called first fruits, but did not include tithe, which, despite good biblical precedent, was nowhere claimed by the church until it was introduced into Gaul by the Council of Matisco in 585. In early days the offerings were the main, indeed the only, form of revenue, but from the time of Constantine endowments rapidly piled up, especially in the greater churches, and in these rents became the principal revenue.[25] Rural churches, on the other hand, often continued to be very meagrely endowed, and here offerings must have always been important. In sixth-century Spain some landlords built churches as a commercial speculation, going fifty-fifty with the incumbent for the offerings – which suggests that they must have been substantial.[26]

Church revenues, like the churches themselves, fell into two classes, those of the episcopal church with its *tituli*, and those of the *parochiae* or *dioceses*. With the *tituli*, *parochiae* and *dioceses* may be classed the various charitable organizations, hospitals, orphanages, almshouses for the aged or for widows, hospices for strangers. Some of these were financed and staffed by the bishops, but most had their own endowments and clergy. Episcopal churches tended on the whole to be richer than *parochiae*, and it might be a financial loss for a *cardinalis* or *canonicus*, a priest on the bishop's *canon* or *cardo*, to be appointed to a parish or even to be promoted to a poor bishopric. The Council of Orleans in 538 enacted that *de his vero clericorum personis quae de civitatensis ecclesiae officio monasteria, dioceses vel basilicas in quibuscumque locis positas, id est sive in territoriis sive in ipsis civitatibus suscipiunt ordinandas, in potestate sit episcopi si de eo quod ante de ecclesiastico munere habebant aliquid aut nihil exinde habere voluerit, quia unicuique facultas suscepti monasterii, diocesis vel basilicae debet plena ratione sufficere*,[27] and in 482 when Gregory, a priest of Ravenna, was against his will made bishop of Mutina, he demanded and received a Ravennate church estate worth 30 solidi a year in compensation.[28] This incident serves to show that bishoprics were of very unequal value. Justinian, in one of his Novels, classified episcopal incomes (apart from patriarchates) in six categories, over 30 lb. gold, from 30 to 10 lb., from 10 to 5 lb., from 5–3 lb., from 3–2 lb., and under 2 lb. (144 solidi).[29] We know of one bishop who got only six solidi a year, rather less than a private soldier's ration and clothing allowance and donative.[30] In these circumstances it is not surprising that three British bishops who attended the Council of Rimini in 359 were so poor that they had to accept the government's proferred *annonae et cellaria* – bishops were, it may be noted, fed on officers' scale of rations – to avoid burdening their richer colleagues with their upkeep.[31]

The poorest class of the clergy were the village priests. Those who built churches were indeed compelled to endow them. From the end of the fifth century the popes forbade the bishops in their jurisdiction to consecrate a new church unless provided with rent sufficient to cover its upkeep and lighting and the maintenance of its clergy,[32] and in Gaul the same rule was enacted by the Council of Orleans of 541,[33] and in Spain by the Council of Bracara of 572.[34] But the endowments which Gregory the Great passed as adequate were many of them very exiguous, ranging from ten down to three solidi per annum tax paid.[35]

In the area under their jurisdiction the popes from the latter part of the fifth century enforced a scheme whereby the revenues of episcopal churches, both rents and offerings, were divided into four equal parts, one of which went to the bishop, one to his clergy, being subdivided among them according to their grade and seniority, one to the upkeep and lighting of the buildings, and one to the poor.[36] In Spain a similar rule was introduced in 572, but here there were three portions only, the poor being omitted.[37] In Gaul the bishops had much wider discretion, controlling all rents and taking half of the offerings, the other half going to the clergy; this rule was enacted in 511.[38]

In Gaul and Spain the bishop also had the legal control of the endowments of the parishes. The first Council of Orleans in 511 ruled that gifts to parochial churches which were in the nature of capital – lands, slaves and cattle – were to be vested with the bishop,[39] and the third and fourth Councils of Toledo in 589 and 633 insisted that the founders of parochial churches must hand over their endowments to the bishop.[40] The bishop was, however, generally expected to devote their revenue to the churches for whose benefit they had been given. It was enacted by the third Council of Arles (538) that in the case of town churches (*basilicas in civitatibus constitutas*) the bishops had full discretion as to how much of their revenues be devoted to the upkeep of their buildings and the maintenance of their staff – they could in effect be converted into *tituli* – but that with rural churches (*de facultatibus paroeciarum vel basilicarum in pagis civitatum constitutis*) local custom must be observed.[41] The Council of Carpentoratum ordered that if the episcopal church was adequately endowed, the revenue from bequests to parishes must be spent on them, but that if the cathedral were poor the bishop might, after allowing sufficient to the parish to maintain its buildings and clergy, transfer the rest to his fund.[42] The Fourth Council of Toledo reproved bishops for taking away all the revenue of parish churches, so that they fell into ruin and their priests had no pay.[43] The bishop also enjoyed a third of the offerings in parish churches; this rule was enacted in 511 for Gaul and in 516 for Spain.[44] In both canons bishops were also instructed to repair parochial churches. The Second Council of Bracara declared that the third of the offerings must be spent on lighting and repairs, and not taken by the bishop,[45] but the Fourth Council of Toledo allowed the bishops to take a third both of the offerings and of the rents.[46] Italian and Spanish bishops also exacted fees, called *cathedratica*, at their annual visitations; these were limited by popes and councils to two solidi, a substantial sum for a village priest whose endowments brought in five solidi or less.[47]

Bishops were elected by the clergy and people of their city, and consecrated by – or with the consent of – their metropolitan and a majority of the provincial bishops. The clergy probably in effect usually meant the city clergy, though in deference to complaints Pope Gelasius on one occasion ordered all the priests and deacons from the parishes to be summoned.[48] The people is specified to be the *ordo et plebs*, or the *honorati ordo et plebs* or *honorati et plebs*.[49] On occasions the common people might have a decisive influence,[50] but in the *Epistola ad Gallos* the pope condemns elections made '*favore populi*'; 'for what is sought for is not what the people wishes but what evangelical discipline desires; the plebs bears witness only as often as it regards the merit of some worthy man and so lends the ear of favour.'[51] How an election went depended very much on circumstances. A forceful and authoritative presiding bishop might impose his will. Thus Sidonius Apollinaris found so many candidates at Bourges that they filled two benches, but he rejected them all in favour of a man of his own choice, and at Cabillonum the metropolitan set aside the three candidates, a dissolute nobleman and two others who had been guilty of corrupt practices in their canvas, and persuaded the meeting to elect the local archdeacon.[52] On the other hand, the election by the clergy and people was often important. Several Gallic Councils denounce those 'who obtain the patronage of influential persons, and with underhand cunning induce some to sign the *decretum* by gifts and intimidate others,'[53] or by whom 'the citizens or, sinful though it be to say it, the clergy are impelled by the presence of influential persons to make the *consensus*.[54] Pope Gelasius, however, allowed reasonable election expenses, including 'twenty-two and two thirds solidi on food and forage for the decurions whom he had produced for the election to the bishopric.'[55] An attempt was made by the Council of Arles in the middle of the fifth century to lay down a regular procedure to avoid canvassing and corruption; the bishops were to propose three candidates of whom the clergy and people were to select one; but there is no evidence that this canon was ever put into effect.[56]

The lower clergy were appointed and promoted by the bishop, but he was expected to pay due regard to the wishes of the founders of parish churches and their heirs. The Council of Orange (441) dealt with the delicate case where a bishop had built a church on an estate belonging to him in the territory of another bishop.[57] The first bishop was not to presume to consecrate the church he had built or to ordain clergy for it, but the second bishop was to ordain men of the first's choice, or to accept already ordained clergy whom the first bishop appointed. Bishops had also, if they were wise, to pay regard to recommendations of their protégés by powerful persons.[58]

The numbers of the clergy increased rapidly from Constantine's time onwards. In the year of the Great Persecution the bishop of Cirta, the capital of Numidia, had 16 clergy (3 priests, 2 deacons, 4 sub-deacons and 7 readers) and there was evidently no other church in the town.[59] Under Pope Felix IV (526–30) the clergy of the cathedral of Ravenna – the royal capital it is true – numbered 60,[60] and there were, of course, many other churches in the city. At Carthage the total number of clergy was over 500 in A.D. 484.[61]

Men were ordained at every age. Pope Siricius fixed minimum ages for deacon and priest at 30 and 35 respectively, but infants were often offered to the church and held minor orders up to the rank of reader in childhood. Some took orders as young men after completing their education, but a substantial number did so after finishing a secular career as a civil servant or in the professions.[62] The clergy were drawn from almost every class. It was very rare for a high-ranking senator, such as the former prefect of the city, Sidonius Apollinaris, to take orders, and if he did it was to become a bishop forthwith. It was less uncommon for men who had held a provincial government and thus became *clarissimi*, like Germanus of Auxerre, to be ordained, or more often consecrated bishops: Pope Siricius and Caesarius of Arles disapproved of such candidates. Civil servants of all grades from *palatini* to *cohortales* often took orders – they too fell under the disapproval of Popes Siricius and Innocent and of Caesarius – but soldiers very rarely. From the professions, doctors and professors were rare, but barristers very common; even the law was in Pope Innocent's severe judgment an unfitting prelude to holy orders.[63]

Bishops fall into three categories. The popes and the clergy naturally favoured regular promotion from the lower ranks of the clergy; Pope Zosimus thought that the civil service, with automatic promotion by seniority, should be a model for the church.[64] Many bishops were in fact chosen from among the senior priests or deacons of the cathedral church.[65] But laymen often preferred a real holy man, whose *suffragia* would be effective with God, or an eminent layman, whose *suffragia* would be useful with the imperial or royal government. So we find on the one hand monks being consecrated bishops, and on the other senators, civil servants or lawyers, neither having held any minor orders.[66] And despite the opposition of the imperial government and the disapproval of the popes a large number of the clergy seem to have been drawn from the middle class of landowners, the decurions of the cities.[67] Such men naturally secured positions in episcopal or at any rate urban churches. The country clergy were normally peasants; if they were *coloni* their landlord's permission was required, if slaves they had to be manumitted first.[68]

One gains a strong impression that by the fifth and sixth centuries the churches had become conspicuously wealthy in the western parts as in the eastern. We have no details except for the Roman See, which was obviously *sui generis*, and the see of Ravenna, which as an imperial and then a royal capital from the early fifth century was also exceptional. But it is worth noting that the bishop of Ravenna had an annual salary in gold rents, apart from his share of the offerings and dues in kind from the church estates, of 3000 solidi:[69] which is more than the 40 lb. of gold which Justinian allotted to the Augustal Prefect and Dux of Egypt and twice what the proconsuls of Palestine and Cappadocia received.[70] But even without figures the wealth of the church in Gaul is sufficiently attested by the canvassing and bribery in episcopal elections, already denounced in the *Epistula ad Gallos*, by the assignment of rich sees to their ministers and favourites by the Frankish kings,[71] and by the constant attempts of powerful laymen to obtain grants of church lands.[72] In Britain the accumulation of wealth had begun later and doubtless did not go so far, but there is reason to believe that it was already considerable before the end of Roman rule.

How far the work of conversion had gone by then it is difficult to say. There were still in the latter part of the sixth century a substantial number of rural pagans in the western provinces. Pope Gregory the Great found that in Sardinia many peasants, including tenants of church lands, were openly practising pagan worship, bribing the governor of the province to turn a blind eye.[73] In 589 the Third Council of Toledo declared that 'the sacrilege of idolatry is rooted in almost the whole of Gaul and Spain,'[74] and a series of Gallic Councils in 533, 541, 567, 578 and 625 denounced pagan practices, such as the worship of holy trees and holy springs.[75] Martin of Bracara in the latter part of the sixth century wrote a tract '*de correctione rusticorum*,' in which he denounces among other pagan practices the observance of Thursday, the day of Jupiter, instead of Sunday.[76] Anecdotes in Gregory of Tours show that the survivals of paganism were not merely witchcraft and superstition, but regular worship of the old pagan gods – Jupiter, Mercury, Minerva, Venus.[77]

Others will deal more competently than I can with the growth of monasticism. I would only emphasize that it was long before it acquired momentum in the west. The movement started early in the fourth century in Egypt, Syria and Palestine, and spread to Cappadocia a generation later. It was not until yet another generation that it took root at Constantinople. The first western monasteries of which we know are Martin's house at Tours and Ambrose's at Milan. Augustine seems to have introduced monasticism into Africa, and we hear of no more foundations in Gaul until Cassian's two houses of monks and nuns at Marseilles and Honoratus' famous house at Lérins in the early fifth century. Gallic monasticism was directly inspired by contemporary Egypt, of which Sulpicius Severus and Cassian wrote long and detailed accounts in Latin.[78]

Notes

1. *LRE*, 874–8
2. Codex Justinianus, I, iii, 35
3. Only in Gaul do we possess a fifth-century register of units of government, the Notitia Galliarum, printed in O. Seeck, *Notitia Dignitatum* (Berlin, 1876), against which we can set the lists of episcopal signatures at councils. This has been done by L. Duchesne, *Les fastes épiscopaux de l'ancienne Gaule* (Paris, 1900–15)
4. Gregory the Great suppressed a number of Italian sees; see Gregorius, *Epistulae*, I, 8; II, 44, 48; III, 20; IX, 60 (*MGH Ep* I, II). But this was because the cities concerned had been destroyed by the Lombards
5. Mesnage, J., *L'Afrique Chrétienne, Évêchés et ruines antiques* (Paris, 1912). We know of only one African *municipium* which was not a bishopric (Augustine, *de cura gerenda pro mortuis*, 15). For bishoprics on estates see the *Collatio Carthaginiensis*, I, 181–2 (Mansi, IV, 136)
6. Vives, J., *Concilios Visigoticos et Hispano-Romanos*, (Barcelona-Madrid, 1963)
7. Pliny, *Natural History*, III, 7, 18; IV, 117
8. Hilarus, *Epistulae*, 14 (Thiel), *cum ecclesia eius municipii in qua ante fuerat ordinatus semper huius civitatis ecclesiae fuisse diocesis constet*
9. *Concilium Hispalense II*, canon 2 (Mansi, X, 557)
10. *Ibid.*, canon 7 (Mansi, X, 559). For *chorepiscopi* see *LRE*, 879. The only *chorepiscopi* known in the west are at Salona (*CIL*, III, 9547) and, as a special and exceptional case, in Gaul in 439 (Mansi, V, 1192). It is of interest that at the Council of Sardica a canon (No. 6) was proposed by Hosius of Corduba, that bishops should not be consecrated in villages or small cities, 'that the name and authority of bishop may not be cheapened' (Turner, C. H., *Ecclesiae Occidentalis Monumenta Iuris Antiquissima*, Oxford, 1939, I, 499–500)
11. *DEB*, 3 (28.7–29.2), cf. Stevens, C. E., 'Gildas and the Civitates of Britain,' *EHR*, L (1937), 193–203
12. *LRE*, 880–1
13. Leo, *Epistulae*, 46 (*PL* LIV, 883–6)
14. *LRE*, 883–8
15. *Ibid.*, 888–9
16. Zosimus, *Epistulae*, 1, 4–7, 10–11 (*PL* 20, 642–5, 661–9, 673–5).
17. Symmachus, *Epistulae*, 16, Simplicius, *Epistulae*, 21, Hormisdas, *Epistulae*, 24, 142 (Thiel)
18. Bruns, H. T., *Canones Apostolorum et Conciliorum* (Berlin, 1839), I, 155 ff.
19. Valentinian III, *Novellae*, 17
20. Epiphanius, *adversus Haereses*, lxix, 1–2
21. Athanasius, *Apologia contra Arianos*, 63, 85
22. *Ibid.*, 20
23. Jones, A. H. M., 'Church Finance in the Fifth and Sixth Centuries,' *JTS*, 1960, 86–89
24. Sulpicius Severus, *Epistulae*, I.10 The first mention of a *parochia* seems to be in 439, also in Gaul (Mansi, V, 1192), where it is implied that it might be a place *quem curiae et civitatis species aut ordo nobilitat*
25. *LRE*, 894 ff.
26. *Concilium Bracarense II*, canon 6 (Barlow, C. W., *Martini Bracarensis opera omnia*, New Haven, 1950, 120–1)
27. *Concilium Aurelianense* III, canon 21 (*MGH Conc.* I, 79–80)
28. Simplicius, *Epistulae*, 14 (Thiel)
29. Justinian, *Novellae*, 123, §3

Notes

30. Brooks, E. W., *The Select Letters of Severus of Antioch* (London, 1903–4), Book I, Letter 4
31. Sulpicius Severus, *Chronica*, II, 41. For *cellaria* see *LRE*, 396–7
32. Gelasius, *Epistulae*, 34, *Fragmenta*, 21 (Thiel); Loewenfeld, S., *Epistulae Pontificum Romanorum Ineditae* (Leipzig, 1885), nos. 2, 15; Gasso, P. M. and Batlle, C. M., *Pelagii I Papae epistulae quae supersunt* (Montserrat, 1956), no. 86
33. *Concilium Aurelianense IV*, canon 33 (*MGH Conc.* I, 94–95)
34. *Concilium Bracarense II*, canon 5 (Barlow, *op. cit.* 120)
35. Gregorius I, *Epistulae*, II, 9; IX, 58, 71, 180 (*MGH Ep.* I, II)
36. Simplicius, *Epistulae*, 1, Gelasius, *Epistulae*, 14 §27, 15, 16, *Fragmenta*, 23, 24 (Thiel)
37. *Concilium Bracarense I*, canon 7 (Barlow, *op.cit.* 112)
38. *Concilium Aurelianense I*, canon 14 (*MGH Conc.* I, 6)
39. *Ibid.*, canon 15 (*MGH Conc.* I, 6)
40. *Concilium Toletanum III*, canon 19, IV, canon 33 (Mansi, IX, 998; X, 628)
41. *Concilium Aurelianense III*, canon 5 (*MGH Conc.* I, 74–75)
42. *Concilium Carpentoratense* (*MGH Conc.* I. 41)
43. *Concilium Toletanum IV*, canon 33 (Mansi, X, 628)
44. *Concilium Aurelianense I*, canon 15 (*MGH Conc.* I, 6)
45. *Concilium Bracarense II*, canon 2 (Barlow, *op. cit.* 119)
46. *Concilium Toletanum IV*, canon 33 (Mansi, X, 628)
47. Gelasius, *Fragmenta*, 20 (Thiel). Gasso and Batlle, *op. cit.* nos. 32, 33, *Concilium Bracarense II*, canon 2 (Barlow, *op. cit.* 119)
48. Gelasius, *Fragmenta*, 4 (Thiel)
49. Bonifacius, *Epistulae*, 12, Caelestinus, *Epistulae*, 4 §5, Leo, *Epistulae*, 10 §6, 40 (*PL* 20, 772; 50, 431; 54, 634, 815)
50. As in the case of Ambrose (Paulinus, *Vita S. Ambrosii*, 6–7) and Martin (Sulpicius Severus, *Vita S. Martini*, 9)
51. *PL* 13. 1191
52. Sidonius Apollinaris, *Epistulae*, IV, 25; VII, 9
53. *Concilium Arvernense I*, canon 2 (*MGH Conc.* I, 66–67)
54. *Concilium Aurelianense V*, canon 11 (*MGH Conc.* I, 104)
55. Loewenfeld, *op. cit.*, no. 22
56. *Concilium Arelatense II*, canon 54 (Mansi, VII, 885)
57. *Concilium Arausecanum I*, canon 10 (*MGH Conc.* I, 437–8). For lay patrons see *Concilium Aurelianense IV*, canon 7 (*MGH Conc.* I, 89) and Gelasius, *Epistulae*, 41 (Thiel)
58. Agnellus, *Liber Pontificalis Ecclesiae Ravennatis*, 60, (*MGH Lang.* 319)
59. Optatus Milevitanus, *de schismate Donatistarum*, Appendix 1
60. Agnellus, *loc. cit.* (*MGH Lang.* 321)
61. Victor Vitensis, *Historia persecutionis Africanae Provinciae*, III, 34
62. *LRE*, 912–4
63. *Ibid.*, 920–7
64. Zosimus, *Epistulae*, 9 §1 (*PL*, 20, 671); cf. Leo, *Epistulae*, 12 §4 (*PL*, 54, 659–61)
65. As recommended by Leo in *Epistulae*, 14 §6 (*PL*, 54, 673)
66. *LRE*, 923–5
67. *Ibid.*, 925–7
68. *Ibid.*, 920–2
69. Agnellus, *loc. cit.* (*MGH Lang.* 319)
70. Justinian, *Novellae*, 30 §6, 103 §1, *Edicta*, 13 §3
71. Gregorius Turonensis, *Historia Francorum*, V, 45; VI, 7, 38; VIII, 20, 22, 39 (*MGH Merov* I)

Notes

72. *Concilium Arvernense I*, canon 5, *Concilium Aurelianense IV*, canon 25, *Concilium Parisiense III*, canon 1 (*MGH Conc.* I, 63, 93, 142–3), Gregorius Turonensis, *de Virtutibus S. Iuliani*, 14, *in Gloria Confessorum*, 70 (*MGH Merov* I)
73. Gregorius, *Epistulae*, IV, 23, 25–7, 29; V, 38; IX, 204; XI, 12 (*MGH Ep* I, II)
74. *Concilium Toletanum III*, canon 16 (Mansi, IX, 996)
75. *Concilium Aurelianense II*, canon 20; IV, canons 15–16, *Concilium Turonense II*, canon 23, *Concilium Autissiodorense*, canons 1, 3, 4, *Concilium Remense*, canon 14 (*MGH Conc.* I, 64, 90, 133, 179–80, 204–5)
76. Barlow, *op. cit.* 183–203
77. Gregorius Turonensis, *Historia Francorum*, VIII, 15, *Vitae Patrum*, XVII, 5 (*MGH Merov* I); also *Vita S. Caesarii*, II, 18 (*MGH Merov* III, 490)
78. *LRE*, 929–33

The Archaeological Background on the Continent

C. A. Ralegh Radford

Conversion is an evocative word. The vision that confronted St Paul on the road to Damascus is the pattern of conversion and Christian thought has rightly emphasized this facet of the spread of the Gospel. But for the majority conversion was less spectacular – the customs and the background of the older way of life were taken over into the Christian community and profoundly influenced its development. The letters which passed between Ausonius and Paulinus illustrate the difference. The master, absorbed in the elegant literary pursuits of the retired and scholarly civil servant, vainly awaited the return of his brilliant and beloved pupil, unable to comprehend the overwhelming splendour of his new vision:

Et sua praeteriens iam iam tua limina pulsat.
Credimus? An qui amant ipsi sibi somnia fingunt?

Paulinus, governor of a province and consul at an early age, had sold all to become the priest and guardian of a rustic shrine. The old interests no longer held him:

Negant Camenis nec patent Apollini
Dicata Christo pectora.
Breve quicquid homo est est corporis aegri
Temporis occidui, et sine Christo pulvis et umbra.[1]

It is the spirit of Ausonius rather than that of Paulinus which can be traced in the archaeological record.

In the fourth century Britain was a province of the Roman Empire. The more civilized lowlands – the area lying south and east of the great military bases at York, Chester and Caerleon – were under civil rule and conditions differed little from those in Gaul and in the provinces further to the south and east. Beyond the great bases stretched a wide zone administered by the army and gradually shading into the territories of the federate peoples, beyond which lay the unconquered territories in Scotland and Ireland. In the early fifth century the barbarian sweep across Gaul cut the customary links across the narrow seas and left Britain virtually isolated and open to raiders and settlers from beyond the frontiers. At the same time a reactivation of the Atlantic sea routes opened the way to closer contacts between the federate states and the unconquered lands of the north and west and the Mediterranean world. Relations between the Insular Celts and this Mediterranean world changed both in kind and in degree between the fourth and fifth centuries; it is the former connections to which the present paper is relevant.

The archaeological evidence for Christianity in the early centuries comes from two main sources. The churches, including the cathedrals, are places for common worship, above all for the celebration of the Eucharist. The cemeteries are burial places, connected with the cult of the martyrs. Since Roman law forbade burial within the city limits the two types of site are separated topographically. In origin their functions were different and the structures found are expressed in different idioms. It is only in the fourth century and more particularly towards the end of that century that the two architectural forms begin to coalesce into a standard type of building. The date is important in relation to the history of Roman Britain.

Christianity arrived in Gaul at an early date. The authentic record of the persecution at Lyons in 177 discloses an organized Christian community already in existence[2] and similar communities are attested not only further south but even in the Rhineland (p. 33) at a date not much later. After the Peace of the Church in 313 such communities multiply and evidence is accumulating which enables their extent and distribution to be assessed. This evidence is fullest for the Rhineland[3] but what is known from the rest of the Seven Provinces bears out the conclusions that will now be summarized. The distribution of the Christian communities of the fourth century is essentially urban; the dwellers in the countryside – the *pagani* – continue to follow the older cults. Typical are the rural parts of the great metropolitan diocese of Tours in Central Gaul, which still lay outside the sphere of the church when the bishop, St Martin,[4] undertook his vigorous campaigns against heathen shrines in the last quarter of the fourth century.

The earliest church building of which a clear picture can be obtained lies at the other end of the Roman Empire, at Doura on the Euphrates.[5] The building was designed as a normal private house with four ranges enclosing a courtyard. Certain alterations were made when it was adapted for use as a church. A date corresponding to 232 A.D. was scratched on the wet plaster, probably at the time of these alterations. Some years later the building was partly demolished and partly embedded in a great ramp added at the back of the city wall to strengthen it against the attack of the Persian artillery, before which the city fell in 256.

A doorway from the street led into a vestibule which gave access to the courtyard. On the south side of this courtyard the main room of the house and an adjacent room had been thrown together to form a single hall measuring 45 by 16 feet. At one end a low rectangular platform had been added, a feature not usually found in houses. In the northwest corner of the house was a room with a basin covered with an aedicula at one end; the walls of this room were decorated with Christian paintings, including a representation of the Good Shepherd on the wall at the back of the aedicula, episodes from the life of Christ and Old Testament scenes. The west side of the courtyard was filled by a room with a central entrance and side doors leading to the rooms already described. On the east side was a columned portico. Stairs alongside the vestibule led to an upper floor, of which no part remained.

The basin in the smaller room with the Christian paintings must be interpreted as a font. It shows that the Christian community at Doura was presided over by a bishop, for baptism was administered by the bishop in the early church. This hall was probably both catachumeneum and consignatorium, the paintings serving for instruction. The main hall with the raised platform for the episcopal seat or throne is the place for the liturgical celebration of the Eucharist; in accordance with the stricter precepts of the early Church it lacks sacred paintings.[6] The rest of the building served as a dwelling for the bishop and his familia and as offices. It is not too much to say that Doura represents in embryo the cathedral and its associated buildings; it is probably typical of the small provincial Christian communities of the early third century; in this case it must have numbered less than 100.

The same type of church is seen in a more developed and elaborate form at Mérida in southern Spain. Emerita was a colonia founded by Augustus. In 252 it was the seat of a bishop, Martial by name, who apostasized in that year.[7] The most famous martyr of Emerita was St Eulalia, who suffered in 304. She is commemorated in a poem by Prudentius,[8] in whose day her tomb was shown in a basilica outside the west wall of the city on the site of the present church named in her honour. The earliest remains on that site go back to the fourth century.[9]

The early church at Merida lay (p. 22) inside the city alongside the Theatre.[10] It is ruined with the walls standing to a maximum height of about 10 feet. The house was elaborate and opulent with good mosaic pavements. There is a basin in the corner of the courtyard. Two large apsidal halls open out of the courtyard, the larger decorated with paintings of *Orantes*. The rest of the building, in so far as a detailed description is published, presents no unusual features. The formal linear character of the paintings would indicate a date in the late fourth or fifth centuries, which is that of the house, or possibly of its conversion into a church. The use of sacred paintings became normal in churches in the course of the fourth century and does not preclude the identification of the larger hall as the place in which the Eucharist was celebrated.

It remains to consider whether this building is the fourth-century Cathedral of Emerita or a subsidiary church akin to the Roman *tituli* shortly to be considered. The basin, if serving as a font, would suggest the former solution. Paul the Deacon of Mérida, writing in the seventh century describes the Cathedral of St Mary, known as Jerusalem, with its baptistery standing under the same roof and adjacent to the bishop's palace.[11] It is possible that, as at

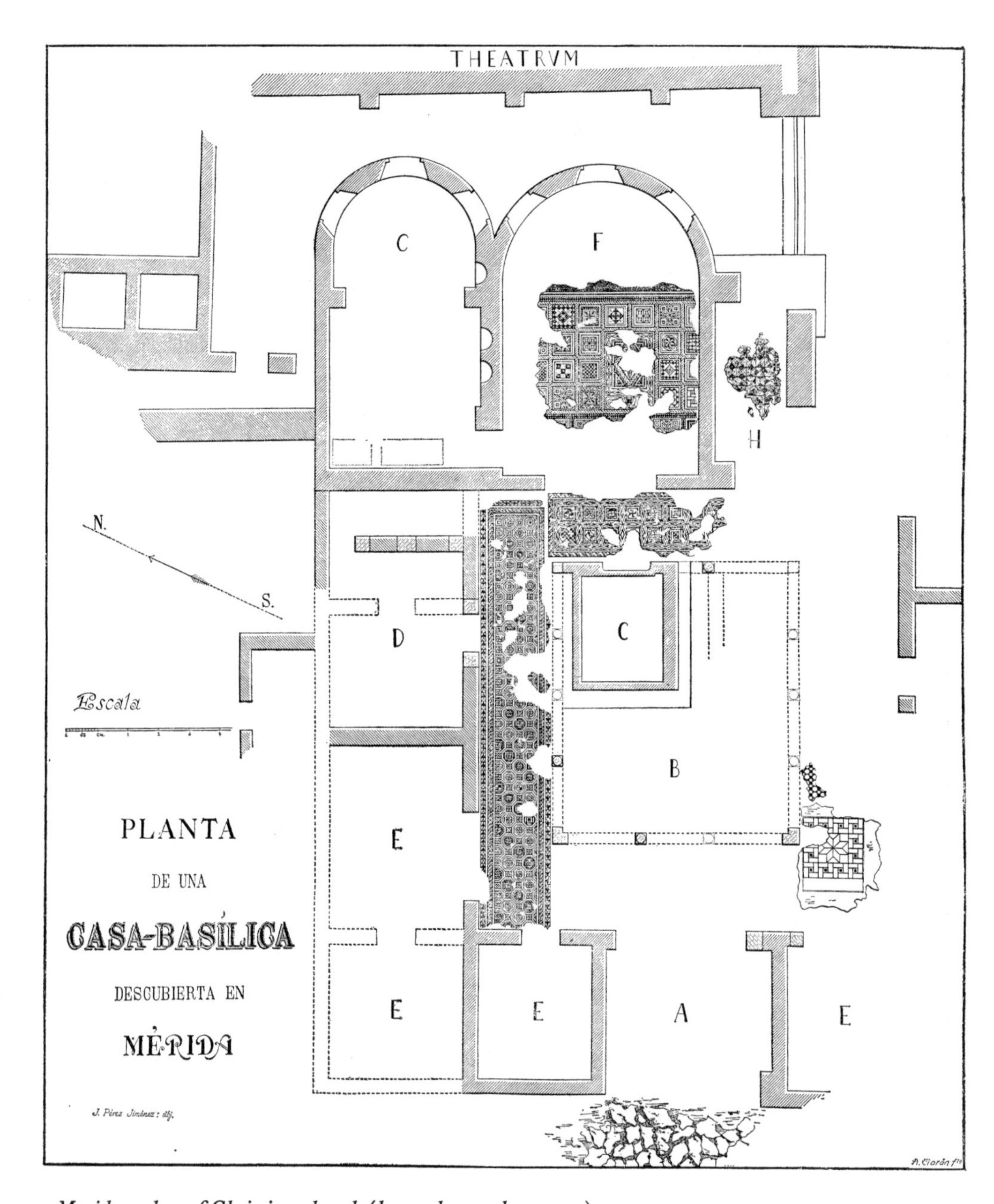

Merida: plan of Christian church (late 4th or 5th century)

Salona (see p. 23), the earlier cathedral complex survived in the bishop's palace alongside a new cathedral built on more spacious lines and to a more usual plan. That the house already discussed survived into the seventh century as the Cathedral of Emerita is borne out by no comparable evidence.

The development of a building of domestic character, forming the early cathedral, into a more normal type of layout may be studied at Salona. This great city was deserted early in the seventh century in the face of Slavonic invasions. The remaining inhabitants withdrew into the fortified palace of the Emperor Diocletian at Split or across the sea on to the islands or to Italy. The episcopal palace[12] is an immense private house, occupying the whole of a large block in one corner of the city and served by a special branch of the aqueduct. Only the ground stage survives with store rooms, olive presses and other evidence of domestic occupation. To the south, across a former street, then blocked, a great complex with two basilicas and a baptistery was built about 500. The earlier cathedral must have lain within the area of the palace which continued to be occupied; it was perhaps on the upper floor, in a large room to which led an external stair rising from the garden. Two small oratories lay within the garden. They dated from the early fourth century and one was perhaps even older. These can never have sufficed for the Christian community of Salona in the later fourth and fifth centuries, the importance of which is demonstrated by the growth of the extensive cemeteries at Manastirine, Kapljuc and elsewhere.

The great complex at Salona and a similar palace adjacent to the cathedral at Aquileia (p. 25) illustrate the provisions of the fifth century Imperial rescript dealing with the right of sanctuary attaching to the churches of God (*magni Dei templa*).[13] This right, it is decreed, shall apply not only 'to the altars and in the oratory (*oratorium*) surrounded with its fourfold limit of walls but in what lies beyond as far as the furthest gates of the church' (*ad extremos fores ecclesiae*) so that sanctuary should extend to 'all that lies between the temple (*templum*) . . . and the first gates of the church (*primas fores ecclesiae*) after the public places, whether it be houses or gardens or courtyards (*atria*) or baths or corridors' (*porticus*).

The buildings already studied are basically private houses – at Salona a palace – with one or more rooms adapted for liturgical purposes and the most important, the palace at Salona, suggests that the provision of a separate building, readily recognizable as a church, might be delayed until the fifth century or even later. There are a number of similar instances at Rome, where there is only the continuous tradition of Christian worship to lead to the identification of a particular building as a Christian church. The Severan building beneath the church of S. Anastasia may serve as an example.[14] The ground floor consists of long vaulted rooms with open fronts surmounted by mezzanine chambers; the form is typical of shops found in many great houses or house blocks of this age. A great stairway leads to an upper floor, which has a purely domestic appearance as far as the façade has been preserved. The incorporation of this façade into the north wall of an aisled basilica with an apse took place only in the sixth century, when the south side of the hall was extended across a street. Since the *Titulus Anastasiae* is known to have been in existence as early as the fourth century this house must have served the needs of the Christian community for at least 200 years after the Peace of the Church; the upper floor was probably designed for this purpose in the third century.

The *Titulus Equitii*, also a Severan building and lying alongside the Church of S. Martino ai Monti,[15] is even more interesting. On the ground stage the central part of a rectangular block forms a two-aisled hall of three bays covered with groined vaults. Rooms open out on either side. Near the entrance a stair in a projecting turret leads to an upper floor, of which the arrangement is uncertain. This was the church associated with St Sylvester before he became Pope; it was replaced by a new basilica built alongside by Pope Symmachus about 500. The titulus of the third century occupied the Severan building. The liturgical hall for the celebration of the Eucharist was almost certainly on the upper floor; the aisled hall at ground level may be compared with the atria in front of many early Roman basilicas. The whole arrangement suggests a building erected early in the third century with a specialized layout designed for the needs of the church.

Regard must also be had to the *Titulus Clementis* beneath the church of S. Clemente, by some regarded as the original cathedral of Rome, replaced when Constantine built the Lateran Basilica. Though the name was connected with St Clement, Bishop of Rome at the end of the first century, as early as 400, such an origin of the *Titulus* is unlikely. These churches normally acquired their names from the original proprietors or donors. It has been suggested that the *Titulus Clementis* owes its name to the Consul Flavius Clemens, a relative of the Flavian house, who, with his wife Domitilla, was charged with atheism, a synonym for Christianity, and condemned to death. The architectural history of the building is consistent with such an origin.[16]

In Flavian times a palatial dwelling arose in the valley running from the Colosseum to the area where the Lateran now stands.[17] Only the ground stage, forming a podium, remains. A building, of domestic character was erected on this foundation early in the third century; the lateral walls still stand and show no trace of internal divisions. This would suggest that the new layout included a large hall, probably larger than any room yet indicated in the other buildings found beneath or incorporated in early titular churches. Late in the fourth century the property was enlarged by extension across a narrow alley to incorporate a second house which had contained a Mithraeum. An aisled basilica with an apse extending into the second building was then erected, the side walls incorporating those of the Severan structure. The *Titulus Clementis* is well attested on this site early in the fourth century and there can be little doubt that the Severan building housed it. That the Flavian podium formed part of the palace of Flavius Clemens and was devoted by him to the use of the Christian community is an attractive hypothesis, which lacks proof.

It is probable that the apparently domestic buildings of the *Titulus Equitii* and the *Titulus Clementis* already shewed a certain specialization as Christian churches as early as the first half of the third century. In particular the vaulted hall on the ground stage of the former and the large hall which has been postulated in the latter would be unusual features in a purely domestic arrangement.

After the Peace of the Church in 313 the evidence becomes fuller and more widespread. The older form of church, a building including a liturgical hall, continued in use and examples have already been cited. But the hall within a wider complex was gradually replaced by a separate building designed for the liturgical celebration of the Eucharist and distinguished by its architectural form. These are churches in the more modern sense of the word. The initiative seems to have come from Rome, where the Emperor Constantine erected a great cathedral, an immense aisled hall with an apse at one end on the site that has remained the Lateran basilica, together with a great memoria on a similar plan over the tomb of St Peter on the Vatican Hill. The emperor was also responsible for a number of buildings in the east, in particular for memoriae at Jerusalem and Bethlehem. To survey the whole field would transcend the limits of this paper and it will therefore be convenient to concentrate attention on areas comparable with Roman Britain – the frontiers along the Rhine and the Upper Danube and their hinterland.

Aquileia was the centre which deeply influenced a great zone stretching from the head of the Adriatic north and east across the Alpine passes to the upper and middle Danube, which formed the frontier of the Empire in the fourth century. Paganism survived late in this region, as it did in Gaul. When the Emperor Theodosius visited Aemona (Ljubljana) in 388 he was met by the city dignitaries, including the priests of the pagan cults in full regalia.[18] Even later, about 400, St Sisinnius and his companions suffered martyrdom when they attempted to suppress the cult of Saturn at a holy well on the Nonsberg in modern Tyrol.[19]

At Aquileia attention must be directed to the complex dating from the episcopate of Bishop Theodore (*c.* 308–19), which straddles the Peace of the Church. The complex (p. 26) forms a block near the Imperial Palace.[20] The north and south sides are entirely filled with aisled halls, each over 100 feet long. On the west side they are connected by a narrower hall, also aisled. The space enclosed by these halls is filled with a number of smaller rooms with a courtyard in the centre; a part of this area and of the north hall are inaccessible by reason of the foundations of the late medieval campanile. That the whole complex was in use as a church as early as *c.* 320 is not open to doubt. The main southern hall was begun by Bishop Theodore and completed after his death. The eastern bay, separated from the rest of the hall by low balustrades and paved with a magnificent mosaic of Jonah, formed the part reserved for the clergy; there is no structural synthronon, indicating the use of movable seats. The position at which the altar was set for the Eucharist is in the centre of the next bay; it is marked by a mosaic panel with a winged victory standing behind the altar in the position of the celebrant – *absorpta est mors in victoria* – with smaller panels

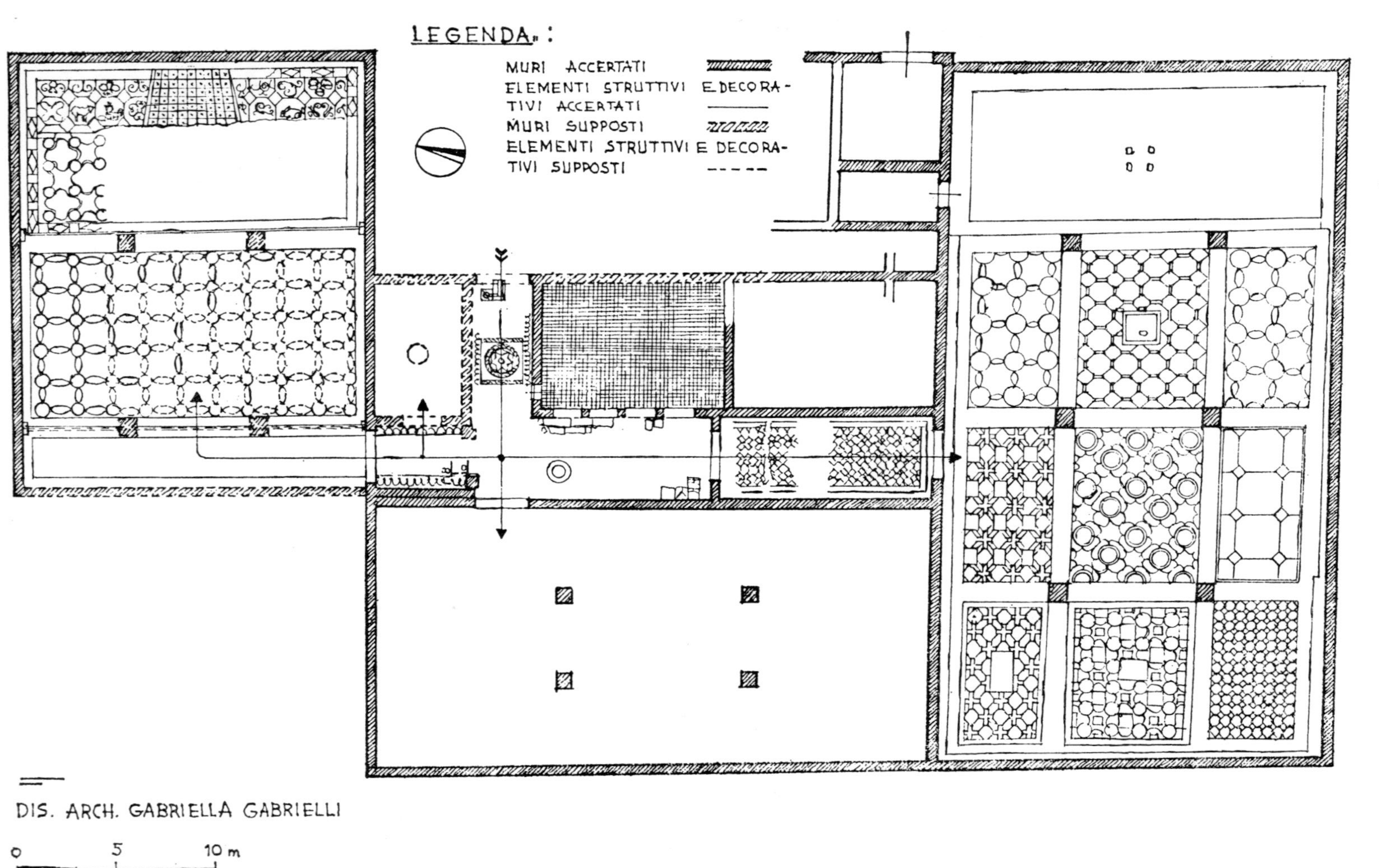

Aquileia : plan of Constantinian Cathedral

showing the offering of bread and wine. The walls were decorated with landscape paintings of no particularly Christian significance. The smaller northern hall has a similar enclosure at the east end, within which a central panel of mosaic with crosses stands out against the elaborate and opulent geometrical and animal pattern; it was probably covered with a rich carpet on which the episcopal chair would be placed during the liturgy. The part corresponding to the position of the altar in the southern hall lies within the area of the campanile.

It has been shewn that the eastern part of the north hall is the oldest part of the complex and argued that it represents the pre-Theodoran church of the third century; on style the mosaics could be as early as the third quarter of the century. The existence of such an oratory serving the Christian community of that date may be deduced from the inscription *Theodore felix Theodore hic crevisti* found in a later part of the pavement. A room containing the font has been postulated in the area beneath the campanile, but there seems no reason why it should not have stood in the west hall as in the following stage. The significance of the halls in the full Constantinian plan may be accepted, reading from north through west to south, as catachumeneum, consignatorium and basilica.

The later fourth century saw the enlargement of the north hall to more than double its size, the installation (or renewal) of a font in the west hall and the provision of a narthex connecting all three halls. In the later fifth century the south hall was in turn enlarged and the badly damaged north hall abandoned. A baptistery was built west of the great church and on its axial line. This stage represents the final triumph of Christianity when the need for a large catachumeneum had passed.

Two points should be stressed. There is no trace of an apse, a feature in church planning that only became common in this region in the sixth century. The decoration of the Constantinian and later fourth-century churches, though rich in Christian associations and definitely Christian as regards the inscriptions, contains little that need offend the pagan. The Eucharistic panel with the victory as celebrant forms the best illustration of this.

The rectangular plan of the churches at Aquileia and the absence of an apse have been stressed. This plan predominates in the region influenced by the city. The church in the lands that are now Austria and Slovenia was poor and its buildings simple. The church at Lauriacum (Lorch) is (p. 28) an example;[21] it dates from *c.* 400 or rather later. The simple rectangular hall is divided by a balustrade and the 'eastern' part has a semi-circular bench or synthronon serving as a seat for the clergy – at Aquileia movable chairs used for the same purpose must be assumed. This synthronon becomes a more or less constant feature in the churches of the late fourth and fifth centuries in this area. Later, following the southern fashion the synthronon will move into the apse, when this architectural form is adopted. A second example, approximately contemporary, may be noted at Aguntum.[22] There is no essential difference, but the example is of

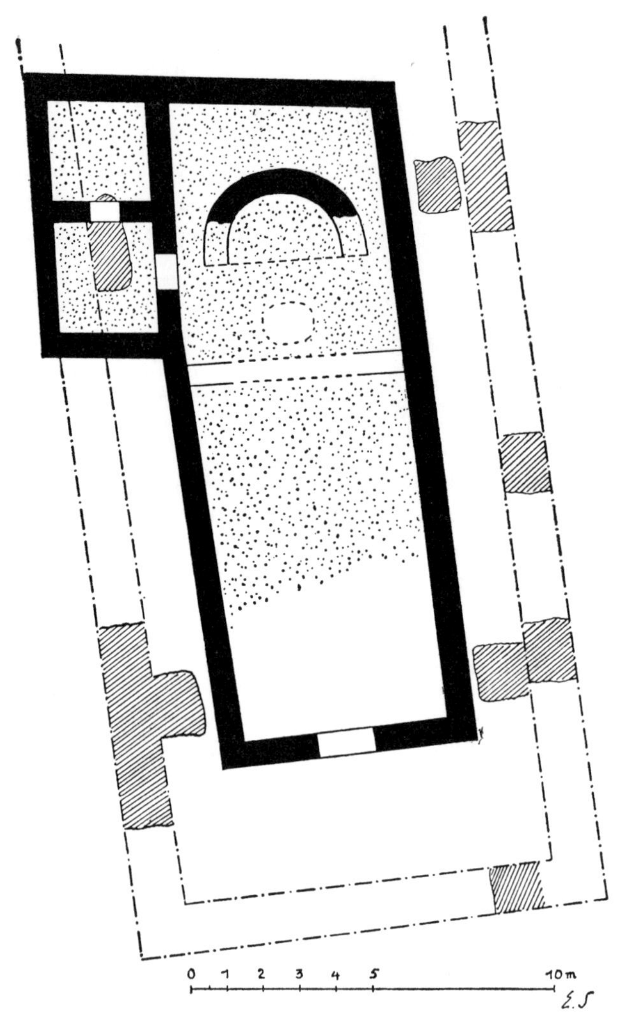

Lorch, Upper Austria : Christian church (late 4th or 5th century)

some interest. The churches already discussed have all been congregational halls designed for the liturgy, above all for the celebration of the Eucharist. Aguntum was, in origin, a cemetery church, a memoria, behind which lay a different architectural and liturgical tradition. It is only late in the fourth century that the two traditions begin to fuse in Rome and the great cities. The provinces adopted the same ideas at an even later date and Aguntum is an early example.

The cathedral at Lavant (p. 29) in Tyrol[23] follows the same tradition. It dates from the fifth century and is larger than the churches at Lauriacum and Aguntum. Behind the synthronon is a large chapel with its own synthronon, probably the place in which the clerical body celebrated its private liturgy. At

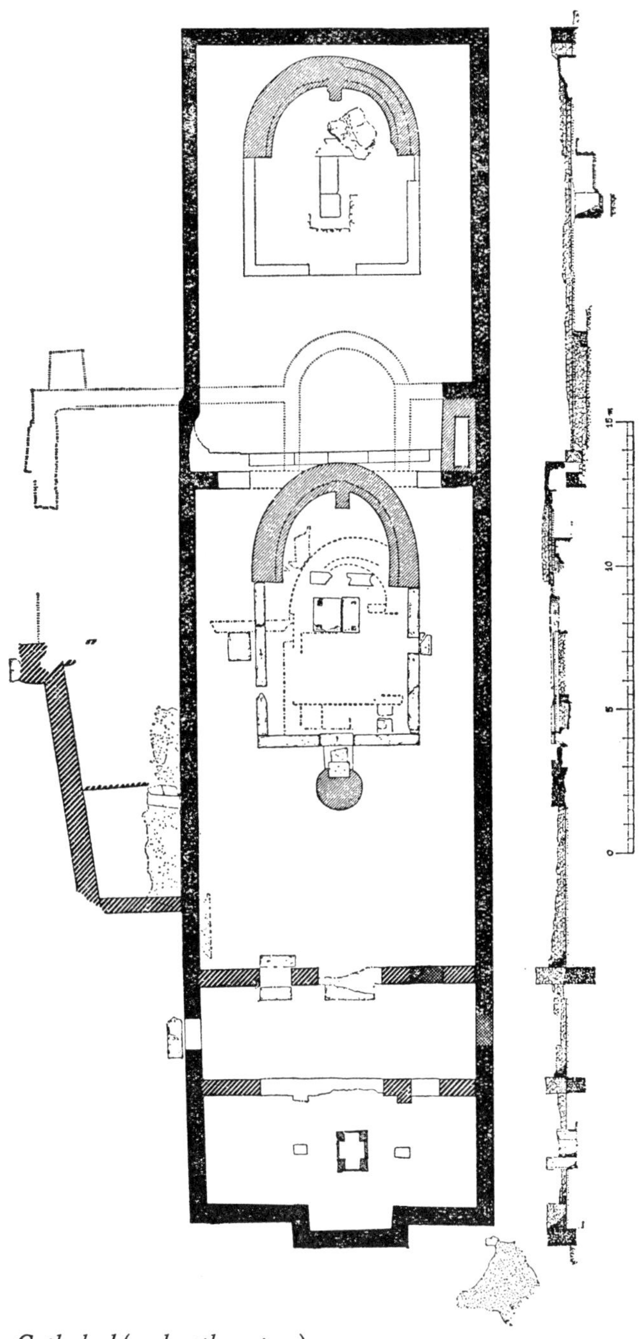

Lavant, Tyrol: Cathedral (early 5th century)

the 'west' end and separated from the church by a vestibule is the baptistery with a small font. The complex of two churches with a baptistery on the

Hemmaburg[24] illustrates both traditions. The whole complex is dated to the first half of the fifth century. But the general layout and the more conspicuous

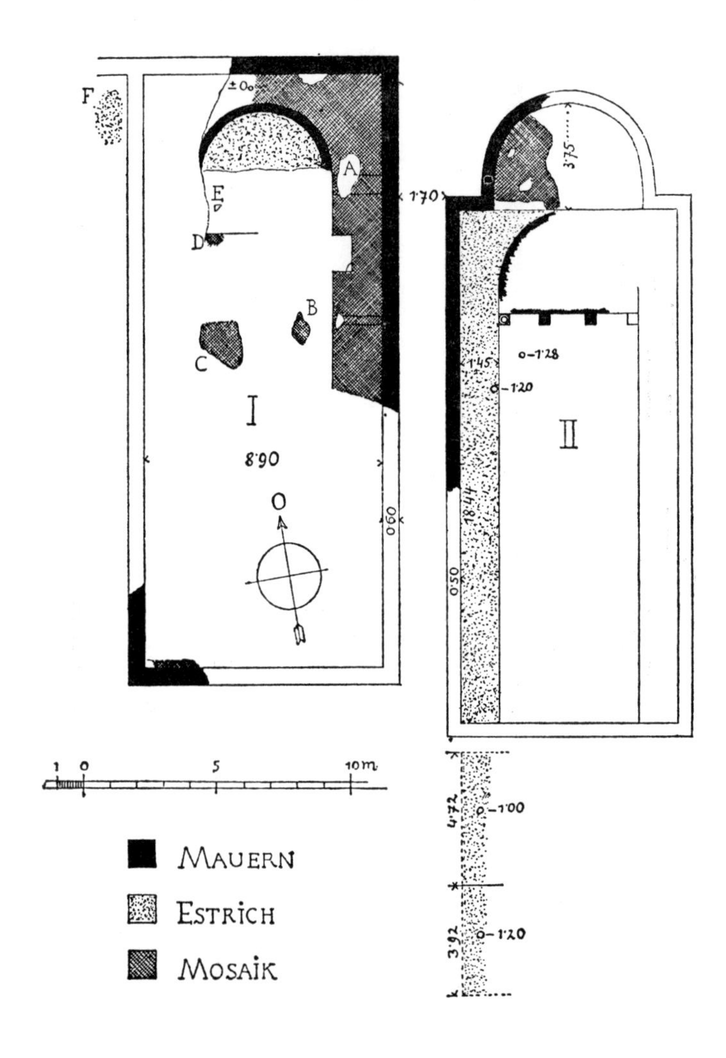

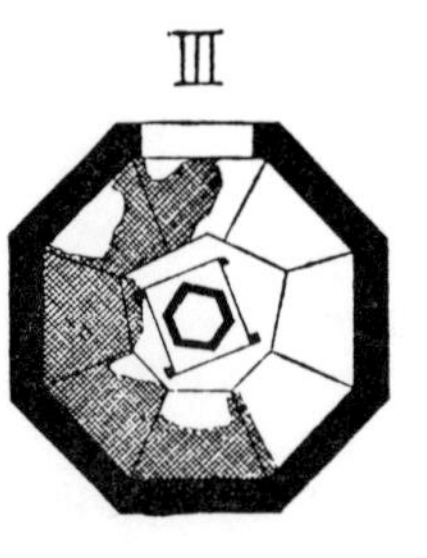

Hemmaberg, Carinthia : churches and baptistery (probably late 4th and 5th century)

survival of good classical traditions in the rectangular hall suggest that this is the earlier element in the complex.

The evidence from the Rhineland falls into the same pattern. At Trier – in the fourth century Augusta Trevirorum, an Imperial capital – there has been recovered beneath the medieval cathedral and the adjacent Liebfrauenkirche the plan of two great parallel halls with associated rooms.[25] The complex, which is on a larger scale than the contemporary cathedral at Aquileia, dates from the second quarter of the fourth century, probably from the decade 340–50. Late in the same century a massive tower-like structure was erected at the east end of the northern hall. This structure, which still stands to eaves level, was probably intended to house a memoria for relics.

A number of lesser churches are also recorded from the Rhineland and the upper Danube. The rectangular hall at Abodiacum (the Lorenzberg by Epfach)[26] may serve as an example. These buildings seldom show markedly Christian characteristics. Their function as churches is established either by a continuous Christian tradition or by their association with inscriptions or other objects, which seldom date before 400.

The second type of Christian centre – the memoria or martyrium – was from very early times associated with the cult of the martyrs. It arose primarily in the cemeteries, above the grave of the individual martyr, though orthodox practice allowed the erection of memoriae at other places; *e.g.*, at the place of the actual passion. The normal connection between the grave and the memoria meant that these cult centres lay outside the cities of the Roman world and therefore in places ill suited for congregational worship. The practice of recurrent commemorations of the dead was not unknown to the pagan world and the adoption of this custom by the Christian communities need cause no surprise. An early and well authenticated example is the simple shrine erected on the Vatican Hill about 170 above the traditional burial place of St Peter. This lay in an enclosed area within the great Roman cemetery.[27] The shrine itself has no marked Christian character and could be paralleled in a number of pagan cemeteries. The fostering of this cult by the Emperor Constantine and the erection of a great basilica ensured that the development of this site would be exceptional and its further history is irrelevant to the present theme.

More illuminating for the problems of Roman Britain are the developments in the Rhineland and other transalpine areas. Topographically two contrasting patterns may be distinguished. At Andernach the late Roman walled settlement survived and the great church of the Middle Ages arose alongside the Frankish villa regalis within the area of this settlement. The establishment of this church goes back to Merovingian days, though there is an even earlier Christian cult centre outside the walls.[28] At Bonn the medieval town grew up round the church which arose above the memoria or martyrium in the cemetery alongside the road outside the fortifications.[29] Xanten (see p. 32) is another example of the second sequence, which is relevant to the problem of Verulamium. The early structures forming these memoriae also have a bearing on developments in Roman Britain; three examples may be noted in brief.

Xanten – the form *ad sanctos* is attested as early as 864 – lies on the west bank of the Rhine, outside the walls of the Roman Colonia Ulpia Traiana;[30] the Roman road running south-east from the city gate crossed the site of the medieval town and the legionary fortress lay about one mile beyond. The collegiate church stands less than 100 yards east of the line of the road, which was here bordered by a small industrial settlement. The earliest burials under and around the church are cremations going back to the third century or even earlier.

The beginnings of Christianity in Xanten[31] are linked with the legendary Theban legion and more particularly with St Viktor, in whose honour the collegiate church is named. Gregory of Tours, writing about 590, mentions an oratory of St Mallosus and adds that his relics were translated after it had been enlarged. He goes on to say that the martyr Viktor is buried there, but that his grave has not yet been recognized.

The cremation cemetery was abandoned and forgotten in the fourth century. Oriented skeletons with and without grave goods were buried and a new cemetery arose on the site of the medieval collegiate church. Its focus was a double coffin of wood containing the bodies of two men aged between 35 and 40, who

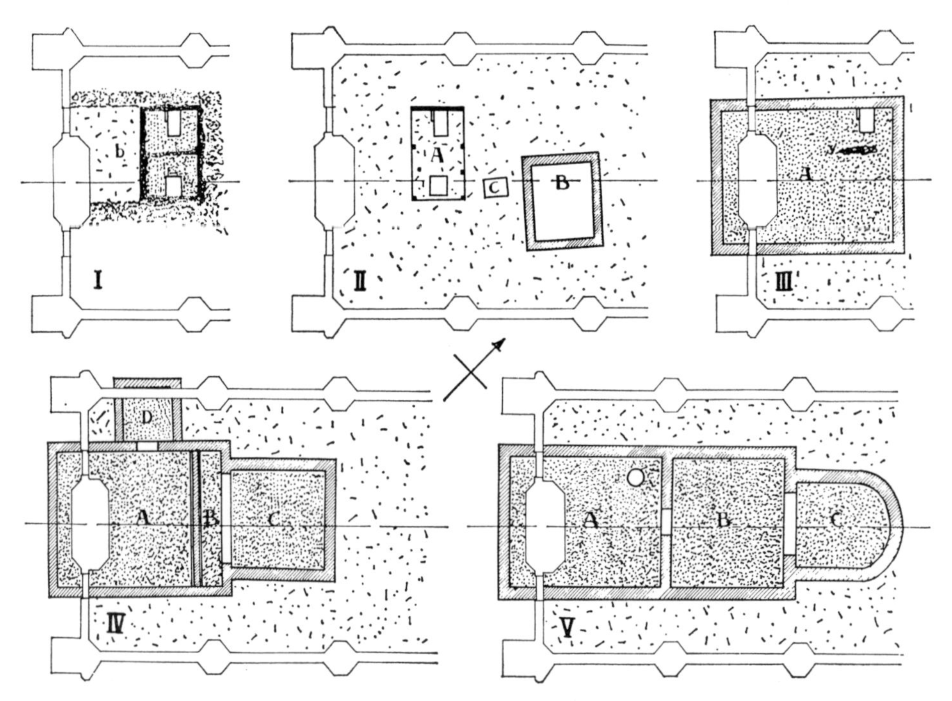

Xanten, Rhineland : succession of memorial chapels (late 4th to late 8th century)

had met a violent death. The burial took place after 348, probably in the years 361–3. The later graves around this focus were oriented and without grave goods. A stone reused to cover one of these graves bore a Christian inscription of *c.* 400. About 385 a small wooden cella with two rooms and a forecourt with a floor of beaten earth was built above the double grave. From the beginning meals were eaten in this area. The cella was burnt about 400 and replaced with an open enclosure of posts having a solid wall on the north side only. Similar structures rose round about, while a Frankish cemetery with rich grave goods developed in the area to the north of the medieval church. The wooden structure was replaced with a larger rectangular oratory of stone before the middle of the fifth century, when Roman administration ceased in the town. Frankish burials of the sixth and seventh centuries are found south of the central area. That the double grave with its cella represents a cult centre connected with Christian martyrs can hardly be doubted. It had throughout the Middle Ages formed the focus of successive churches of St Viktor. The first of these, dating from the eighth century, had a rectangular nave and north porticus with a small square chancel. This was replaced in turn by the Carolingian minster of *c.* 800.

The church and cemetery of St Severin lie outside the walls of Cologne (p. 34) by the road to Bonn.[32] Oriented inhumations without grave goods begin to appear in this cemetery as early as *c.* 160; it is possible that they represent the burials of Christian community, since St Irenaeus records the existence of such communities in lower Germany in the last quarter of the second century. Within this area a small rectangular hall (36 by 30 Roman feet) with a western apse was built early in the fourth century. There was no trace of an altar, but two undisturbed burials lay under the floor of the chord of the apse. They are credibly identified as the Diocletianic martyrs Asclinus and Pamphilius who are commemorated in the Martyrologium Hieronymianum on 30 June. The martyrium is not exactly oriented but set at right angles to the Roman road and subsequent burials follow the same alignment. Aisles and a narthex were added to the hall late in the fourth century, while graves and other memorial structures witness to the continued use of the cemetery. A small tomb chamber inserted into the narthex lay disturbed and empty. It has been convincingly identified as the tomb of St Severin, Bishop of Cologne and a prominent figure in the last years of Roman Cologne. The discovery of his tomb and the subsequent translation of his relics is recorded in 948. The cult centre continued in use after the Frankish conquest, when a small walled court was added at the back of the memoria.

The growth of medieval Bonn round a focus in the Roman cemetery has already been noted (p. 31). The oldest remains beneath the Münster consisted of a small cella with libation tables of the period *c.* 260–300.[33] This formed the focus of a Christian cemetery above which the medieval church developed. Technical reasons prevented the excavation of a possible grave or graves beneath the cella, but tradition records the martyrdom of St Cassius and St Florentius and the cella can credibly be connected with this tradition. The cella was

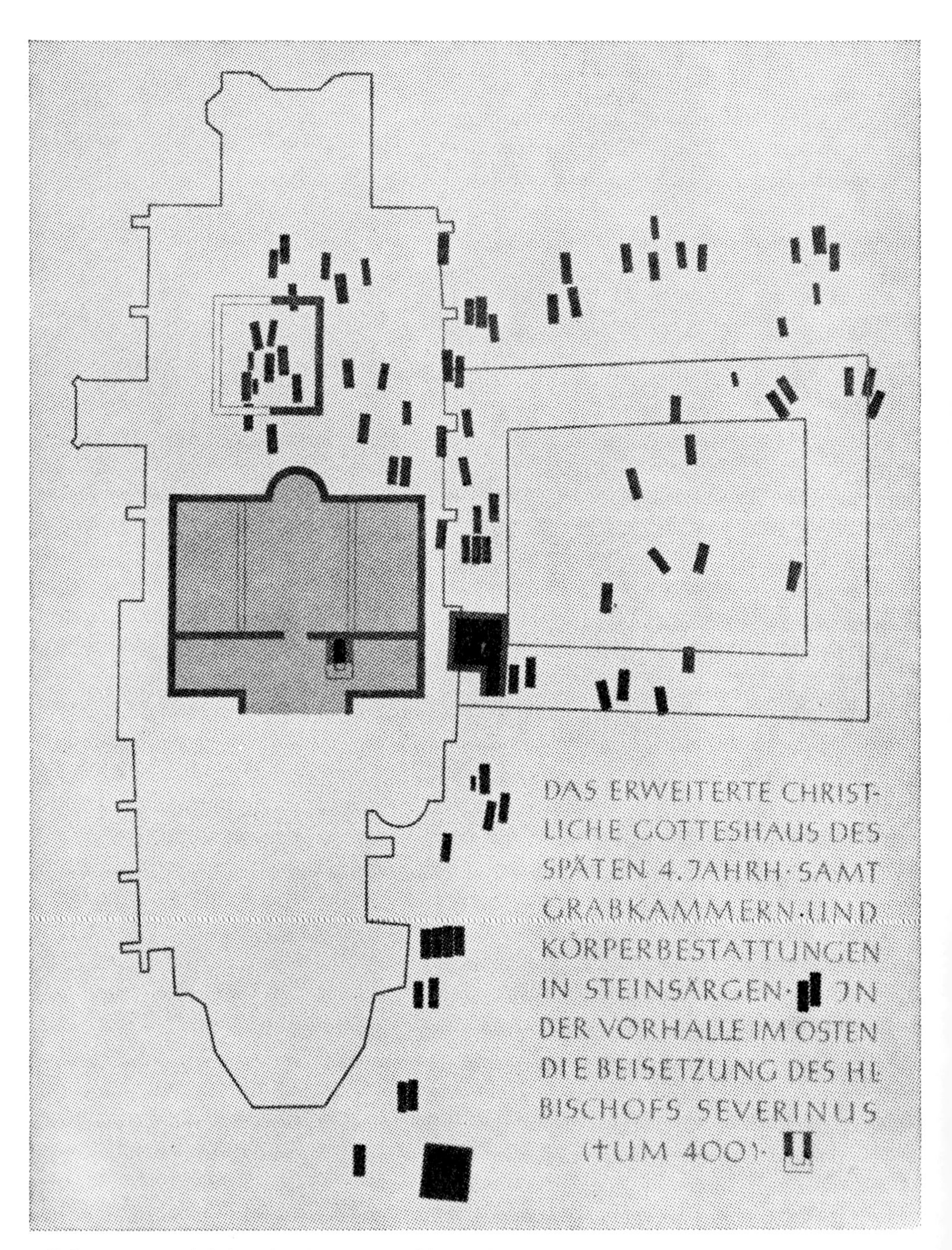

Cologne : memorial chapel and cemetery of late 4th century

enlarged at the end of the fourth century; a basilica is first recorded in 691.

Finally a word should be said about the connection of Christianity with the villas. A Roman villa at Donnersheim in eastern Austria[34] shews no architectural anomaly, but broken fragments of a Christian altar indicate the existence of a Christian community. If the mid-fourth-century date ascribed to the villa really applies to the altar this would imply a church not a memoria. But it is difficult to place this type of altar so early and a considerably later date, probably in the early sixth century, is to be preferred. An earlier connection is attested at Salona where the focus of the cemetery at Monastirine lies in a small suburban villa, in which burials were placed and over which the memoria developed.[35]

Notes

1. The personalities and correspondence are sympathetically summarized in Waddell, H., *The Wandering Scholars* (London, 1927, 7th ed. 1934), 1–12. For the passages quoted see D. Magni Ausonii, *epistula* xxv, 131–2 (*MGH*, Auct Ant, V, ii, 190–4) and Paulini Nolani episcopi, *carmen* X, 22–3 and 288–9 (*CSEL*, XXX, ii, 1894, 26–9)
2. Eusebii, *HE*, V, I
3. Friedrich, H., 'Die Anfänge des Christentums and die ersten Kirchengründungen in römischen Niederlassungen im Gebiet des Nieder und Mittelrheins und der Mosel,' *Bonn Jahrb*, 131 (1926), 10–113
4. Sulpicii Severi, *Vita sancti Martini*, capp. 13–5 (*CSEL*, I, 1866, 122–5); Jullian, C., *Histoire de la Gaule*, (Paris, 1926), VII, 264–73
5. Hopkins, C. 'The Christian Church,' in *The Excavations at Doura-Europos; Preliminary Report of the Fifth Season of Work October* 1931 *March* 1932 edited by Rostovtzeff, M.I. (Newhaven, 1934) 238–89
6. Canon 36 of Council of Elvira (*c.* 300) in von Hefele, C. J., *Conciliengeschichte*, (Freiburg im Breisgau, 1855, 2nd ed. 1873), I, 170
7. Caecilii Cypriani, *epistula* LXVII (*CSEL*, III, 1868, 735–43)
8. Prudentii, *Peristephanon Hymnus* III, 186–215 (*CSEL*, LXI, 1926, 324–5)
9. *Catálogo Monumental de España: Badajoz* 1907–10, II, (Madrid, 1926), no. 2001
10. *Ibid.*, I (Madrid 1925), no. 753; Ramón Melida, J. 'Una Casa romana cristiana' in Junta superior de Excavaciones: *Memoria* no. 12 (Madrid, 1917)
11. *Acta Sanctorum*: Novembris, I (Paris, 1887), 326 (de vitis Patrum Emeritensium, cap. VIII)
12. *Forschungen in Salona* (Vienna, 1914), i, 100 sqq.; Dyggve, E. *History of Salonitan Christianity* (Oslo 1951), 29–30
13. *Corpus Juris civilis*, I, 123 (ed. Kraeger, II, 65)
14. Junyent, E., *Il Titolo di San Clemente in Roma* (Rome, 1932), 115–21 (*Studi di Antichità cristiana*, VI)
15. Vieillard, R., 'Les Origines du Titre de Saint Martin aux Monts à Rome' (Rome 1928), *Studi di Antichità cristiana*, IV)
16. Junyent, E., *Il Titolo di S. Clemente*, 131–40
17. Junyent, E., *ibid.*, 35–81
18. Latini Pacati Drepanii Panegyricus Theodosio Augusto dicatus, cap. XXXVII in Baehrens, A., *XII Panegyrici Latini* (Leipsic, 1874), 305: among those greeting Theodosius were: *reverendos municipali purpura flamines, insignes apicibus sacerdotes*

Notes

19. *Vita S. Ambrosii a Paulino . . . conscripta*, cap. LII (*PL*, 14, 44)
20. Brusin, G. and Zovatto, P. L. *Monumenti paleocristiani di Aquileia e di Grado* (Udine, 1957), especially plans II–VII
21. Noll, R., *Frühes Christentum in Oesterreich* (Vienna, 1954), 82–5
22. Noll, R., *ibid.*, 91–2
23. Noll, R., *ibid.*, 92–5
24. Noll, R., *ibid.*, 108–12
25. *Neue Ausgrabungen in Deutschland*, ed. W. Krämer (Berlin, 1958), 368–79
26. *Ibid.*, 409–24
27. Kirschbaum, E., *The Tombs of St Peter and St Paul* (London, 1959), 63–94
28. Friedrich, H., *ut supra* n. 3, *Bonn Jahrb*, 131 (1926), 107
29. Lehner, H., and Bader, W., 'Baugeschichtlicher Untersuchungen am Bonner Münster,' *Bonn Jahrb.*, 136–7, i (1932)
30. *Sechszehnhundert Jahre Xantener Dom*, ed. W. Bader (Cologne, 1964), 99
31. *Ibid.*, 65–84
32. *Neue Ausgrabungen in Deutschland*, 329–39
33. Lehner, H., and Bader, W., *ut supra*, n. 29, *Bonn Jahrb*, 136–7 (1932), 38–45 and 192–206
34. Noll, R. *Frühes Christentum in Oesterreich*, 73–5
35. *Forschungen in Salona* (Vienna, 1926), II, 9–11 and 40–2

The Christianization of Roman Britain

W. H. C. Frend

The stages by which the Greco-Roman world became Christian still provide an important field for research. Since Harnack and Deissmann first opened up the subject at the beginning of the century much work has been done. The researches, notably of the late Professor A. D. Nock, have illustrated how religions spread from one end of the Mediterranean to the other, conveyed by families of traders who took their gods with them to their new homes, by soldiers, travellers and even slaves.[1] Thus Mithraism spread along the trade routes and military frontiers of the Empire in the late second and early third century, a world-religion in the making, that left the same characteristic shrines and symbols on the Wall and in London as at Dura-Europos on the Euphrates frontier.[2] This was the route taken also by the cults of Isis, Serapis and Jupiter Dolichenus. Religious movement, however, was mainly a movement from the east, the far northwestern provinces of the Empire being affected last and perhaps least.

The spread of Christianity was aided by the same means, but with the powerful addition of the influence of the Jewish settlements. In the second century wherever these were located the traveller would, like as not, encounter the Christians. The latter were often regarded as a dissident sect of Jews[3] though repudiated by these and feared and hated by the populace.

In the West, apart from Rome and some of the larger towns in north Africa, there were few Jewish centres, and consequently few Christian centres in the first two centuries. The churches at Lyons and Vienne on the main trade routes leading northwards from Marseille seem to have been exceptional, and most of their members appear to have belonged to immigrant trading groups from Asia Minor.[4] To these Christians the ordinary native provincials were 'wild and barbarous tribes' with whom they had little dealing.[5] Even in the next century when the Church was making great strides in the East, a foreign, Greek-speaking element seems to have played a considerable role in establishing Christianity in western towns. Occasionally, as at Aquileia where the earliest church was built within a stone's throw of a large synagogue, association with Judaism may also have assisted the process.[6] In Britain the earliest references to Christianity found in Tertullian *c.* 200 and Origen *c.* 240 may be derived from travellers' tales. 'The parts of the island inaccessible to Rome have been subjected to Christ'[7] has the sound of an exaggerated story circulated among the Christians of Carthage by some returning merchant. The name Aaron,[8] however, as one of the two confessors allegedly martyred at Caerleon also suggests a Jewish influence on the mission to these islands. But Origen's suggestion *c.* 240 that 'Christianity was a unifying force among the Britons' could have had little basis in fact.[9] Christianity in Britain was not in the first place an indigenous movement.

The first tangible evidence for Christianity in Britain may well be the traditions surrounding the martyrdom of the soldier Alban at Verulamium. Alban's death is attested in four independent sources, namely his *Acta Martyrum*, the *De Excidio Britanniae* of Gildas, the *Vita Germani*[10] of Constantius, written in Gaul *c.* 475, and a reference in the sixth-century Gallic poet, Venantius Fortunatus.[11] If the last two entries are too late to carry conviction, the *Acta* have the merit of showing detailed knowledge of the topography of Verulamium, and must be taken seriously. The cult of Alban can also be traced back at least to 429. The martyrdom however can hardly have occurred as Bede suggests[12] in the Great Persecution under Diocletian and his associates (303–12), for contemporaries were unanimous that Constantius I in whose dominions Britain lay, took practically no part in the persecution.[13] Levison's tentative arguments in favour of the period Decius–Valerian (250–60) are not supported by anything much more tangible than inherent probability. Recently, Dr John Morris has pointed to the description in the *Acta* of Alban's judge as 'Caesar' in the earliest MS. This could be merely fantasy on the part of the author designed to increase the importance of the martyr in the eyes of his readers, but it could also refer to Geta Caesar who in 208–9 was left as the governor of the civil province of Britain while his father Septimius Severus and his elder brother Caracalla were campaigning against the Picts. The view that a governor might order the cessation of persecution on the ground that it was simply aiding the spread of Christianity could correspond to an early-third century situation when 'the blood of martyrs' was 'seed', and when the lot of the Christians was very much at the mercy of individual governors.[14] We would be wise however to admit with Levison, '*ignoramus* and *ignorabimus*.'[15]

The third century is almost a blank in the story of the Church in Britain. By 312, however, the date of Constantine's victory of Maxentius, organized Christianity in Britain was represented by three bishoprics at York, London and perhaps Colchester, of which the last-named, whose bishop was accompanied to the Council of Arles in 314 by a priest and deacon, may have been the senior.[16] Elsewhere, Cirencester (Corinium) is the only town to have produced evidence for Christianity at this period, for as Sheppard Frere points out the famous word-square (*Rotas opera tenet arepo sator*) now known to be a Christian cryptogram, is incised on wall-plaster which to judge by its technical quality is of third- or even second-century date.[17] Christianity in Britain, however, seems if anything to have been less advanced than elsewhere in the Celtic provinces[18] and no more significant at this stage than other mystery cults brought in from the East.

The situation does not appear to have changed much in the first half of the fourth century. During his stay in the West in 341–6, Athanasius preserves vivid recollections of large new churches being built in Aquileia and Trier to accommodate increasing numbers of Christians.[19] There is no evidence as yet of this happening in Britain. Where the British bishops took part in the general affairs of the Church they acted in concert with the other Westerners. Athanasius lists Britain among those provinces that accepted the decrees of the Council of Nicaea in 325[20] and supported the demand of the Western bishops at the Council of Serdica, 342–3, for his acquittal.[21] At the Council of Ariminum in 359 the Britons were still pro-Nicene and resisted the attempt of the Constantius II to impose a compromise-Arian formula on the West. Though, at the time, the acceptance by three of their number of the emperor's offer to pay their way home out of the Imperial treasury aroused resentment, it was conceded a generation later that the poverty that they pleaded may have been real.[22] Though the context indicates that there were other British bishops who refused Constantius' offer, the incident does perhaps reflect the depressed situation of the Church in what was generally regarded as a very wealthy island.[23]

In contrast, however, there is little doubt that the Constantinian era was a flourishing one for paganism of all types in Britain – except perhaps for Mithraism on the Wall. In an article published twelve years ago, I suggested how this was the case, and the many discoveries and excavation of temple sites since that time have tended to confirm this view.[24] Lewis' survey of Romano–Celtic temples suggests that very few of these are known to have fallen into disuse before the fourth century except where one site seems deliberately to have been replaced by another.[25] Equally rare are cases of disuse during the first half of the fourth century. Where evidence is available it would seem that in this period existing temples were extended and new temples built, and built well in stone and brick. At Brean Down in Somerset, for instance, the temple shows two periods of building, both Constantinian.[26] Those at Worth in Kent,[27] and Pagan's Hill in Somerset, also indicate a good deal of modification and enlargement after the death of Constantine.[28] Though Constans in 341[29] and his brother Constantius in 357[30] might order the closure of all shrines, their words fell on deaf ears in the Romano–British countryside.

The pagan reaction under Julian 361–3 was followed by fourteen years of religious toleration under Valentinian I. The latter, though himself a Catholic Christian, was disposed to allow all religions except Manichaeism free rein. His views were eloquently summed up in a statement he is supposed to have made to a semi-Arian council at Lampsacus in 364, 'I am a layman and should not interfere in such matters [details of the Faith]. Let the priests, whose concern these things are, assemble where they please.'[31] They might, but they could not call on the assistance of the state in suppressing pagan worship. It is against this background that one may visualize the construction of the great pagan health and cult centre at Lydney sometime after 364, apparently with some form of official aid,[32] and the continuing prosperity of long-standing centres of pagan cults and custom such as the temple and fairground at Woodeaton,[33] the similar site at Frilford,[34] and the temples at Yatton[35] and Pagan's Hill[36] in Somerset or Harlow in Essex.[37]

However, at this stage changes in the religious picture of Roman Britain in favour of Christianity were beginning to show themselves. First, let us take the military zone, and particularly the Wall. In the third century Mithraism, though depending perhaps to some extent on the personal preference of some individual commanding officers,[38] and local cults held sway. The number of dedications by legionaries from overseas and their officers show how great was the reliance placed on the local gods of health and the chase at this period. Then came the great Pictish invasion of 297, and thereafter the 58 known temples in the vicinity of the Wall show an astonishingly lame-duck existence. Only Coventina's Well continued to attract offerings down to the end of the fourth century. A bare 200 yards away a Mithraeum had been sacked and not re-built some 50 years before.[39] It would seem a reasonable supposition that the advance of Christianity was a cause of this decline of interest. Ever since he ordered his troops to inscribe the Chi-Rho on their shields before the battle of the Milvian Bridge, Constantine had favoured Christianity in the Roman Army. Even pagan troops were obliged to recite a prayer to the *summus deus*.[40] His policy was continued by his successors, except Julian, and its effectiveness may be illustrated perhaps by the fact that Jovian and Valentinian, both Westerners and officers in Julian's army, were nonetheless devotedly Christian. Later, Magnus Maximus, the commander on the Wall to 383, was a fanatical upholder of Nicene orthodoxy and the last usurper whom Britain provided, Constantine III, was also a Christian.[41] If therefore the impact of Christianity was to be felt anywhere in Britain in the fourth century one would expect it on the Wall and at other military sites, such as Richborough or Caernarvon (Segontium), and at Richborough two Romano-Celtic temples near the fort seem deliberately to have been destroyed in about the middle of the fourth century.[42] The treatment of the fine examples of pagan statuary at Corbridge where they formed the bedding for a military road built *c.* 369[43] is paralleled in other parts of the Empire where Christians asserted themselves. At Gaza, for instance, this was one of the ways in which a Christianized population demonstrated its rejection of the past.[44] On the other hand, no churches have yet been discovered in the Wall area, though the Christian graves at York and the existence of a bishopric there[45] provide positive evidence for Christianity in the northern centres of military occupation.

In two other sides of Romano-British life the Church was making ground, namely in the cantonal towns and among the villa-owning aristocracy. It is noticeable that a number of town temples seem to have enjoyed a shorter life than those in the countryside.[46] Of the five discovered in and around Colchester, one only (Colchester 2) has provided tangible evidence of use after *c.* 350, and comparatively early abandonment seems to be true of the three temples at Caister by Norwich.[47] In London it can fairly be argued that the threat of trouble which caused the Mithraists on the Walbrook site to bury their treasures came from the Christians,[48] and evidence, though scattered, for the existence of the latter in the towns now begins to increase. At Corinium (Cirencester), where the Sator–Arepo graffito came from, as Toynbee has pointed out with justice, one may infer the strength of Christianity in the town by 360 from the fact that as part of the aftermath of the pagan revival under Julian, the *praeses* and *rector* of *Britannia prima*, L. Septimius, restored there a column dedicated to Jupiter and referring to the *prisca religio* – the old (or pagan) religion.[49] At Silchester, the church which recently has been re-examined occupies a prominent position immediately southeast of the forum with streets on three sides. It was not an impressive building, its overall length of 42 feet comparing poorly with urban churches in other parts of the West. There was a rough, tesselated floor in the narthex, and a finer mosaic with a black and white chequer pattern placed centrally in the apse. The remainder was probably covered with boards or paving-stones. The apse was flanked with two transepts. The date at which this building was erected can hardly be earlier than *c.* 360 to judge by a somewhat worn coin of FEL. TEMP. REPARATIO type (minted therefore between 348 and 353) found in the floor-mortar underlying the nave.[50] From Bede one learns also of the existence of a number of churches in and around Canterbury which Augustine and his monks repaired and re-used when they landed in England in 597.[51] Perhaps a fragment of evidence pointing to the spread of Christianity among the urban poor is a Chi on a late sherd of coarse black pottery from Exeter,[52] and a similar find has been made at Verulamium.[53] It must be admitted, however, the archaeological harvest from the well-excavated Romano–British town-sites accords with the literary evidence that points to the poverty of the new religion even in the towns of Roman Britain during the fourth century.

Romano–Celtic paganism was still an active force. In Silchester and Verulamium, to name two sites where excavations have been thorough enough for conclusions to be arrived at, Christians and pagans co-existed for another generation at least. The two Silchester temples seem to have been in use *c.* 370,[54] while the large temple associated with the theatre on Insula xvi at Verulamium seems to have been re-furbished as late as 400.[55] At Bath also, the temple of Aquae Sulis and the baths seem to continue in use until the second half of the fourth century.[56] One does not want to over-draw the picture and co-existence is probably the right term, for, at Verulamium, indications point to the rise of a Christian area around the shrine of Alban on the hill south of the Roman city, just as at Cologne, or Bonn, or Salona, new Christian settlements developed in the fifth and following centuries independent of the former pagan town. At Verulamium, and perhaps elsewhere, this settlement may have provided a tenuous link with the medieval town.

A number of Roman villas provide evidence for Christianity in the fourth century. To the chapel at Lullingstone, brought into use as a Christian centre perhaps *c.* 360[57] one must add now the mosaic from the northwest room of the large villa at Hinton St Mary.[58] There would seem to be little doubt that the splendid head of the fair-haired and clean-shaven man with a Chi-Rho monogram behind his head is Christian, and may even represent Christ himself. A young figure representing Christ either in the form of the Good Shepherd or as a young man with radiant countenance carrying a baton has been found in north Africa.[59] The Hinton St Mary and Frampton mosaics, to which may be added some of the Orpheus mosaics, from great houses like Woodchester or Horkstow, the Mildenhall treasure, as well as the large and costly lead water tanks found near villa sites in southern and eastern England bring us face to face with an educated and wealthy Christianized society which was making its presence felt in the Romano-British countryside in the second half of the fourth century.[60]

It is difficult, however, to say how far the influence of these wealthy Christian families extended among the rural population as a whole. Some of the Romano-Celtic temples show a marked diminution of activity after the reign of Valentinian I (*ob.* 375). The Brean Down temple, for instance, built only *c.* 340, seems to have gone out of use by *c.* 370. The interior was ransacked and a smelting furnace was constructed in the north annexe.[61] The temple complex at Springhead in Kent which had gradually developed over the years, reaching a maximum use in the early fourth century, was also declining.[62] Their excavator considers that coin deposits in Temple v of Valentinian I had been the gift of an adherent when the temple itself was already in ruins.[63] A smithy had been established in the remains. At Jordan Hill near Weymouth the last phase of the temple probably as late as the fifth century may also have been domestic.[64] The shrine seems to have ceased to be used as such. Other sites, however, such as those already mentioned at Frilford, Woodeaton, Bourton Grounds, Farley Heath and Pagan's Hill enjoyed a long life into the fifth century,[65] while that at Maiden Castle was not built until the reign of Theodosius and seems to have enjoyed the support of wealthy patrons half a century later to judge by the gold coins of Honorius (395–423) found on its site.[66] Altogether, the evidence does not lead to any clear-cut conclusions. Temples were obviously not immune from the general decline in material standards that set in at the end of the fourth century, though it is worth remembering that the last phase of the church at Silchester was also one of slow decay under squatter occupation.

At the end of the fourth century religion in Roman Britain was developing on similar lines to that prevailing in the other Celtic provinces. Christianity was established with episcopal government in the towns. The armies and their leaders were Christian, and some of the wealthy families on the land were also Christian or at least favourable to the new faith. Britain, moreover, was fully part of the Latin-Western tradition. This was not merely a matter of following episcopal colleagues at councils and adopting a common episcopal organization. One of the most interesting features of the Lullingstone wall paintings is how the roofed colonnade with the human figure standing between the columns resembles other examples of Christian art in the West. The figures face front and have their arms outstretched in prayer. They wear rich flowing tunics with pearl-edged stripes and roundels woven into or embroidered on the long sleeves, characteristic of the nobility, even the Roman nobility, of the fourth century.[67] Two of the figures that have been preserved have the wide, deep-set eyes (as does the head at Hinton St Mary's) which one associates with late-Roman artistic traditions. The *Orante* attitude, too, is typical of catacomb and sarcophagus art of this period. The mosaic at Hinton St Mary also invites continental parallels of the youthful Christ, while the curious panel of figures on the Walesby cistern, standing in their short tunics and cloaks suggests similarities with groups of figures on Gallic sarcophagi of the fourth or early fifth centuries.[68]

At the same time the persistence of rural paganism may be paralleled by what is known from literary and archaeological sources of the remainder of the West, except north Africa. The Rhineland temple and settlement at Pesch also seems to have been extended in the Constantinian era and to have continued in use until the first quarter of the fifth century with a coin series including Honorius.[69] In the Danube provinces, Rudolf Egger describing his excavations of the temple to Latobius in the Lavental (Austria) gives as his view that while the towns of the province were being Christianized in the fourth century, the countryside remained firmly pagan.[70] The resistance of the dwellers in the Alpine passes to the efforts of Bishop Vigilius of Trent and his clergy to send missionaries among them may not have been untypical,[71] for 70 years later in 460 Maximus, Bishop of Turin still describes the surrounding countryside as pagan.[72] There were many pagan survivals even in sixth-century Gaul.[73] Britain was not alone in the West in giving Christianity what Gildas describes as a 'tepid reception.'[74]

The turning-point in favour of Christianity in northern Gaul and perhaps in Britain too was brought about by the mission of Martin of Tours. This intrepid man, who had once been a soldier, then a hermit, and who as bishop was to voice his disapproval at Magnus Maximus' judicial murder of the eccentric Christian Priscillian, was not to be daunted by the age-old paganism of northern Gaul. His mission, documented admirably by his biographer, Sulpicius Severus, was as vigorous as it was effective.[75] Neither threats nor assaults nor imprecations could deter the saint, and the destruction of major shrines such as Bibracte in the territory of the Aedui is perhaps confirmed by the sudden ending of some of the coin series of Norman temple sites with Magnus Maximus (383-8). In the decade following Martin, his disciple Victricius, another former soldier, who was Bishop of Rouen, continued harrying the remains of paganism along the Channel coast.[76] By the last years of the century Rouen appears to have been an entirely Christian city, and the remotest parts of the diocese Christianized.[77]

Did Martin's zeal inspire a similar movement in Britain? One can perhaps point to a direct contact in the life and work of Ninian, for it is difficult to disbelieve entirely the tradition preserved in Bede that Ninian was also a disciple of Martin.[78] The finding of early Christian inscriptions, dating in all probability to the fifth century together with the discovery of the Celtic monastery at Whithorn suggests that the tradition of missionary activity among the Picts of Southern Scotland at this time was not ill-founded.[79] If this were the case, it would indicate the emergence of a strongly monastic type of Christianity even though episcopally organized, in some parts of Britain, parallel to that which was now developing in northern Gaul. There is the reference too, to Constans, son of the usurper Constantine III, 407–11 being a monk, whose promotion to Caesar by his father caused horror among orthodox Christians.[80] It is also difficult to regard the dedications to Martin such as existed at Canterbury in 597 as being solely Frankish importations.[81]

In view of the part which Britain was to play in the Pelagian controversy in the first decades of the fifth century one must accept the probability of a fairly rapid expansion of Christianity at least among the lettered classes in the period that saw the withdrawal of the legions. Pelagianism, with its intermingling of Pauline teaching and Roman Stoicism, could only have flourished in an environment in which both had taken root. This is not as improbable as it might seem at first sight. It is generally agreed that Pelagius himself must have had a good education before he left Britain probably soon after 380 to study law in Rome, and a fair level of interest in Latin and Roman culture is attested by fourth-century mosaics from wealthy villas such as Low Ham in Somerset or Lullingstone and especially by the magnificent fresco at Otford in Kent which illustrates part of the *Aeneid*.[82] At Silchester some townsman ended his complaint against the *perfidus campester*, Pertacus, with the opening words of Book ii of the same work (*conticuere omnes*).[83] The glimpse which St Patrick's *Confession* gives of a Christian family proud of its Latin culture, and providing clergy for three generations is perhaps indicative of the existence of scattered but tenacious communities of Christians whose leaders were now to come to the fore.[84] One additional fragment of evidence may be quoted that points to an increased vigour in the Church in Britain at the turn of the fifth century. Victricius of Rouen writing his *De Laude Sanctorum* in 394–5 describes how he had just been sent to Britain at the request of some of his colleagues to settle ecclesiastical disputes.[85] This suggests a certain liveliness in the Church as well as its close links with Christianity in northern Gaul.

Whatever the background, Pelagianism was to be a force in Britain for 30 years or more. Outside south Italy, Britain, as J. N. L. Myres has pointed out, was where Pelagius' notions had their profoundest effect.[86] In south Italy it was attracting the traditional leaders of society, families like that of Bishop Memor near Beneventum or for a moment Paulinus of Nola, who for generations had given an example to their people by wealth and public spirit. Among such as they Pelagius' teaching, with its emphasis on the possibility of human perfectibility through the right use of free-will, found ready response. Despite their new Christian allegiance, their ideal remained the *boni mores Romanorum* which, as

Augustine taught, now belonged to a bygone age. Pelagius awoke in them a sense of challenge against the Gothic invaders and the now predominant but fatalistic theology of north Africa.

In Britain, the astonishing outburst of energy that characterized the few years following the great Germanic invasion of Gaul in 406 may have owed something to Pelagian inspiration.[87] Some background of political and religious thought must be conceded to a situation which the plain, factual historian Zosimus, *c.* 460, regarded as a revolutionary one that first engulfed Britain and then spread to Armorica.[88] 'The Britons,' we are told, 'were living on their own no longer obeying Roman laws,' and that 'fighting for themselves they had freed the cities from the attacking barbarians.' This was a unique display of energy by the provincials of the Western empire in the crises of the first decades of the fifth century, a contrast to the tame surrenders of the Romans to Alaric and the north Africans to the Vandals. Moreover, the cities, which were the hotbeds of Pelagianism, took the lead, and Britain in the person of Gratian II produced the only usurper in the history of the Empire who was described as a *municeps*.[89] It is difficult not to accept Myres' suggestion that Pelagian ideology was somehow involved, but Zosimus' statement does not carry the argument very far.

It is evident, however, that in the next quarter of a century that constitutes the twilight period of Roman Britain, the existing ecclesiastical links with Gaul were maintained, and that Pelagianism continued to flourish among the educated Roman-Britons. We hear from Prosper Tiro of a Pelagian bishop named Severianus whose son, Agricola, was among the leaders of the movement in the 420s.[90] The orthodox opposition found help from Gaul as it had in the time of Victricius, and in 429 the deacon Palladius persuaded the Gallic bishops to send St Germanus, Bishop of Auxerre, to crusade against the heresy. From his *Life* written by Constantius nearly 50 years later we learn that the Pelagians he encountered were among the island's leaders, and for the benefit of one of these he performed a miracle of healing.[91] In Rome too, Pope Celestine angrily denounced 'certain men' in Britain 'who were enemies of grace and had taken possession of the land of their birth,' and he set about their removal.[92] Even if the account of Germanus' second visit to Britain in 447 is a double of the first, there is no doubt about the strength of the intellectual current among the higher ranks of society even at this time. On these grounds alone, the archaeologist would do well to weigh his evidence carefully before suggesting the end of Romano-British urban and villa-culture before the second quarter of the fifth century.

At this period one senses rather than is able to prove that Britain was mainly as Christian a country as northern Gaul had become a generation before. The career of Fastidius, described briefly by Gennadius of Marseille[93] at the end of the century, as *episcopus Britannorum* is not an isolated phenomenon. His letters to Fatalis on 'the Christian Life' and on 'preserving widowhood' may be paralleled by the strong Christian moralism displayed by an anonymous young

Briton who had undertaken 'a perilous journey to Sicily' against his father's wishes and now writes back assuring his father that he would eventually return but urging him to practise in the meantime the Christian virtues, particularly of chastity and continence.[94] If the monastic tradition was not by this time firmly entrenched, the ground was being well-prepared.

Christianization, however, had come too late. Whatever the allegiance of Vortigern,[95] it is clear that the Celtic tribalism that he represented had little sympathy for the intellectual and episcopally organized Christianity that had been consolidating its position in southern Britain in the previous 30 years. Nor, of course, had the rebellious Germanic *foederati* and invading Jutes and Anglo-Saxons. In the subsequent clash of forces Romano-British Christianity and the urban culture that sustained it were among the sufferers. Church organization failed to survive the crisis, and for the first time in four centuries the history of Britain parted company with that of Gaul and the Rhineland. The age of the Celtic saints opens an entirely new chapter.

Notes

1. Nock, A. D., *Conversion*, (Oxford, 1933), Ch. vi
2. See Vermaseren, M. J., *Mithras, the Secret god* (Eng. tr. by T. and V. Megaw, 1963) 30–43, and in general, the exhaustive study by E. and J. R. Harris, *The Oriental Cults in Roman Britain* (Etudes préliminaires aux religions orientales dans l'empire romain 6), (Leiden, 1965)
3. See for instance, Celsus, cited by Origen, *Contra Celsum* ii. 2 and ii. 4
4. Eusebius, *HE* v. 1. See also Ch. i of my *Martyrdom and Persecution in the Early Church* (Oxford, 1965)
5. Eusebius, *HE* v. 1. 57
6. See my 'The Influence of Greek Immigrants on the Spread of Christianity in the West,' *Mullus* (Festschrift Th. Klauser, Stuttgart, 1964), 124–29
7. *Adversus Iudaeos* 7, *Britannorum inaccessa Romanis loca Christo vero subdita.* See Toynbee, J. M. C., 'Christianity in Roman Britain,' *JBAA*, xvi (1953), 1–24
8. Gildas, *De Excidio Britanniae* 10 (31, 20–21). *Aaron et Iulium Legionum urbis* . . . . Bede (*HE*.1.7) makes them both *cives* of their city
9. *Hom. in Ezekiel* iv (*PL* 25. 723)
10. *Vita* 16. (*MGH*, *Merov*, vii, 262)
11. See Levison, W., 'St. Alban and St. Albans,' *Antiquity* xvi (1941), 337 ff., and Morris, J. R., *Transactions of the St. Albans and Herts Architectural and Archaeological Society*, 1967 (forthcoming) also, Stevens, C. E., 'Gildas Sapiens,' *EHR*, LVI (1941), 373
12. *HE*, 1. 7
13. Augustine, *Ep*.88.2 citing a letter from Donatist bishops to Constantine in 313, Lactantius, *De Mortibus Persecutorum*, 15, and Eusebius, *HE* viii, 13, 12
14. As shown by cases quoted by Tertullian in *Ad Scapulam* written in 212–3
15. Levison, W., *op. cit.*, 350
16. Richmond, I. A., *Arch. J.* iii (1947), 67. For a convincing argument that the bishoprics represented three of the metropolitical churches of the four British provinces of the day, Mann, J. G., *Antiquity*, xxxv (1961), 316–20

Notes

17. Frere, S., *Britannia, a history of Roman Britain* (London, 1967), 332. On the Rotas square, see Toynbee, J. M. C., *op. cit.* 3 and pl. i. For its Jewish origin, however, see Meyring, J., *Rev. des Sciences religieuses*, XL (1966), 321–352
18. One indication of the comparative insignificance of Christianity in the Celtic provinces at this time is that Irenaeus the bishop of the important centre of Sirmium on the Danube was described in his *Acta Martyrum* as a young man, whose parents and relatives were pagan. *Acta Sancti Irenaei* iv. 5. (ed. Knopff-Krüger).
19. Athanasius, *Apologia ad Constantium imperatorem* 15 (*PG* 25. 613)
20. *Epistola ad Iovianum imperatorem* 2 (*PG* 26. 816)
21. *Historia Arianorum ad Monachos* 28 (*PG* 25. 725)
22. Sulpicius Severus *Chronicon* (ed. Halm), ii, 41
23. It was the main source of grain supplies for the Rhine army at this time. Ammianus Marcellinus, xviii, 2, and Zosimus, *Hist. Nova* iii, 4, 5
24. 'Religion in Roman Britain in the Fourth Century A.D.' *JBAA*, xviii (1955), 1–19
25. Lewis, M. J. T., *Temples in Roman Britain* (Cambridge, 1966), 143
26. *JRS*, XLIX (1959), 129
27. Klein, W. G., 'Roman Temple at Worth, Kent,' *Ant J*, viii (1926), 76ff.
28. Rahtz, P., *Proc. of Somerset Antiq. and Nat. Hist. Soc.*, xcvi (1951), 112ff.
29. *Cod Theod* (MM), xvi, 10, 2
30. *Ibid.*, xvi, 10, 3
31. Sozomen, *HE*, vi, 6, 2
32. Wheeler, R. E. M., and Wheeler, T. V., *Lydney Park* (Reports of the Research Committee of the Soc. of Antiquaries ix 1932), 29–33 and 103–4
33. The coin evidence, however, suggests a falling-off of interest after Gratian (367–83) though the peak distribution of coins is Constantine-Valentinian I, Goodchild, R. G., and Kirk, J. R., *Oxoniensia* xix (1954), 36
34. Bradford, J. S. P., and Goodchild, R. G., 'Excavations at Frilford,' *Oxoniensia* iv (1939), 32
35. *JRS*, LV (1965), 216
36. Rahtz, P., *op. cit.*, 118
37. Wheeler, R. E. M., 'A Romano-Celtic Temple near Harlow, Essex, and a note on the Type,' *Ant. Journ.* viii (1928), 300–26
38. Briefly but comprehensively described by Lewis, *op. cit.*, 102–7. Mithraism 'started modestly and although the signs are that it grew, it did not grow much' (105)
39. Richmond, I. A., and Gillam, J. P., *AA* 4th Ser. xxix (1951), 39
40. *LRE*, 91
41. Paulus Orosius, *Historia Adv. Paganos*, vii, 40
42. Bushe Fox, J. P., *Richborough*, Third Report, 36
43. Richmond, I. A., 'The Roman Legionaries at Corbridge: their Supply-base, Temples and Religious cults,' *AA* 4th Ser. xxi (1943), 127 ff., and 174–5
44. Paul the Deacon, *Life of Porphyry of Gaza* (ed. and tr. Hill, G. F.) 76. At Cuicul (Djemila) in Mauretania Sitifensis, a large number of dedications to Saturn were used similarly in the fourth century town
45. The *Guardian* of 19 June, 1967 reports the possibility of the Christian character of a building excavated near the Minster
46. Lewis, M. J. T., *op. cit.*, 140–1
47. *Ibid.*, Table 7. Dates of Town Temples

Notes

48. Toynbee, J. M. C., in the *Listener*, 11 November, 1954, 801–3. The Mithraeum however remained in use until the middle of the fourth century or later (information from its excavator, Professor W. F. Grimes). See also Lewis, *op. cit.*, 101
49. *Insc. Lat. Sel.* 3435. Toynbee, *op. cit.*, 3
50. Reported in 'Roman Britain in 1961,' *JRS*, Lii (1962), 185–6. In the excavators' view the *terminus post quem* for the construction is 'at least *A.D.* 360'
51. *HE*, i, 26
52. Fox, A., *Roman Exeter* (1952), 92, pl.Xa
53. My attention was drawn to this sherd by the Department of British and medieval Antiquities at the British Museum
54. Lewis, *op. cit.*, 140
55. Lowther, A. W. G., *Ant. J.*, xvii (1937), 28 ff., and Sheppard Frere, 'Verulamium; three Roman Cities,' *Antiquity*, xxxviii (1964), 110
56. Information from Professor B. W. Cunliffe, who is excavating the site
57. Meates, G. W., *Lullingstone Roman Villa*, London, (1955), Chs. xii-xiv
58. Toynbee, J. M. C., 'A New Roman Mosaic Pavement found in Dorset,' *JRS*, liv (1964), 7–14. For a dating of this mosaic not later than 340–50 see Smith, D. J., 'Three Fourth-Century Schools of Mosaic in Roman Britain,' *La Mosaique Gréco-Romain* (1965), 100–1
59. For instance, in Perpetua's dream, *Passio Perpetuae* 10, 4 (ed Knopf-Krüger). For the possible association of the youthful Christ with Sol see my *Donatist Church* (Oxford, 1952), 103 n. 9, and the mosaic from the cemetery beneath St Peter's, Rome, illustrated in Toynbee, J. M. C., and Ward Perkins, J., *The Shrine of St Peter* (London, 1956), pl. 32
60. Listed in Toynbee 1953, 15 ff.
61. It had a brief but intensive period of occupation between 340 and 370. It was perhaps a victim of the raids of 367–8 and never re-used as a temple. *JRS*, xlviii (1958), 146 and xlix (1959), 129. For the significance of the coin finds, Boon, G. C., 'The Roman Temple at Brean Down and the dating of "minimissimi",' *Numismatic Chronicle*, 7th. Ser. i (1961), 191–7
62. Temple ii, ruined *c.* 360. Penn, W. S., 'Springhead, Temples ii and v,' *Arch. Cant.*, LXXVII (1962), 116. Temple i was destroyed at the same time
63. *Ibid.* 121
64. Drew, C. D., *Transactions of the Dorset Nat. Hist. and Arch. Soc.*, liv (1932), 21
65. Typical perhaps of this trend is P. Rahtz' comment on Pagan's Hill (*op. cit.*, 118). The temple was still in use 'at least to the reign of Arcadius (383–408)' and the condition of some of the late fourth-century coins found there, 'postulate an even longer period, perhaps extending into the fifth century as at Lydney'
66. Wheeler, R. E. M., *Maiden Castle*, Dorset (Reports of the Research Committee of the Society of Antiquaries) xiii (1943), 75
67. See *Toynbee* 1953, 9ff. and my remarks, *op. cit.*; for a description of how the rich dressed in Rome at this period, see Ammianus Marcellinus xiv, 6, 9
68. *JRS*, L (1960), 238–9 and pl. xxvi
69. Lehner, H., 'Der Tempelbezirk der Matronae Vacallinhae bei Pesch'; *Bonn. Jahr.* (1919), 78ff.
70. Rudolf Egger, *Römische Antike und frühes Christentum* (Klagenfurt, 1962), 98
71. Vigilius describes the mission in a letter to Bishop Simplicianus of Milan as 'to a barbarian nation where Christian peace was new.' *PL* 13, 549–52
72. Maximus of Turin, *Sermo* ci, *PL* 57, 734

Notes

73. Examples quoted by H. Leclercq in his art. 'Paganisme,' *Dict. d'Arch. Chrét. et de Liturgie*, xiii, 1, 311–29, and 359
74. *De Excidio* 9 (31, 4); *licet ab incolis tepide suspecta sunt* (*praecepta Christi*)
75. Described by his biographer, Sulpicius Severus, *Vita Sancti Martini* 13–15
76. Paulinus of Nola, *Letter* 18.4 to Victricius, written *c.* 400 (ed. Hartel, 131)
77. Paulinus of Nola, *ibid.*, and Victricius, *De Laude Sanctorum*, 1ff. (*PL* 20. 443)
78. Bede, *HE*, ii.4. See the careful study by N. K. Chadwick, 'St Ninian: A preliminary Study of Sources,' *TDGNAS*, XXVII (1950), 9ff., and Owen Chadwick's remarks in *SEBH*, 181, n.2 stating the case against direct continuity between Martin and sub-Roman Christianity in Britain through men such as Ninian, and Thompson, E. A., 'The Origin of Christianity in Scotland', *Scot Hist Rev*, 37 (1958), 17–22 for a more positive assessment of the evidence
79. Radford, C. A. R., 'Excavations at Whithorn,' *TDGNAS*, XXIV (1955–56), 170ff.
80. Paulus Orosius, *Historia Adversus Paganos*, vii, 40, 7
81. Bede, *HE*, i, 26, says that the church was dedicated 'in the time of the Romans.' For the view however that this was not possible, see Owen Chadwick, *loc. cit.*
82. Cited from S. Frere, *Britannia*, 313–4, and pl. 28b
83. Frere, S., *Britannia*, 312 (note 2) and 314
84. Patrick, *Confession* 1 (*PL* 53. 801), and also 4
85. *De Laude Sanctorum* 1. (*PL* 20. 443–4). Victricius himself may have been by origin a Briton
86. Myres, J. N. L., 'Pelagius and the end of Roman rule in Britain,' *JRS*, L (1960), 21–36, at p. 31. This was also what the contemporary Chronicler Prosper Tiro thought. See the lines in his epigram *In obtrectatorem Augustini*, '*Aut hunc fruge sua aequorei pavere Britanni Aut huic Campano gramine corda tumet*', Prosper, *Epigrammata*, *PL* 51. 151
87. Myres, J. N. L., *op. cit.*, 31ff.
88. Zosimus, *Historia Nova*, vi, 5
89. Paulus Orosius, *Historia adv. Paganos*, vii, 40
90. Prosper Tiro, *Chronicon* ad ann. 429 (*PL* 51. 594)
91. *Vita Sancti Germani* 12. See also Evans, J., 'St Germanus in Britain,' *Arch Cant* LXXX (1965), 175–85
92. Prosper, *Contra Collatorem*, LXI, 2 (*PL* 51. 243)
93. *De Scriptoribus Ecclesiasticis* 56 (*PL* 58. 1094)
94. Cited from *SEBH*, 210–11 and see Morris, J. R., 'Pelagian Literature', *JTS*, N.S. XVI (1966), 37ff.
95. C. A. R. Radford believes that 'heresy was probably the real offence of Vortigern' in the eyes of Gildas and Nennius. *Antiquity*, xxxii (1958), 23. I feel less happy that Pelagius would have felt anything in common with Vortigern's 'magi' (Nennius, *Historia Brittonum*, 40) and incestuous customs derived apparently from Celtic tradition

Christianity in the Roman Army in Britain

G. R. Watson

Professor J. M. C. Toynbee, in her illuminating study of Christianity in Roman Britain, summarizes as follows: 'The picture painted by archaeology is admittedly, at present, an incomplete and patchy picture, almost wholly civilian in its context. It is, perhaps, only at the forts at Brancaster in Norfolk, Richborough in Kent, and Carrawburgh on Hadrian's Wall that we have any trace of Christian faith in military circles, if we assume, as we reasonably may, that the Mithraeum near the last-mentioned was wrecked by order of a Christian prefect at some date within the early decades of the fourth century.'[1] Dr Frend, in his subsequent paper on Religion in Roman Britain, was concerned with drawing a distinction, not between civilian and military, as Professor Toynbee had done, but between town, fort, and villa on the one hand and the less Romanized countryside on the other.[2] The army, therefore, by implication should have been more Christian than the greater part of Britain. Yet to Professor Toynbee's list Dr Frend could add little.[3] Most recently, the Rev. John Wall has assembled the evidence for Christianity in the northern counties, including for this purpose the whole of Scotland.[4] This included two small finds made at Catterick in 1959, one a Chi-Rho scratched on the external face of the cold plunge bath, and another inscribed on the base of a glass bottle.[5] The real question is, what is the value of the evidence now assembled? For the most part it consists of the monogram Chi-Rho inscribed on masonry, plaster, tableware, or bowls, spoons or jewelry with a VIVAS inscription.[6]

In the case of portable objects little is proved: we know nothing of the attitude with which the owner regarded the object, the means by which it was acquired, or the circumstances in which he lost it. Certainly the six pieces with Christian associations, out of a total of 110 finds, in the Traprain Law treasure, are not evidence for the presence of Christianity in the vicinity of the find-spot.[7] And if this is true in the case of Traprain Law, we cannot be sure, in the absence of other evidence, that it is no less true throughout the military area generally.

We are therefore bound to consider inscriptions on objects which are not easily portable to be of the first importance. At once we think of tombstones, of which four or five have been claimed to be Christian.

The first is *RIB* 1255, found at Risingham (Habitancum). This was believed by Haverfield to contain the otherwise unknown word REHITIA(VIT), which he supposed to be equivalent to REQVIE(VIT), and therefore Christian.

The style of the lettering was held to support an approximate dating to the fourth century. But Wright has now shown that the so-called REHITIA(VIT) is really a consular date of A.D. 278, and should read: inte]re[u]it iṃ[p(eratore) Prob]o it(erum) co(n)s(ule). The Christianity disappears.

The second is *RIB* 955, found at Carlisle:[8] *D. M. Fla(uiu)s Antigon(u)s Papias ciuis Grecus uixit annos plus minus LX quem ad modum accomodatam fatis animam reuocauit Septimia Do*[. . .]. Here the use of the expression *plus minus* may suggest that the inscription is Christian. One may still have doubts, not only in view of the preliminary D.M., but also on account of the curious sequence *accomodatam fatis animam reuocauit*, which is capable of more than one interpretation.[9] But even if this inscription is Christian, its civilian nature is clear from the words *ciuis Grecus*.

The third inscription is *RIB* 787, from Brougham (Brocavum): *D. C. M. Tittus M*[. . .] *uixit ann*[*is pl*]*us minus XXXII M*[. . .] *frater ti*[*t*]*ulum* [*posui*]*t* Here again it is suggested that the use of *plus minus* makes this a Christian tombstone. That may be so, but there is another feature which is perhaps of even greater interest, the abbreviation D C M. Collingwood held that the C must be an error. It is admittedly hard to see what it could represent. But in that case what are we to make of the suggestion sometimes made that Christian tombstones were occasionally bought in pagan workshops with the D M already in place, the rest of the inscription being added *ad hoc*?[10] Was this one custom-built by a pagan, who thought that the insertion of a C into D M would make the sign Christian? In any case there is nothing to show that the deceased had ever been a soldier.

The next stone is *RIB* 1722, from Chesterholm (Vindolanda): *Brigomaglos iacit* [*qui et Brioc*]*us*. This is probably late fifth century, and the fact that it was found only a short distance outside the fort does not necessarily prove a continuation of Christianity during the sub-Roman period: it could equally well represent the effects of missionary work into the area.

Next we may consider *RIB* 1828, found at Carvoran and now at Newcastle:[11] *D. M. Aur. T. f. Aiae d. Salonas Aur. Marcus 7 Obseq(uentis) coniugi sanctissimae quae uixit annis XXXIII sine ulla macula*. The inscription would appear to be third century: the phrase *sine ulla macula*, may, it has been suggested, be an indication of Christianity. On the other hand there are pagan parallels.[12] If this is a Christian inscription it is of the first importance. Unlike the others considered so far, this one is definitely from a military circle.

One other inscription from the military zone has been thought to be both Christian and military. This is *RIB* 690 from York: *D. M. Simpliciae Florentine anime innocentissime que uixit menses decem Felicius Simplex pater fecit leg. VI V*. But, as is clear on the inscription, the legionary title is, to use Mr Wright's own description, 'a secondary cut in rougher lettering,' and is probably no more than a graffito. If so, there need be no military connection at all. The Christianity is in any case dubious: it is dependent on the employment of the phrase *anime innocentissime*, and to this, as Professor Toynbee has pointed out, there are many pagan parallels.[13]

It would appear then, that apart from such portable objects as rings, spoons and tableware, any of which could be, and no doubt were, taken as loot, the evidence for Christianity in the army of Roman Britain depends essentially on a Chi-Rho monogram at Catterick on stone, and a similar one (now lost) at Maryport, apart from the basically negative evidence of the destruction of Mithraea at Housesteads, Carrawburgh, Rudchester, and Caernarvon.[14] What the monograms prove it is difficult to say, but before we imagine that the soldiers who received the order to destroy the Mithraeum at Carrawburgh were enthusiastic Christians (and we may be sure that the Mithraea were destroyed only after the express command of a senior officer)[15] it is as well to bear in mind what was going on at this time at the nearby Coventina's Well.[16] Offerings continued to pour in. If they are not as numerous as in former times, that is probably rather an indication of economic conditions in the frontier zone than of a general conversion to Christianity. Why then were the Mithraea destroyed so enthusiastically? The answer may be that Mithraism had always been an exclusive religion: of the ten dedicators of Mithraic inscriptions on the Wall at least five, possibly six, were prefects, two were centurions, one a *beneficiarius consularis*, and there was one other, whose name Herion, if not an error for Hieron, at least suggests a Greek provenance.[17] The common soldier may quite possibly have delighted in the sheer destruction of an officers' temple: he may have simply delighted in sheer destruction. He did not need to be a Christian to do that.

Notes

1. *Toynbee* 1953, 1–24, see esp. 23
2. *JBAA* xviii (1955) 1–18, see esp. 7ff.
3. Cf. the distribution map (pl. I). Dr Frend himself comments (7), 'Including every small object on our map, we get a rather thin scatter throughout southern and eastern England, with a few finds in Yorkshire and in the military zone. Obviously the evidence is incomplete, but it seems quite certain that we are not dealing with a great popular movement'
4. AA[4], xliii (1965) 201–24 and xliv (1966) 147–64
5. For the bath see *JRS* li (1961) 193 and AA xliii (1965) 214; for the bottle *JRS* l (1960) 239 and AA xliv (1966) 151ff.
6. Noteworthy is the Chi-Rho reported from Maryport, for which Dr Michael Jarrett has searched without success. Cf. *CW* liv (1954) 269ff.
7. This is recognised by John Wall (AA, xliv 149) who nevertheless concludes (150), 'We cannot therefore rule out the possibility that the objects with Christian associations were owned by an organised Christian community somewhere in the North'
8. Cf. Professor J. M. C. Toynbee, *op. cit.*, 14 and Salway, P., *The Frontier People of Roman Britain* (1965), 216f., no. 20

Notes

9. Dr Salway translates 'at which limit he gave up his soul resigned to its destiny'; Mr Wright's interpretation is 'and gave back to the Fates his soul lent for that extent of time'
10. As suggested by Professor Toynbee, *loc. cit.*
11. Cf. Salway, *op. cit.*, 221, no. 27
12. Cf. *CIL* VI 22657: *Dis M[a]nibus M. Munati Feli[cia]ni qui vix(it) ann(is) LXVI men(sibus) || dieb(us) IIII. Munatia Aph[rodi]te uxor coniugi car[is]simo quae vixit cum eo [a] virginitate sine ulla macula ann(is) XXXIV et M. Munatius Felicianus filius patri piissimo [e]t b(ene) m(erenti) fecerunt.* Cf. also VI 9663: *D. M. in hoc tumulo iacet corpus ex animis cuius spiritus inter deos receptus est. Sic enim meruit L. Statius Onesimus viae Appiae multorum annorum negotias, homo super omnes fidelissimus, cuius fama in aeterno nota est, qui vixit sine macula an(nos) p(lus) m(inus) LXVIII. Statia Crescentina coiux marito dignissimo et merito cum quo vixit cum bona concordia sine alteritrum animi lesionem bene merenti fecit.* Though it contains Christian usages, this loving and ungrammatical epitaph is surely pagan
13. *Op. cit.*, 23 n. 4
14. For Housesteads cf. AA xxv (1904) 255ff; for Carrawburgh AA, xxix (1951) 6–92, esp. 39ff.; for Rudchester AA xxxii (1954) 176f.; for Caernarvon *Arch Cambr* cix (1960) 136–72, esp. 155f.
15. Gillam, J. P., AA, xxxii (1954) 178, commenting on the closely parallel destruction of the several Mithraea on the Wall, wrote, 'Such uniform treatment implies a single wave of feeling along the line of the Wall, or a single general order.' Earlier, in AA, xxix 43, the late Sir Ian Richmond and J. P. Gillam had already recognised that 'it becomes reasonable to see the desecration at Carrawburgh as the work of Christian hands, even if perpetuated on political rather than purely religious grounds'
16. AA viii 45. Offerings appear to have been made right up to the final withdrawal of the Roman garrison
17. Dedications were made by prefects at Carrawburgh (*RIB* 1544, 1545, 1546) and Rudchester (*RIB* 1395, 1396 and possibly 1397), by centurions at Housesteads (*RIB* 1600) and Rudchester (*RIB* 1398), by a *beneficiarius consularis* and by Herion at Housesteads (*RIB* 1599, 1601)

The Literary Evidence

J. R. Morris

The trouble with the literary evidence for fifth- and sixth-century Britain is that there is a vast amount of it, and that it is difficult to know what to make of it. The easiest way to deal with it is to say that half of it is worthless rubbish: what you choose to accept gives you a short cut to a quick answer, and you have a fool-proof excuse for ignoring awkward bits that do not fit, or for explaining them away.

Put so simply, this sounds like a crude and silly approach that any serious historian will naturally and easily avoid; but it is not easy to avoid if you treat these texts as you might treat the evidence for better documented periods, if you aim at achieving a simple clear cut distinction between the reliable and the unreliable, between fact and fancy. Such simplicity is risky at the best, dangerous with these difficult texts. The historian does well to bear in mind the dictum of the late Professor J. B. S. Haldane, challenging the alleged exactitude of the physical sciences, that 'a fact is a theory in which no one has made a large hole for a long time.' The historian's problem was expressed neatly by Professor Ludwig Bieler in a recent article: 'according to a widely accepted view, it is the historian's task to find out "what has actually happened". This, I believe, is impossible. The historian cannot do more than collect, assess and interpret evidence.'[1]

This does not mean that we must wail our sirens in a fog of uncertainty. Though nothing is perfectly certain, we can distinguish the probable from the possible and the unlikely, isolate the extremes of the virtually certain and virtually impossible, and weigh the degrees of probability in between. Our texts have been collected; most of them are printed somewhere in some form. Our main problem is assessment, and here our first concern must be to detect and recognize the bias and purpose of each source before we attempt interpretation. Every text has bias and purpose. All great historians, from Thucydides, Tacitus and Bede to Gibbon, have preached their own beliefs; they are great because they recognize their purpose and make it plain to their readers, and because they found their argument on a careful assessment of their own sources, distinguishing between knowledge and report. If we reject their conclusions, we do so on the basis of their own evidence, interpreting it differently. We need a sharper criticism of more pedestrian writers, ancient or modern, who are less aware of their own bias, who are content to endorse a conclusion because it is 'generally accepted' or 'universally agreed,' and we must be especially wary of the man who claims to set down objective truth free from bias, for the closer he comes to his ideal, the more he is enslaved to the passing prejudice of his own day, uncritically reading present assumptions into the experience of the past.

We are all products of the world we live in, and we cannot hope to escape from its present assumptions. We can try to recognize them, to criticize them, to discount what is not valid for the past. But our world and our experience changes, so that each generation requires a new interpretation of the past. The historians of stable Victorian England could afford to deplore the bellicosity of Greek city states, to bewail the blind decadence of the later Roman Empire; the modern veteran of two world wars has less authority to condemn past follies, but is better equipped to understand them. That is why assessment and interpretation go hand in hand. Each new acceptable interpretation of a period establishes a working hypothesis, that demands and prompts fresh assessment of old evidence, and that assessment modifies or overturns the accepted interpretation.

I have set down elsewhere[2] my present interpretation of the sources for the history of the British Isles in the fifth and sixth centuries, and must summarize it before venturing assessment. We have good contemporary evidence for the beginning and the end of the period. In 400 A.D. the British Isles were divided between the civilized Roman diocese and the barbarians beyond its frontiers, Picts and Scots. Romans and barbarians were a world apart, alien and hostile in speech, culture and interest, in government and in religion. By the seventh century, the whole of the British islands were split into a multitude of small kingdoms, speaking four main tongues, Irish, Welsh and Pictish native and long established, English foreign and recent. But they were comparable kingdoms, sharing a common homebred religion, analogous political institutions, a similar rural economy. There were great differences between the speakers of one language and another, between the individual kingdoms; but these internal differences were much less than those which distinguished seventh-century Britain from its own past, and from contemporary Europe.

At the top of society, the influence of the past was least apparent; unlike Europe, there was little continuity of urban political institutions or of the ownership of large rural estates. But at the bottom, there was less change; unlike Europe, the bulk of the population still spoke essentially the same languages as their ancestors in the Roman and pre-Roman past, and still observed much customary ancient law. Whereas in Europe barbarians settled within Roman society with comparatively little native resistance, to fuse into the society conventionally termed feudal, in Britain 200 years of war left the Germanic immigrants little influenced by native Roman civilization, the natives almost totally unaffected by Germanic custom. The impact of Merovingian Europe and of papal Christianity bore down upon diverse traditions whose interaction at home was more recent in time, and quite different in kind.

Late Roman Britain and the Britain of Bede are relatively easy to comprehend, because they are amply depicted in contemporary records, and because they were relatively stable. The centuries between changed rapidly, and the changes are ill-described. They were initiated by an administrative decision of the year 410. Hitherto the bulk of the day-to-day civil administration of Roman Britain had been the responsibility of the council and magistrates of a dozen or more *civitates*, internally self-governing, and equivalent smaller communities. Defence, finance and the coordination of the *civitates* had been the responsibility of a dozen senior officers, and some scores of lesser officials, appointed by the imperial government in Italy. In 410 the imperial government declined to make further appointments to these posts, or to continue responsibility for defence, finance or any other aspect of central administration. These responsibilities were thrust upon the common council of the British states, hitherto an advisory body and a means of pressure, not a decision-making authority. Now, it had to replace the central functions of the imperial rulers, to make the appointments they had made, to take charge of finance and defence. The ruin of Roman Britain in the next two centuries was in a general sense a by-product of the fall of western Rome; in detail, it stemmed from the failure of the states of Britain to agree upon a central government whose authority all could and would respect.

There is neither evidence nor likelihood that anything else changed in 410 beyond the change in the central administration. There is no evidence for any evacuation of troops or withdrawal of 'Romans'; for all freeborn inhabitants of the diocese had long been Romans, as fully Roman as Spaniards, Italians or Syrians, as Roman as their descendants are today English or British. What army there was remained; nothing suggests that existing posts were abolished or new ones created in or about 410. What changed was the authority that appointed their holders.

There is a little general evidence for the outline of what happened. Procopius,[3] well informed, but writing a century or more later far away in Constantinople, says that the island was governed by 'tyrants'; that is, by local emperors, replacing the authority that the emperor in Italy had abdicated. Various sources indicate who one or two of them were.[4] One text[5] suggests the obvious, that at least at first the British named their own consuls. The British were compelled, as one contemporary observed,[6] to live 'independently,' no longer subject to laws enacted by the emperors in Italy, and the increasing weakness of the emperors soon put much of Gaul in the same position.[7] But the same contemporary noted that British were outstandingly and surprisingly successful in repelling their external enemies.

This success means that at least for a short time the British reached some kind of agreement; for victories cannot be won without soldiers, and soldiers cannot fight unless civilians provide the money for their pay, food, weapons. In Britain in 410, political power lay in essentially the same kind of hands as in the rest of the empire, in the *potentiores*, landed nobility who dominated the *civitates* and the council, and *viri militares*, senior army officers whose power lay in the willingness of their troops to obey their orders. No government could hope to achieve lasting stability without overwhelming support among one of these elements, or the support of considerable sections of both. In Europe, there was commonly a clear cut difference between the outlook of the military and the civilian leaders, but it was rarely that all army officers embraced one side in any given conflict, all civilian noblemen the other; most governments, legitimate or otherwise, rested upon varying combinations of some military and some civil support. Though those that fell were commonly defeated in battle, they retained until defeat the support of soldiers prepared to fight for them and civilians prepared to finance and administer them; they fell because the combination behind their enemies proved stronger.

The little evidence we have suggests that the political conditions of Britain did not differ. One text[8] appears to describe the replacement of one government of *potentiores* by another of different views but similar social composition about 410–11, and implies that at that date neither had elevated an emperor. To survive, the new government must have earned at least passive acceptance by at least one of the main military authorities; the proper institutions of government are headed by an emperor, a *praefectus praetorio*, by definition and tradition civilian, and a *magister militum*, by definition an army officer. The emperor might be either a civilian or a soldier. Some ten or fifteen years later, political authority is said to have been vested in a *superbus tyrannus* named Vortigern and his council; the term *tyrannus* is most commonly and properly applied to an emperor, but does not exclude the possibility that Vortigern was the all-powerful prefect of a military emperor. We do not know and shall not know what titles he or others used, though we do know the range of titles that it was open to him to employ. We are told that he was subject to the same pressures as continental emperors; he employed Saxon, English, *foederati* to repel the Picts; their job done, a decisive section of the *potentiores* refused to continue to finance them or him; and in conflict with the *potentiores* he was driven to hire still larger numbers of *foederati*, who took pains to augment their numbers on their own initiative, until they were strong enough to attack and defeat both parties among their Roman British employers.

The outline of subsequent history is set down by Gildas, writing a century or slightly less after the rebellion; and continued by other writers, British and English. The first Saxon revolt was followed by a long period of war, in which the British were ultimately victorious. For several generations, up till Gildas' day, native British authority prevailed, with the English confined to specified areas, whose limits the archaeological evidence is able to determine. Later, a second Saxon revolt overthrew British authority in the greater part of what is now England in a single generation, annexed, colonized, and changed the language of the rest more slowly over a period of several centuries.

There is just enough evidence to indicate the approximate dates of the main events which divide these centuries into distinct periods. A contemporary

Gallic Chronicle baldly notes the Saxon subjugation of Britain in 441 or 442, and evidently means the first Saxon revolt. It therefore implies that the federate settlements began a decade or more earlier, somewhere about the 420s; and the evidence of many thousands of excavated graves agrees that the main body of federate Anglo-Saxon cemeteries begins somewhere about the 420s, though a small proportion of the grave goods was then anything up to a generation old; while the literary and archaeological evidence argues that the main fabric of Roman British civilization endured and prospered for a generation after 410, until at least the early 440s. The narrative of the wars of Vortigern preserved by Nennius ends with a massacre of the 300 *seniores*, the principal citizens of the civilian *civitates*, followed by a mass emigration to Gaul of their surviving fellow citizens, and by the initiation of a guerilla resistance among the remainder under Ambrosius Aurelianus. Ample contemporary continental evidence witnesses the arrival in Gaul of a large number of immigrants from Britain in or just before 460. The resistance initiated by Ambrosius triumphed at the siege of Mount Badon, something over a generation before Gildas wrote, about or just before 540, and Badon is therefore to be dated about or a little before 500, somewhere in the 490s. Neither English nor British tradition knows anything of war between the two peoples in the early sixth century, but both concur in recording the outbreak of the second Saxon revolt, on a small local scale immediately after the Justinian plague about 550, attaining its decisive victories twenty years later, and permanently securing the future England in the years 570–600. The main periods are therefore: I, the continuation of Roman Britain under its own emperors for a generation, from 410 to about 440; II, the British-Saxon wars between about 440 and about 495, in two stages, (a) the initial success of the first Saxon revolt from about 440 to about 457 and (b) the increasingly successful war of resistance by the British between about 460 and about 495; III, the period of British dominance after the wars, from about 495 to about 570; and IV, the success of the second Saxon revolt, in the years 570 to 600.

The key dates in this broad outline are reasonably secure, for they rest upon contemporary and continental evidence. Anything beyond the broad outline requires close assessment of the individual native sources that concern each period. Those that concern the first period, the early fifth century, are extensive and informative; one of the ironies of Roman Britain is that until the very end it remains voiceless and anonymous, for no single native literary work is known, but that the surviving works of early fifth-century British writers, most of them composed after the end of Roman rule, fill a fair sized bookcase. These works are Christian and controversial; most of them were written by Britons abroad, and most of them are Pelagian. Their assessment means that they must be seen in the context of Latin Christianity, and of the impact of British thinking thereon.

The main stages in Latin Christian evolution during the fourth century are fully recorded. In 311 Christianity suddenly, and somewhat prematurely, became the religion of the government. It had grown first and strongest among the cities of the eastern Greek-speaking provinces, and preserved a strong radical element, exalting the virtues of the poor against the evil of riches; so strong that even in the fifth century, St Augustine had to still the doubts of the last of the pagan aristocrats of Rome, that Christian doctrine threatened the rights of property. Though his argument was and is persuasive, radicalism persisted. By 311 Christianity had grown powerful in the west in Africa and Italy, and had made a considerable impact in Spain and the Rhineland; but in the rest of Gaul and in Britain it remained weak. In the whole of the provinces of Lugdunensis and Aquitania, barely half a dozen sees are known to have existed before Constantine; in a provincial capital of the importance of Tours, the first effective bishop took office in 340, and the Christians were few enough to assemble in a private house, neither rich enough nor numerous enough to afford a church building until about 350, and the see of Orleans was no earlier, that of Angers still later. Throughout the Gallic provinces, Christianity came in as the religion of the government and its officials, strong where they were numerous, weak where they were few; and earned affection or distrust as a government religion. On the one hand, the politically ambitious speedily learnt the practical advantages of conformity with Christian ritual and idiom, and bishops suddenly promoted from the status of persecuted sectaries to that of influential government advisers delighted in the triumph of the church; but other Christians distrusted the influx of time-serving converts, and feared the government's authority over the church, while the bulk of the population of rural Gaul paid little regard to a new government religion confined to the towns.

The sordid wrangles of the Arian controversy at first evoked contempt and disgust among non-Christians. But their outcome demonstrated that in Gaul very small conventicles of plebeian subjects were prepared to risk exile, imprisonment and even life for the sake of beliefs dearly held, and that their perseverance was able to defy government with success. The dispute spurred the Christians to reform; the majesty of Pope Damasus, the stern sincerity of Ambrose of Milan, the simple piety of Martin of Tours revealed the Christian church as an effective champion of human rights, able to restrain and defeat the arbitrary violence of emperors and their officers, while the vigorous promotion of the cult of martyrs made the veneration of men who died resisting unjust rulers a major part of Christian worship. Martin and his pupils began to extend Christianity to peasants and border barbarians, and in the last years of the century, immediately before the break between Britain and Rome, the whole western world became Christian in a generation. Conversion to Christianity did not of course mean that the converts ceased to be pagans; though church fathers might thunder the wishful belief that 'the same mouth cannot utter the praises of Christ and of Jupiter,' the poems of Ausonius, writing hymns to Christ and Jupiter with equal delight in language, proved them wrong; as did the ordinary laity, whose persistent practice of attending mass on Sunday mornings and sacrificing to their Lares in the afternoon long earned censure from church councils.

The triumph of Christianity was immediately followed by the capture of Rome in 410, and the first barbarian federate settlements in Gaul in 418. Disaster forced men to think afresh, and new thought begot controversy, in which British writers were prominent. In the interests of building a disciplined monolithic Christian church able to survive the disintegration of lay society, Augustine of Hippo elaborated the theology centred upon the original sin inherited by all men from Adam, only to be redeemed by the sacramental grace of God. Men trained in the older humanist values of Latin Christianity were deeply offended, and found their spokesman in Pelagius, a monastic Briton then regarded as the most polished writer in Rome. Augustine's views made little headway until after the fall of Rome shocked men's thinking, and then not through the normal processes of a church council or the approval of the Pope, but by a secular edict for the arrest of Pelagius and his colleagues issued by the civil government over the head of Pope Zosimus, who still refused to condemn Pelagius. The government enforced conformity in the Mediterranean, but its writ had ceased to run in Britain, and was already weak in northern Gaul. There, the author of the Chronography of 452 could remark, with casual detachment, that 418 was said to be the year in which Augustine 'invented the heresy of predestination.' In Britain, Pelagian thinking was and remained orthodox, Augustinianism a foreign heresy imposed by a lay government that had no authority in Britain, though its universal acceptance in the Mediterranean made it a foreign ideology of considerable weight.

Pelagianism produced a radical wing of its own, a group of young British writers, the most prominent of whom is termed the 'Sicilian Briton'[9] because he wrote in Sicily in and shortly after 411. His socialist concepts are more advanced than any other of the recorded radical thinking of antiquity; to him 'mankind is divided into three classes, the rich, the poor and those who have enough,' and its problems are to be solved by taking from the rich their excess and giving it to the poor, so that everyone has enough and class distinctions are abolished. But he does not, like most early Christian egalitarians, stop at a single redistribution of wealth; he also aims to end the causes of class difference, with the argument 'Abolish the rich, and you thereby automatically abolish the poor; for the few rich are the cause of the many poor.' The slogan 'Abolish the rich,' *Tolle divitem*, has a rhythm that a formidable crowd might shout; Augustine exploited his outspokenness to the full, and tried without success to make Pelagius responsible for his extreme views; but there is no doubt that the voicing of such views will have helped to induce the government to back Augustine's demands. There is of course no evidence to show whether or not such views were widespread in Britain; but more than a century later, the writings of one of his close associates were cited by Gildas with approval, as the work of 'one of us.' At least that tract had been read and recopied in Britain for four generations, surviving the storms of the Saxon wars; and the thinking of Gildas and of later British and Irish Christian writers shows a total unawareness of the controversy, with the occasional utterance of sentiments that would have angered conscious Augustinians.

These are polemical theologians; though they and others wrote mostly abroad, they were reared in Britain, and their similes and analogies reflect a good deal of the social, political and educational practice and assumptions of early fifth-century Britain. They admired the monastic way of life, preached by Martin's pupil Victricius in Britain about 396. Victricius also zealously propagated the cult of martyrs, champions of conscience against unjust authority. Gildas[10] attests the rapid spread and long persistence of the martyr cult in Britain: 'the splendid lamps of holy martyrs, whose shrines would have inspired divine love in the minds of pilgrims, had not many of them been torn from us for our sins by the miserable partition with the barbarians' (*lugubri divortio barbarorum*). He names two shrines that remained, and the concept took sufficient root for the name 'martyrium' to spread widely, surviving to this day in south Wales as 'Merthyr', though it is unlikely that the *martyria* made any significant impact before 400 A.D., probable that their spread belongs in the decades thereafter. St Patrick's account of his early life and of the British ecclesiastics, whose authority he rejected not far from 440, as well as Constantius' description of Germanus' visits, based on tales told him by the bishop's companions, attest the continuance of the vigorous intellectual and political life, the rich and sophisticated culture of Roman Britain into the 440s. Thereafter, evidence ends.

The sources for the next century are much more difficult to evaluate. There was little continuing written tradition, and virtually no records were preserved; what we have was set down by men who had little understanding of the vanished past they described. Their distorted statements often appear to conflict with one another and with common sense, and it is essential to get our priorities right in assessing them. It is rarely helpful to ask directly of any writer or statement the simple question, do we believe it? Our belief or disbelief has little more value than the statement itself. What we have to recognize is that there is a reason for every statement; it may be that it is true, that its author is a congenital liar, ignorant, ill-informed, or the like; but the first priority is to pinpoint the origin and purpose of the statement as far as we are able, to relate it to the author's bias and circumstances; thereafter to place it in the context of the time to which it relates.

The second priority is to understand the knowledge of the author's first readers. All our sources are either contemporary with the events they describe; or written within living memory; or set down later. A contemporary may misrepresent an event, or invent an obscure incident outside his readers' knowledge, but he cannot foist upon them an important public event which they well know did not happen. So it is with living memory. In ours or any other society, we add to our own experience what our fathers have told us of theirs, but we rarely know our grandfathers well enough to learn more from them than odd disjointed incidents of the distant past. The experience of each of us is much alike. My father's stories of his own life give me some understanding of who Gladstone and Asquith were and when they lived. As a child I was taken to gape at the empress Eugenie, and told something of her life, so that I know that the Franco–Prussian war was about a hundred years ago. My father knew an old lady who had danced in Brussels on the eve of Waterloo, so that I know that Wellington beat Napoleon well over a century ago, and would not confuse the two Napoleons. But that is the limit of living memory; it tells me nothing of the French Revolution, let alone of Cromwell and the English revolution. Its furthest limits lie between a 100 and 150 years back, at most a century before my own birth. Behind it lie a jumble of names of people, events and places, ill-related to one another or to time. They derive not from living memory, but from a historical tradition, that may be oral, or may be written, but is still out of living experience. If our historical record was entirely oral, if we lacked history books and records, a writer or a lecturer might describe how Marlborough beat Gustavus Adolphus at Minden, or explain the Martello towers of the south coast as defences erected against the Spanish Armada, without meeting protest or denial; but if he congratulated his readers on our freedom from war in our generation, or praised the long unbroken democratic tradition of modern Germany, he would be treated as a humorist or a lunatic. So it is with Gildas. He may talk nonsense about Magnus Maximus or the date of the Roman walls in innocence, for these lay outside living memory in 540; but when he complains[11] that the generation which won the war at Badon has died out, so that the country is now run by a generation ignorant of past troubles, that has only known our present security (*illis decedentibus cum successisset aetas tempestatis illius nescia et praesentis tamen serenitatis experta*) he cannot be wrong, because his readers knew, just as modern readers' knowledge prevents us from contrasting the serenity of our own day with the ghastly anarchy of Victorian England. So it is when he says that the Britain of his day is governed by impotent *rectores* and overmighty *duces*, who assume the style of *reges*, by duly consecrated bishops and ordained priests, that the island is partitioned but has been at peace for more than a generation. The assessment of Gildas must concentrate upon what he says of his own day and of the recent past; it must respect his account of Vortigern, a century earlier; but it need not regard his guesses about the more remote past, nor about the relative date and meaning that he gives to a single document incorporated into the early part of his narrative.

It is therefore obvious that the date of a writer is of supreme importance if he is contemporary with the event, or writes within living memory, but is of little moment if he writes later. If a text describing sixth-century events is shown to be of the seventh century, then its early date commands high respect; if its date be later, it matters little whether it belongs to the ninth century or the seventeenth; what matters then is the historical tradition upon which it relies, and this tradition varies with circumstance, not necessarily with time. Thus, Baldwin's life of Samson, written six or seven centuries after the event, is much closer to its near contemporary original than is the eighth-century life of Germanus used by Nennius, three or four hundred years nearer to its original in time. These self-evident priorities in assessment need emphasis, for the cult of the *codex vetustior* has done much to muddle modern studies of these centuries.

Apart from Gildas, the principal written sources for fifth- and sixth-century Britain are the documents collected under the name of Nennius, the Welsh Poems, the Saints' Lives, the Annals, and the Genealogies. Each have their own rules. The purpose of genealogies is to connect living persons with persons at least believed to have been mighty in the past; the two ends are likely to be a great deal more substantial than the links in the middle. National customs vary the method of distortion; since descent through the female was acceptable in Wales, the commonest contrivance of Welsh genealogists is to concoct a marriage between a man and a woman who may have lived centuries apart, so that the two lines connected have greater validity than the marriage. Irish and English custom did not acknowledge descent through the woman, so their genealogists contrive ancestry by allotting an improbable excess of sons to a long dead hero like Ida or Niall; and both not infrequently tack a pedigree whose origin they do not know on to a father of several sons, so that the younger among a group of sons are always suspect if their relationship is not attested outside the genealogical tradition.

Annalists, usually monastic, command a higher respect, for their deliberate distortion is commonly confined to entries enhancing their own house, order, or patron. They require however a more patient critical analysis, for their early form is commonly a relative order, to which later hands have added absolute dates; sometimes an extant text is itself a conflation of two or more earlier annals, and its author slots his sources together in the wrong places. These however are the routine problems of textual criticism, arduous, but in themselves easier to sort out than conscious manipulation.

Nennius' documents each require separate study; some are contemporary or near contemporary, others within living memory, others later. Some have been closely studied; Kenneth Jackson[12] has established the early date of some northern documents, within living memory of their later entries; the Kentish Chronicle is a rational narrative out of keeping with known British writing significantly later than the sixth century, with a close knowledge of the British toponomy of Kent; the list of Arthurian battles reads like an epitome of a lost poem. On the other hand, the stories of Ambrose and Vortigern draw upon the story teller rather upon historical record, and are of more interest to students of literature than of history; the accounts of Patrick and of Germanus rest on devolved, perhaps even vernacular, saints' lives, and other sections are transcriptions and epitomes of Irish legend. The essential fact is that Nennius in himself is no authority, and has no entity, and the differences between the manuscripts is of marginal importance; some of his texts have high historical value, some negligible, and the whole collection is in urgent need of close study.

Historical study of the Welsh poems has begun, but only begun; and is unlikely to be as thorough as the texts deserve until the critical discussions, at present only published in modern Welsh, are translated for the attention of a wider range of scholars. Sir Ifor Williams' conclusion that the core of the *Gododdin* was composed very soon after the campaign it describes is not likely to be overset; but since a large number of verses concern heroes who lived a generation before or after that campaign, the study of the poem's growth during the seventh century, the detection and explanation of the added stanzas, invites further study. So do the later poems; a few lie so close in content and concept to events much earlier than their present form that they may be modernizations of earlier poems, or even of translations from British, while many preserve twisted allusive fragments taken from older traditions and from poems not preserved. The essence of the matter is that the older poems, preserved entire, are versions of works first composed in honour of living men, or of their immediate ancestors, and that many of the later poems make use of similar lost originals. The poet's bias is to honour his patron for the virtues that the patron esteemed; like all government propaganda, it is excellent evidence for the aims and intentions of government, and is necessarily concerned with the misrepresentation of actual events.

I have discussed elsewhere[13] the Saints' Lives, the bulkiest group of documents, and the main conclusions must here be summarized. In general, most extant lives rest ultimately upon an original composed either just before the saint's death, or soon after. But unlike most other sources, they were popular literature, widely read for centuries; they were therefore altered more often, and more drastically, than other sources, in order to bring them into line with changing taste. The nature of the changes is therefore fairly uniform, and adequate texts survive to show what kind of changes were commonly introduced at what period. The grammar of the critical evaluation of these texts is not hard to discover; it has however as yet been little employed, and most lives lack detailed study. Reeves' critical edition of Adamnan's Columba, published 110 years ago, remains a model of the type and scale of treatment which each life deserves, and which no other has yet received. Later editions of the same life, and most studies of other lives, compare with it as a first year undergraduate's essay compares with a doctoral thesis.

The evidence upon which assessment of the normal behaviour of the hagiographer rests consists of a relatively small number of key texts. A few surviving texts are contemporary with the events they describe, or were written within living memory, among them the pioneer works of Athanasius, Jerome and Severus, Jonas' Columban, Adamnan's Columba, the first life of Samson. A number of later lives, as Wrmonoc's Paul Aurelian and Wrdisten's Winwaloe, reproduce the orthography of primitive Welsh or even British names of people and places that are certainly not the product of scholarly archaism; others, like

Richemarcus' David or Jocelyn's Kentigern, are conflations of earlier lost versions of diverse date, and occasionally incorporate an incident or cite a document written down in or near the saint's lifetime. More important is the study of the evolution of those few lives which exist in successive versions, notably the lives of Samson; unfortunately many later versions remain unpublished, disregarded as epitomes or devolved accounts that add nothing of value to the biography of the saint concerned.

The detectable changes in such successive versions are few and simple. If the cleric commissioned to copy or edit an old life had a sense of purpose or a delight in literary achievement, he tended to insert names and incidents that honoured his hero or his monastery and to suppress what he considered uninteresting or unedifying. Fortunately, the majority of such clerics had less ambition, and were content to transcribe what they found mechanically into the normal language of their own day, omitting or awkwardly adapting only the most grossly offensive incidents, retaining a great many names of people and places, that can have held little interest for their readers, often epitomizing the story to the point of obscurity, sometimes expanding it or replacing it with an edifying homily annexed from one of the fathers of the church, or with a colourful miracle borrowed from the lives of other saints or from the repertoire of the story teller. The result is that a few great names appear in many lives out of due time and place, Patrick, Germanus, Martin, Arthur and the like; otherwise, names are taken over from version to version, or else omitted; they are not inserted unless they give honour to the saint or the monastery. When Glastonbury tradition brings Patrick, Gildas, or Joseph of Arimathea to Glastonbury, it is to be discounted; but when Bangor tradition places Daniel's first monastery at Pembroke, with no kind of reference to David, it serves no Bangor interest. When the Irish life of Abban sends its hero to the pagan English king at Abbandune (Abingdon) in the late fifth century, it claims Abingdon for its own on the strength of a similarity of name, and raises suspicion; but when Columba Terryglass is made to visit an unnamed English kingdom where cremation is practised in the mid-sixth-century, no monastic interest is served, and the passing reference to cremation, not exploited to the saint's credit, argues a near contemporary source, for cremation at that date was rare and remote from Ireland. The life of Berachus is mainly concerned with a juridically interesting law suit with a *magus* over title to land; the numerous monks and kings named were contemporaries with one another, but two nuns who lived long after are imported as witnesses; they play no further part, but are involved because their houses were neighbours, with a potential interest in the property concerned. Likewise, the unedifying incident discreditable to the hero, often adapted or omitted in later versions, belongs to the near contemporary account; but the miracle attending the saint's illegitimate birth is usually imported for the gratification of the reader, and his royal parents are almost always suspect or demonstrable inventions; for, since a few saints were of royal or noble origin, royal rank became a fashionable prerequisite of very many biographers, and inspired in Welsh an elaborate tract on the genealogies of the saints. Though there is very rarely reason to credit the saint's paternity, the majority of the royal pedigrees to which they are attached are valid, an important contribution to the corpus of genealogies.

The enormous mass of trite miracles sometimes discourages the unwary modern reader. The miracles themselves are commonly of more interest to the student of literary tradition than to the historian; but the persons and the circumstances involved are of great interest, for a very high proportion of the people occur also in genealogies, annals and other sources, and very rarely occur in the lives at a discordant date; while the attendant circumstances commonly find their parallels in legal and social tracts, sometimes in archaeology. The miracles are there because the authors and the readers automatically assumed that a supernatural was more probable than a natural explanation for many ordinary phenomena; and because the credit of the saint rested on the quantity and quality of his miracles. Saints appeared as powerful protectors in an age when mere men seemed impotent, and their divine *virtus* is manifest from the earliest known lives. Jerome's Paul, Severus' Martin relate quantities of miracles for which the modern critic may easily discern more human explanations: the source of one of the more striking Irish water-working wonders is the *Dialogues* of Gregory the Great, who heard the story 'the day before yesterday,' soon after the event; no account could be more contemporary, and, though the human explanation is plain to the reader, embellished later versions of such tales turn wonder to absurdity. The commonest miracle is the resurrection of the dead, and in late versions few saints are worth venerating unless they can resurrect more corpses than Christ. The stories are of two main kinds, revival from a faint or coma, or the personified consolation. Earlier versions make plain that the invalid 'is not dead but sleepeth,' but repetition swells the wonder until the decapitated hero picks up his severed head and replaces it on his shoulders, and delivers a homily lifted from Gregory the Great. Usually he dies again soon after, occasionally he enjoys long life. In the consolation miracle, the saint's comforting assurance, usually addressed to bereaved parents, is personified by reviving the dead child to let him explain in person the delights of heaven, and to end with a plea to be permitted to return thereto, a plea that is soon granted with a speedy second death. Later lives are often swollen, their deleted incidents replaced, with stock miracles that reappear again and again; the future saint who in boyhood carried live coals in his apron without burning it, to relight his master's fire, a tale harking back to an age when fire lighting was difficult, occurs in something over 70 lives. The broken cup miraculously mended, the gifts given away and miraculously replaced, the ring swallowed by a fish caught by a fisherman, the bull that gave milk and many other stories occur with varying frequency, in lives early and late, of good bad and indifferent validity, and neither the nature nor the quantity of the miracles has any bearing on the historicity or otherwise of the persons, places, and events narrated in the life. These events however are of outstanding importance for political and social history.

Various groups of lives share important differences from each other. In general, British lives are varied, often extant in extremely devolved versions, so far removed from the originals that the remnant of historical information is extremely small, so corrupt in detail that it is hard to extract from the surrounding banal marvels. Many lives are products of the eleventh and twelfth centuries, edited from decayed manuscripts, difficult to trace, hard to decipher and unedifying in content, that had mouldered for centuries when no one wanted to read a life of the saint concerned; some, however, were preserved within the sacred covers of a gospel book, and with them are preserved, as at Llancarfan and Llandav, records of charter grants made to the monastery and rated as least as valuable as the life, of high importance for the modern historian. The Irish lives are however much more homogenous. They are preserved in two main medieval collections, conforming to a standard pattern of a *Liber miraculorum* set between an account of the saint's youth and of his old age. Exceedingly few earlier texts survive, but the main corpus is much less devolved than most of the British lives, and is much richer in the recorded names of people places and events. In Ireland, the Latin lives are supplemented by a large number of vernacular lives, most of them so contaminated by the story teller that little can be extracted from them beyond a very few names of persons and places; by contrast, Welsh vernacular lives are fewer in number, and less notably devolved from the Latin originals. A comparison of the two traditions prompts comparisons between the intellectual life of the two countries between the eighth and the twelfth centuries.

The saints' lives, the genealogies, and the annals constitute an interlocking corpus of information; the same persons, the same events the same relationships, the same evolution in political government and in economy occurs in each. Though it is plainly unwise to study them in isolation, it is as yet difficult to study them together, for the necessary works of reference are lacking. No dictionary of persons exists for either country, and Hogan's *Onomasticon*, a comprehensive dictionary of Irish place names, is nearly 60 years old, requires replacements by a modern edition with more exact references, and needs to be matched with a corresponding geographical dictionary of early British place names. Until these elementary tools of study exist, critical editions of individual texts is a labour too daunting to be undertaken with serious success. Though at present essential initial problems of person, place and time claim highest priority, the ancient laws of Wales and of Ireland, whose only comprehensive publication is also a hundred years old, and rests on imperfect texts, need re-editing with ample commentaries, that their information may be related to that contained in the saints' lives and other sources.

These heavy labours are unlikely to be undertaken until their value is more widely appreciated than at present. Their greatest single importance lies in their account of the Irish and Welsh ecclesiastical reforms of the sixth century; and the purpose and nature of these reforms cannot be understood without a clearer grasp of the political society whence they sprang and wherein they grew. Kathleen Hughes' recent work has made clear the existence and extent of the episcopalian diocesan church, with its married clergy, but its relations with the monastic reformers is still imperfectly understood. The episcopate of Patrick was followed by the creation of ten or twelve late fifth-century sees, but attempts to establish a metropolitan hierarchy, under the leadership of Armagh or Saul, of Kildare, or of British bishops, wholly failed. Rapidly the concept grew, with the wide spread of the new religion, that each small state, each *tuath*, should have its own bishop. The British church evolved towards the same principle from a different starting point; a normal diocesan organization based on towns, under the metropolitan authority of the bishops of provincial capitals, emerged while Roman Britain endured. Its ideas survived, but not its roots, for the towns withered; only Bishop Dubricius, of Caerwent, of Gloucester or perhaps of Ariconium, has left a mark on later record. Elsewhere, the all powerful *duces* left over by the fifth-century wars turned their commands into *de facto* independent states, divided them into still smaller units among their sons, some of whom reunited their father's dominions by the slaughter of brothers and uncles on a Merovingian scale. Each king sought his own bishop, so that diocesan boundaries change with each political change, and without an independent ecclesiastic hierarchy the bishops of the small kingdoms became the creatures of the kings; and the kings became bloodier and more oppressive, freed from even the limited moral authority that the church of Europe was able to bring to bear upon its lay governments. This was the situation that Gildas' tract described and denounced.

The cure came from the monks. Hitherto, Latin monasticism had been confined to the individual monastic dedication of wealthy citizens, housing a few poorer fellows in their great houses; to the cathedral monasteries designed to impose monastic discipline on ordained and trained diocesan clergy; to one or two seminaries devoted to the training of a scholarly and ascetic elite who might fill the bishoprics and provide the theologians of Gaul; and to a few quieter retreats for men of substance anxious to escape the chaos of Roman collapse. Martin, the cathedral monasteries, and a few noblemen like Iltut in Wales, and later Cassiodorus in Italy, kept schools, but the mass migration to the desert of the Egyptian and Cappadocian monks found no parallel in the west until the publication of Gildas' book. That book gave a voice to the reformers, taught them cohesion and confidence, so that when a generation of young ascetics, headed by a number of Iltut's pupils, pioneered a personal escape from the corruptions of their society into the uninhabited wastes of southwestern Britain and of Brittany, they were immediately followed by a mass of converts to monasticism, and also by lay emigrants, as eager to escape the oppression of the *duces*. Within a decade, the movement grew to massive proportions. In

Wales, several hundred *Llans* and the bulk of ubiquitous early *Tre-* names attest a very large movement of men from their former homes to new settlements, whose security was protected by religious respect for the abbot. Others moved to Cornwall and Devon, more still to Gaul; there emigrants of the late 450s, and perhaps survivors of Magnus Maximus' army before them in 388, had established homes within the northern Gallic states from Belgium to Brest. In Normandy and eastward their numbers were few enough for them to be absorbed among the native population, but the lay and monastic migration of the mid sixth century to Armorica, northwestern Gaul, reinforcing the earlier settlers, was large enough to displace the name and speech of the previous inhabitants, and to turn the peninsula into lesser Britain, Brittany. The emigrants opened new lands; but their withdrawal from their own homes deprived the kings of taxpaying subjects and infantry soldiers. The bishops of the weakened kings disappeared, and in the course of time the British monastic reformers were able to establish the general principle that the abbots of half a dozen principal monasteries were simultaneously bishops of larger kingdoms, and maintained their dioceses intact, whatever the shifts in political frontiers.

Monastic reform grew to a mass movement at almost the same time in Ireland; and there too Irish tradition acknowledged Gildas as its inspiration, its theoretician, and its spiritual guide. The multiplicity of local bishops prevented a simple identification of greater abbots with the bishoprics of large states, though a few greater abbots became the spiritual guides of some of the greater kings. Instead, an increasing number of the local bishops were drawn from the ranks of the monks. In both countries, kings stood in awe of great abbots; in Brittany and Cornwall, King Mark, also called Cunomorus, faced powerful opposition among the monks, whose pressure at the court of Paris contributed to his downfall and death at the hands of Clothaire in December 560. His son Tristan, turned in story to his romantic nephew, succeeded him in Cornwall, but has left no trace in Brittany. In Ireland, a bitter struggle broke the rising power of the central monarchy, complicated by the accidental circumstance that the greatest of the monastic leaders of the second generation, Columba, was also an heir to the throne and a potent force in lay politics. Columba's energetic combination of his lay military strength and his ecclesiastical authority culminated in a major battle of unparalleled ferocity, and occasioned his migration to Iona, on the borders of the heathen Picts, whom he speedily converted, and of the Irish Scot colonists in Pictland. Bishops were yet few among either people, and as their number increased they were regularly taken from the monks of Iona. The sovereign authority of abbot Columba over his monks made the creation of a diocesan hierarchy unnecessary, and produced the form of organization that puzzled Bede, that an abbot who was but a priest should be master of bishops who knew no metropolitan.

In Britain, Cadoc is said to have exercised the double authority that Columba did not attain, ruling as king and abbot over much of southeast Wales; and when a different dynasty succeeded, its monastic bishop was strong enough to exile kings who murdered their rivals. But in Britain the monastic movement split into two wings, aristocratic abbots in the tradition of Cadoc and Gildas, hostile to ascetic extremism, dominant in the former villa lands of Monmouth and Glamorgan, and determined plebeian ascetics headed by David, strong in the southwest and in the uplands of Brecon, where men were poorer and Irish settlers more numerous. Similar divisions were reproduced in Ireland, but in Ireland they engendered an extraordinary and enduring blend of scholarship and piety, initiative and authority, ideally adapted to the aspirations of the rural kingdoms of the English and of barbarian Germany. When the death of Edwin and of Aethelbert ended the authority of Augustine's Roman mission outside Kent, Irish monks converted the bulk of the English, in the north, the midlands, and the south, and though the English early accepted the organizational supremacy and hierarchical structure of the church of Rome, they kept a church rooted on monasteries of Irish inspiration. Irish energy and English discipline proved an ideal combination; in the seventh century Irish and English monks found a massive and widespread response in eastern Gaul and northern Italy, far exceeding that which peninsular Italy accorded to Benedict and Cassiodorus, and carried Christianity, in monastic form, to the heathen Germans beyond the Rhine, to some of the Slav peoples. Their numerous seventh- and eighth-century foundations within the frontiers of the former empire formed the basis of the future Benedictine order.

This is the story of the saints' lives. Its impact upon England and Europe is well known, less intelligible than it should be because the genesis of the movement in Ireland and Wales is less observed, its nature still very inadequately studied. This is the importance which justifies and indeed demands the laborious compilation of the necessary works of reference, the meticulous critical examination of the saints' lives and related sources, which alone can explain the birth and early growth of mass monasticism in Europe.

At present, the contribution of archaeology to our understanding of fifth- and sixth-century Britain is comparatively slight; the great quantity of grave goods interred with pagan English bodies serves to delimit the advance of the English in space and time, but, with little historical context behind it, reveals less than it might of the evolution of their society. The archaeology of the British, who used no grave goods, is very much harder to understand, but the advances of the last few years have been relatively great, and promise rapidly expanding knowledge. Growing archaeological knowledge will greatly enrich, deepen and enliven the story that the texts can tell; but until the overdue parallel work is put into their study, the archaeology will be lamed. The state of the texts is comparable with that of the Greek and Roman writers in the early sixteenth century; a very large number of texts have been printed, even though many of them can only be found in a few large or specialized libraries. They still await the thorough systematic commentaries that Stephanus, Gronovius, Valesius,

Godefridus and their many colleagues supplied to classical texts in the late sixteenth and seventeenth centuries, themselves the inescapable prelude to the synthetic researches of a Gibbon, a Grote, or a Mommsen, on which modern learning builds. When printing was young and the tools of scholarship primitive, the literature of a thousand years of classical civilization required several centuries of protracted study before we could reach our present level of understanding. The literature of two or three centuries of the British Isles, vastly less in size, undertaken with modern equipment and modern understanding, will be the work of as many decades. Able scholars are to hand, and the relatively small sums needed will not be wanting once the full value of the study is widely understood.

The value of the study of these centuries lies in their unique contribution to the future of Europe. The different history of Britain, where alone among the peoples of western Rome the natives for a period contained the Germanic invaders, produced a society where native and newcomer did not fuse, whose evolution provides a laboratory control upon the validity of our judgements upon European feudalism, distinguishes that which arises from the nature of subsistence rural economy from that which may be attributed to the laws and institutions of Rome or of the Germans; while in the British Isles, the survival of the old languages preserved something of the poor man's culture of the Roman and pre-Roman period, and in Ireland alone preserves the literature of an iron age barbarian society virtually unaffected by civilised Roman thought. The peculiarities of British history produced vernacular literature several centuries earlier than in Europe, and also begot much earlier a consciousness of national identity, rooted on a common language, and overriding the political frontiers of small states. The formative centuries between 400 and 600 are neither Roman, nor yet medieval. They constitute a period in their own right, whose changing institutions, economy and ideas merit study on their own, independently of our ideas about Europe in their day, or to the compartments and labels used to classify and identify them. These centuries produced two major contributions to the thought and practice of medieval Europe. The monastic impulse that began in south Wales under the impact of Gildas' book, that spread to Ireland, thence to northern England and to Gaul and central Europe, is the principal point of origin of the monasteries of medieval Europe. It was the product of the three generations in which the British mastered their country, keeping the Saxons of the east under control. The military victory and political failure of the British became the hope of Europe. From among the many possible heroic tales that might have served their purpose, much of Europe selected the splendid failure of king Arthur as the pattern of a golden age of good government, using sovereign power to protect the weak and right injustice. That men might comfort their misfortunes with empty dreams of the great king's return is of lesser moment; but their assertion of their ideal, their belief that it had in the past existed, and would and could come again, urged chivalrous restraint upon the crude authority of arbitrary governments, and gave courage to their subjects to struggle for a just and free society of peace and ease. The concepts formed in and about the centuries that Arthur spans inspired the egalitarianism of the monks. They also fired laymen, and especially in England and France contributed to the early stages of independent thinking that emboldened subjects to rebel. The strength of the Arthurian legend is that it is rooted in factual history, whose meaning and moral survives where the detail is lost. That is why the centuries that produced Arthur and the monks deserve and demand a long overdue study.

Notes

1. *Irish Ecclesiastical Record* 107 (1967) 2
2. *Britain and Rome* (Essays presented to Eric Birley), ed. Jarrett, M. G. and Dobson, B., (Kendal, 1966) 145ff.
3. *De bello Vandalico*, 1, 1
4. The parents of Ambrosius Aurelianus, *purpura induti*, Gildas, 25 (40, 13); his father was probably the elder Ambrosius, Vortigern's rival. On Vortigern's status, see p. 58–9 below. Welsh texts apply the term *imperator* to Arthur. The term remained in use in Britain. Though it is never applied to any European ruler except a Roman emperor, it was used of English supreme kings by Adomnan, Boniface and occasionally in charters, and twice of Irish High-Kings. The usage, peculiar to the British Isles, suggests that it had been regarded by the British of the fifth and sixth centuries as the proper term for a ruler of the whole island
5. The Sicilian Briton, *Ep.* 2, 7, *PL* Sup. 1. 1380
6. Zosimus, 6, 5
7. Both the Germanic kingdoms and the territories of Aegidius became in fact independent principalities
8. *De Vita Christiana*, *PL* 40. 1031=50. 383, cf. *JTS* 16 (1965) 32–35
9. Migne, *PL* Sup 1. 1687ff; 1375ff; cf. *JTS* 16 (1965) 27–41; 43–50
10. 10 (31, 17, 18)
11. 26 (41, 1ff.)
12. *Celt and Saxon*, ed. Chadwick, N. K. (Cambridge, 1963) 20ff.
13. *JTS*, 17 (1966) 342ff.

Some Linguistic Evidence Relating to the British Church

D. Greene

'Linguistic evidence does not tell lies, as hagiographical documents and annals sometimes do. But it cannot go so far as to prove certain dates to be exact and correct; it can only confirm or refute the general course of historical facts, recorded by tradition or reconstructed by modern scholars'. These are the words of Professor Christine Mohrmann in her detailed study of *The Latin of St Patrick* (Dublin 1961), and I may perhaps offer them in defence of my temerity in addressing a public which includes historians, even if I am somewhat less confident than Professor Mohrmann that confirmation or refutation of historical theories by linguistic methods will carry conviction to anybody except the linguist. Most of the subjects which are discussed in this volume do not lend themselves to linguistic treatment and so I have confined myself in this paper to three topics where such a treatment may prove useful. These are the nature of the Latin culture of Britain in the fifth century, the first coming of Christianity to Ireland, and the relations between the Irish and British churches in the period between, say, 450 and 600 A.D. All these topics have been discussed by Professor Kenneth Jackson in his masterly survey of *Language and History in Early Britain;* the first of them was dealt with by Mohrmann in the lectures I have just mentioned, and the other two have been studied in recent publications by Professor D. A. Binchy.

Historical fashions change, and the same evidence can be interpreted in quite different ways at different periods; the question of the status of Latin in Roman and sub-Roman Britain is one of the most striking examples of this. As Jackson has pointed out, scholars up to about 50 years ago tended to assume that Roman Britain was Latin Britain too, and that Latin reigned supreme there except among a few backward peasants and, of course, in remote areas such as the modern Wales and Cornwall. Since then the pendulum has swung violently in the opposite direction, and the fact, first established by Jackson, that Old English shows no certain signs of contact with spoken British Latin has been taken as an indication that British was the vernacular everywhere in the fifth century, although Jackson himself nowhere says anything of the kind.

The internal evidence of the neo-British languages, as I will call Breton, Cornish and Welsh, points clearly to a period when the dominance of Latin in

Britain was overwhelming. Consider, for example, the evolution of a pluperfect tense, formed by adding the terminations of the imperfect to the preterite stem; this has no parallel in Irish, which uses quite different devices, traces of which survive in early Welsh too, and which we may legitimately conclude were part of the system of Common Celtic. Not only that but, just as the forms of the Latin pluperfect have survived into some Romance languages, but with a loss of their original function, so the Welsh pluperfect forms, where they survive in speech, are mere variants of the imperfect or conditional tenses; that is to say, we can see a movement in British which is parallel to that from Classical Latin to Vulgar Latin. The same phenomenon can be observed in the phonology; thus Welsh *fydd* 'faith' has a vowel the quality of which reflects the short *i* of Classical Latin *fides*, but which is now long because it stands before a single consonant, in exactly the same way as the *i* of *fides* was lengthened in Vulgar Latin. Again, Irish preserves the older system of independent vowel length. Another striking morphological parallel, this time with Vulgar Latin only, has been pointed out by Sommerfelt: the existence in both languages of compound prepositions, which are foreign to both Classical Latin and Irish.[1] Modern Welsh *oddiwrth* 'from' contains three prepositional elements, as does Modern French *devant*, from *de ab ante;* Sommerfelt cites examples such as *de ante cruce* 'from before the cross' from the fifth-century *Itinerarium Etheriae*, and concludes that the British usage, which we find in our oldest sources, 'must have been modelled on that of Late Latin' – and, it is hardly necessary to add, spoken Late Latin. Finally, since these phonological and morphological arguments may seem too technical to carry conviction, consider the number and nature of the Latin loanwords in neo-British, which include not only the terminology of a superior civilization, but the elementary vocabulary of everyday life – *pysg* 'fish,' for example, and *braich* 'arm'; even in modern spoken Irish and Welsh, which are under enormous pressure from English, borrowings of this type are rare. All this points to a vigorous Latin speech, both classical and vulgar, and massive bilingualism on the part of the speakers of British. Had the process continued, another Romance language would have been evolved in Britain. The collapse of the imperial power in the island prevented this happening, but the British language which again became dominant in the fifth century had been materially altered by its long contact with Latin.

That there was a distinctive British variety of Latin seems to me to be beyond doubt. The common word *planta*, for example, has been borrowed into both Welsh and Irish in the meaning 'children,' and the Irish form *cland* points to a date of reception certainly not later than the fifth century and perhaps earlier. This was an extension, not a change, of meaning, for W. *plant* and Ir. *cland* were also used in meanings close to those of English *plant*, but the important thing to note is that this colloquial extension is not attested from any Latin document; British Latin *planta* must have been a word like modern English *kids*, which has quite different connotations in written and spoken usage. Another word of not dissimilar meaning in Classical Latin, *scopa*, must have meant 'sheaf' in colloquial British Latin, and had a derivative *scoparium* 'storehouse for sheaves, barn' formed from it, for these are the forms from which W. *ysgub* 'sheaf' and *ysgubor* 'barn' derive; the latter Welsh word was borrowed into Irish in that meaning not later than the sixth century. But the British knew perfectly well that the proper meaning of *scopa* was 'twig, broom,' and that is the meaning it has in Insular Latin texts and in the Irish loanword *scuab*. We may add to these the British Christian **premiter*, from which OIr *cruimther* was borrowed not later than the fifth century; again, this form does not occur in Latin texts. Putting together the evidence we have collected, we might construct a highly speculative sentence of British Latin: *premiter misit plantam de ante scopario* 'the priest sent the children away from the barn'! It is certain that a Gaulish Latin speaker of, say, the fifth century would have made nothing of this; he might have made a shot at *premiter* on the basis of his own *prester* and *de ante* would, as we have seen, be familiar, but the two nouns, though impeccably classical in form, would have defeated him. But he could only have heard a sentence like this, for, as I have said, all the distinctive features of it were avoided in writing the language.

It will be seen that, combining this evidence with Jackson's carefully considered opinion that the correct date for the beginning of the final collapse of Roman Britain is probably as late as the middle of the fifth century, Mohrmann's somewhat dogmatic statement that living Latin in the fifth century means continental Latin cannot stand up. And I think that Jackson's much more tentative suggestions that British Latin would have seemed stilted and pedantic, or perhaps upper-class and 'haw-haw,' to a continental speaker of Vulgar Latin convey the wrong impression, for they are based almost entirely on the conservative nature of the sound system of British Latin and take no account of the local developments I have mentioned. We are not, in any case, entitled to set up the terms 'archaic' and 'colloquial' in opposition to one another; the speech of an Icelandic trawler-man may sound very archaic to his Norwegian counterpart, but it is none the less colloquial. I find myself in agreement with Professor Richard Hanson when he says: 'For at least 350 years traders and soldiers' families, shopkeepers, craftsmen and schoolmasters lived in Roman Britain, and for the last hundred of these clergy too. Did they all speak literary Latin? This is inconceivable. Did they all disappear in 410 when the Roman government left Britain? This is an equally absurd hypothesis.'[2] I cannot follow him all the way, however, when he asserts that Patrick's writings are 'prime evidence' for the British Latin of his time. They are, of course, better than nothing; but it must be said that a writer who explicitly complains of the difficulty he finds in expressing himself in a given language can hardly be regarded as a completely reliable source. It is quite clear that he was not a native speaker of the language; none of the local developments which have been noted occurs in his style and I may remind you that one of these, the use of compound prepositions, occurs precisely in the *Itinerarium Etheriae*, which Mohrmann uses as the type of colloquial Latin of the period. It seems more probable that his style represents the school Latin of Britain at the time, in which the innovations of popular speech were avoided, but the niceties of classical Latin forgotten. That there was interference from Irish – which he probably knew much better than Latin by the time he came to write the works which survive to us – is now generally admitted in respect of the idiom *sugere mammellas eorum* 'to submit to them,'[3] and Irish probably lies behind the phrase *mensura fidei Trinitatis*, which Bieler explains as a *genitivus identitatis* and translates 'the measure which is belief in the Trinity,' for this use of the genitive is common in Irish at all periods.[4] There are other features which are probably to be ascribed to the influence of Celtic syntax, whether British or Irish, such as the use of the dative or a preposition to indicate the subject of the infinitive; Fr Diarmuid Ó Laoghaire S. J. has called my attention to the constructions *opto fratribus . . . scire* 'I wish my brothers to know' (*Conf.* 6) and *ab illis . . . speravi venire* (*Conf.* 18), where there are clear parallels in both Irish and Welsh for the former and in Welsh for the latter. A third case, [*seniores*] . . . *qui venerunt et peccata mea contra laboriosum episcopatum meum*, also noted by Fr Ó Laoghaire, while very strange in Latin, has an exact equivalent in Welsh, but we must suspend judgment here in view of doubts as to the antiquity of the construction in Welsh itself.[5] On the whole, it is probably safe to say that there is interference from British in Patrick's Latin, though that does not necessarily mean that this reflects his own imperfect command of the language; just as British had at one time been deeply penetrated by Latin words and idioms, so, no doubt, Latin in turn began to be penetrated by British as its connections with Rome were cut, and it is quite possible that what Patrick wrote would have been accepted as reasonably correct by his Latin-speaking fellow-countrymen. In the absence of documents for comparison this question must remain unsettled; all we can say is that, though Patrick was a native speaker of British, there is every reason to suppose that his Latin was acquired in Britain and nowhere else.

I now turn to the second problem I wish to discuss, the earliest origins of Irish Christianity. The linguistic material available here consists of the Latin loanwords in Irish which, though far less numerous than those in Welsh, still make up a respectable part of the vocabulary, and in dealing with this period we must study the first stratum, for it is generally accepted that two distinct stages can be distinguished. The first consists of words which have undergone a number of phonetic changes which occurred in Irish between the stage of the language attested in the Ogam inscriptions and that found in the early manuscript sources; broadly speaking, we can say that these changes were as massive as those which took place in, say, the transition from Vulgar Latin to Old French. It is generally believed that *Cothirche*, a traditional name for Patrick, is one of these, though, as we shall see later, there are difficulties about this; it does, however, demonstrate a number of the phonetic changes which apply to words of the first stratum – substitution of *qu* for *p*, unknown in the oldest Irish, with resultant changing of the following *a* to *o* and assimilation of *q* to *c*, internal *t* and *c* changing to *th* and *ch*, and final *-ius* appearing simply as *-e*. These were changes which all native words underwent during the same period so that, in one sense, we possess no dating for them at all; a word like *caisel* could have been borrowed from Latin *castellum* at almost any period before that at which Irish evolved the consonant group *-st-*. The second stratum of loanwords is of clearly British origin; these words show phonetic developments which are British rather than Irish and they continue in Irish with little or no further modification. Here the example *Pádraig* is a certain one; this is identical with W. *Padrig*, showing a series of changes foreign to Irish. This class includes both words borrowed directly from Latin, such as *scuab* from *scopa*, and words of Latin origin borrowed from British; scholars are not in agreement as to the relative importance of the two sources.

What we might call the orthodox historical explanation of this linguistic evidence was first developed by Eoin MacNeill over thirty years ago.[6] He took it that the early loanwords were introduced by the Patrician mission in the middle of the fifth century, while the British loanwords arose from the close contacts between the monasteries of Ireland and Wales in the sixth century; the phonetic processes in Irish which had affected the first stratum were completed by the time the second stratum came in. It is a simple and attractive picture, though it asks the linguist to believe in very massive changes in a period of less than a century – changes which took place in British as well as in Irish. However, the next attempt to draw historical conclusions from linguistic data was even more daring, for twenty years ago T. F. O'Rahilly assigned the first group of loanwords to a continental Palladius–Patrick, who worked in the Irish mission field between 431 and 461, and the second to Patrick the Briton, the author of our documents, who succeeded him, and died about 492.[7] Fortunately it is no part of my task here to discuss the general theory of the two Patricks, for which there are other arguments; as far as the linguistic justification is concerned Jackson is, if anything, too mild in dismissing it as 'scarcely credible,' for it would be totally impossible for a language to alter its phonological system so radically in a period of sixty years. No scholar would now accept O'Rahilly's theory; a by-product of its general rejection, however, is a tendency to accept MacNeill's chronology as completely established, and it is only in the last few years that it has been challenged once more.

In his refutation of O'Rahilly's theory, Jackson pointed out that missionaries coming from Gaul or Northern Italy in the fifth century would have had quite different pronunciations of Latin from those required to account for the early loanwords; the *-c-* of *Patricius*, for example, had become *-ts-* by the fifth century even in the most linguistically conservative levels of society in those areas. This is no doubt true, though I am not sure that everybody would be quite so certain as to the phonology of Gaulish Latin at this period, but the fact that several words in this early stratum have clear connections with Britain points even more strongly in the same direction. We have already seen that *planta* 'children,' from which Irish *cland* is derived is a uniquely British development and Irish *cruimther* 'priest' derives neither from classical *presbyter* nor from Gaulish Vulgar Latin *prester*, but from British Latin *premiter*; it was a hazy memory of this that caused Cormac Ua Cuilennáin to say, over a thousand years ago: '*cruimther* is not a correct version of *presbyter*; it is a correct version of *premter*. The Britons who accompanied Patrick in preaching, it is they who translated it, and what they translated was *premter*.'[8]

MacNeill would have agreed with Cormac's view that it was from Patrick's British missionaries that the Irish heard the word *premiter* for the first time, and so would Jackson. It was in a review of Jackson's *Language and History in Early Britain* that Professor D. A. Binchy put forward a new interpretation of the evidence; he suggested that, while the early loanwords do indeed derive from Britain, they are pre-Patrician, a few perhaps pre-Christian, but the great majority those adopted by the *Scoti in Christum credentes* to whom, as we know, the missionary Palladius was sent from Rome in 431.[9] He developed this argument further in his masterly survey of the Patrician problem,[10] where he pointed out that, while the early loanwords, helped out with some elements of the native vocabulary, constitute the bare minimum of a religious terminology, there is one important vacancy – the word for a bishop, which should have been **echscech* or the like. This led him to suggest that the first stratum of loanwords was already established in Ireland 'when the first bishop (*epscop*) was sent by Pope Celestine.' That bishop was Palladius, about whose fortunes in Ireland we know nothing; on the other hand, it is certain that Patrick, who was also a bishop, was working in Ireland in the fifth century and Binchy's statement implies that his Irish title would have been *epscop*, which is uncompromisingly British, or indeed Welsh, so that the second stratum of loanwords is as old as Patrick himself.

There are several difficulties about this theory. In the first place, it would be unwise to attach too much importance to the absence of a word for bishop in the first stratum of Latin loanwords; it is certain that there was an early borrowing of *Christus*, and the surviving *cresen* 'Christian' indicates that it should have had the form **Criss* or **Cress*, but no trace of it survives and the only form found is *Críst*, which bears unmistakable marks of British origin. Then we have the form *Cothriche* which has already been mentioned; if Patrick called himself *Padrigius* when speaking Latin, and *Padrig* when speaking British, how could *Cothirche* have been evolved? It is true that Professor James Carney has suggested that *Cothirche* is a native word which was later associated with Patrick,[11] but the balance of the evidence seems to be against this view, and the ingenious suggestion of Dr Seán de Búrca that the adjective *patricius* was an early borrowing with the meaning of 'bishop'[12] would carry more weight if there were any example elsewhere of such a usage.

Yet it must be said that the chronology which Binchy's theory would suggest is a great deal more acceptable linguistically than that which Jackson elaborated on the basis of the MacNeill theory; it allows a much more reasonable time for phonological changes which must be assigned to the second period, such as the shortening of long vowels in unstressed syllables (e.g., *eclais* from **eclēsia*) and syncope of post-tonic syllables (*Notlaic* from *Natalicia*). If the second stratum begins about the middle of the fifth century, the beginning of the first stratum can hardly be placed later than the middle of the fourth. The historical implications are that Latin-speaking missionaries from Britain had succeeded in establishing scattered Christian communities in Ireland during the fourth century, but that no episcopal organization was set up until the period in the middle of the fifth century traditionally associated with Patrick, and that from that time onwards the British churchmen who were in contact with Ireland were British-speaking – indeed we might say Welsh-speaking. It should be noted, too, that even if the religious vocabulary which belongs to the early stratum of loanwords is somewhat skimpy, there are other words which point to cultural contacts – *clúm* (*pluma*), *cann* (*panna*), *corcur* (*purpura*), *sorn* (*furnus*), *siball* (*fibula*) all belong here. That there was trade between Britain and Ireland during the fourth century seems probable, and that British Christians took advantage of these contacts to spread their faith to Ireland certainly not impossible.

When we turn to the last century and a half of the period with which this volume is concerned, there can be no doubt of the close contacts of the churches of Ireland and Britain; they form a single unit with many similar institutions and a common ecclesiastical language – Latin with a distinctive British pronunciation. This latter fact is not in dispute, but it has sometimes been made to carry more weight than it will bear; because Christian Ireland pronounced its Latin with British values attached to the consonants we must not assume that every Latin word which belongs to the second stratum of loanwords was borrowed direct from Britain. This reservation might appear to be so obvious as hardly to be worth making, but there is so much confusion of thought on the subject that it must be developed. Thus Jackson says that 'it is well known that the spelling of Old Irish derives from the orthographical ideas of the British monks whose relations with the early Irish church were of such importance in the sixth century.'[13] One might think that there was some direct evidence for these orthographical ideas, but there is in fact none. On the contrary, all the evidence points to vernacular literature in Irish being far older than that in the neo-British languages. The reasons for this are obvious: in Ireland, Latin was confronted by a rich and highly organized native oral tradition and never became widely known outside the Church; in Britain, on the other hand, the writing of the vernacular in the sixth century is as improbable as it would be in Gaul of the same period, for both countries had been part of the Empire and the prestige of Latin was still immense – *nostra lingua* to Gildas, as it certainly was not to his Irish contemporaries. Since we have at least one Irish text of monastic origin, the *Aipgitir Chrábaid*, which can hardly be much later than 600 A.D., written in an orthography which was clearly well established, and since no vestige of such a thing exists in any neo-British language at such an early period, it seems to me highly likely that, if British monks during the sixth century had any ideas on writing their native tongue, they had derived them from their Irish colleagues. It is significant that a recent detailed study of Old Welsh and Old Irish orthography has demonstrated that there is much in the Welsh system which can be satisfactorily explained only on the assumption that Irish models were being followed.[14]

Another example of the unjustified equation of British Latin pronunciation with British origin is the discussion by Vendryes of the old Irish ecclesiastical term *andóit*.[15] He explains it correctly as 'church,' adding that its oldest meaning is 'part of the church containing the relics'; he then goes on to derive it from the late Latin word *antitas* listed by Ducange – apparently a contraction of *antiquitas* – and says that it came into Irish 'par l'intermédiaire du brittonique.' One might think from this that the word was attested in some neo-British language, but it is not; we have no evidence for either word or institution outside Ireland and Gaelic Scotland. If it really comes from *antitas*, all that can be said about it is that this word was taken into Ireland during the later period, when the British pronunciation of Latin was being used; that is not by any means the same thing as saying that it came from a British source.

However, the relations at this period were so close that sometimes it is impossible to decide how a term used in both countries was originally evolved. Take, for example, the word for Maundy Thursday which occurs in Irish, Welsh, Breton and Cornish and therefore cannot be later than the sixth century. *Geiriadur Prifysgol Cymru*, the standard Welsh dictionary, explains the Welsh form *cablyd* as a loanword from Irish, ultimately from either *capitilavium* or *capillatio*. Binchy objected to this that Ir. *caplait* and W. *cablyd* could not have both evolved independently from *capitilavium*, and said there was not a shadow of doubt that what he calls 'the drastic streamlining' of the original word took place in British, perhaps through confusion with *capillatio*.[16] Jackson defended the *GPC* explanation, and offered good reasons why the streamlining could not have taken place in British;[17] he did not, however, deal with the equally good reasons why it could not have taken place in Irish either. There are equally serious problems with Ir. *corgus*, W. *carawys*, Br. *koraiz* 'Lent', from *quadragesima*. Thurneysen listed these Irish forms, together with others which undergo 'drastic streamlining' of a similar kind, as being of monastic provenance and I think this gives us a hint of the only possible explanation; these words arise from the debased Latin jargon of monks whose native tongues were Irish and Welsh, and the forms which have come down to us arise from the mutual interaction of the three languages.

In some cases, of course, the direction of linguistic borrowing is clear; thus, when we find just three examples in early Irish of *Spirut Glan* for 'The Holy

Ghost,' instead of the normal *Spirut Noeb*, we may well agree with Fr Ó Laoghaire that the term used by the Patrician missionaries has been preserved, for *glan* in Welsh means both 'holy' and 'pure,' but in Irish only 'pure.'[18] On the other hand, the devotion consisting of the recitation of Psalm 119 is known in Irish as *biait* and in Welsh as *bwyeit;* both words derive from Latin *beati* (the first word of the psalm), and, since Latin *-t-* appears as [d], from a British pronunciation of Latin. And yet the Welsh form is quite inexplicable as a native development, for the Latin penultimate syllable *-āt-* regularly gives *-awt-* in early Welsh. Both the Irish and Welsh forms go back to a Latin one in which the classical quantities of the first two vowels have been transposed, from *bĕāti* to *bēăti*, and this is just what we expect in Ireland, for Irish has the accent on the first syllable of the word and at one period reduced all long vowels after the accent, as in *treblait*, from *tribulatio*, which is a loan word of the second stratum, evolved from Latin with a British pronunciation, but certainly not from British itself. We may conclude that *beati* was pronounced [be:adi] in Ireland in the sixth century, and this is the form from which the Welsh word derives; it is, I think, legitimate to conclude that the devotion was imported from Ireland too.

What is perhaps a more important example of this process is the borrowing by British of the Irish term *secundus abbas* 'prior' and, no doubt, of the institution as well. The recognition of the identity of Irish *secndap* and Welsh *segynnab* is due to Binchy who, however, explained it in terms of an Irish borrowing from Latin through British.[19] As in some of the other examples I have discussed, there is no reason for regarding it as British apart from the British treatment of *-c-* as [g] and there are strong arguments against it; one is that the Irish word for 'abbot' *abb* derives from the Latin nominative *abbas*, but the Welsh *abat* from the oblique cases, so that the second element in *segynnab* is isolated in Welsh. These are linguistic considerations; I speak with less confidence about institutions, but I do not think that *secundus* in the meaning of 'deputy with right of succession' occurs in ecclesiastical Latin outside Ireland and Wales. It seems to me that the explanation of this usage is to be found in institutions and terminology which are purely Irish. The terms *toísech* 'leader' and *tánaise* 'deputy with right of succession' are deeply embedded in the Irish legal system and the etymology of the former, which is cognate with W. *tywysog*, is not in doubt. The other word, *tánaise*, has not been explained; Thurneysen suggested that it contains the preverbs *to-ad-* and a participle of the verb **ni-sed-*, but offered no comment on the semantic problem.[20] Now this verb forms at least two other compounds which have the meaning 'await, expect' (*indnaide* and *irnaide*) and this reminds us of the explanation of *tánaise* given in the legal text *Críth Gablach:* 'The *tánaise* of a king, why is he so called? Because the whole people looks forward to his kingship without opposition to him.'[21] The *tánaise*, then, is the 'expected one', the equivalent of the Welsh *gwrthrychiad*.

But the words *toísech* and *tánaise* are much more than purely legal terms in

Old Irish; they have come to mean simply 'first' and 'second,' and, indeed, those are the primary meanings assigned to them in the standard lexicographical work.[22] Bearing this in mind, we can reconstruct the whole process. Beside the *tánaise ríg*, the expected successor of the king, there was evolved the parallel office in monastic life of the *tánaise abbad*, a term which is well attested in later documents. This had to be translated into Latin, and the obvious equivalent for *tánaise* was *secundus*, so that we get *secundus abbas*, and, since this happened in the post-Patrician period, the Latin had its British pronunciation. This common monastic term was borrowed back into Irish by the usual process of dropping the final syllables and treated as a single three-syllable word **secund-abb*, of which the second vowel was elided regularly at some period in the sixth century, thus giving *secndap*, the form attested in Old Irish, from which W. *segynnab* (where the *-y-* represents a secondary vowel of the same kind as in *barywhaud*) was borrowed. I think it is more than likely that the two meanings of *secundus* have been responsible for a good deal of confusion in some of our early documents; one might suspect, for example, that the *Ailill primus* and *Ailill secundus*, both from the same place, who are recorded as successive coarbs of Patrick in several lists[23] represent merely the succession of *one* Ailill who had been *secundus abbas*, but to follow this would take me too far from my theme. Binchy has already pointed out that Welsh uses the word *eil* 'second' for 'heir' and that Asser's use of the word *secundarius* may have been influenced by this; he thought this might point to a common Celtic practice of using the word meaning 'second' in the special sense of 'heir' or 'successor.' It seems more likely to me that we should put it the other way round, and take it that these British developments, as well as the word *segynnab*, have their original in linguistic developments which were purely Irish.

I need hardly say that what I have been saying serves only to strengthen the view stated by O'Rahilly, that 'throughout the sixth century the closest relations existed between the Irish Church and that of Wales';[24] from a linguistic point of view, the large number of not only British Latin, but Welsh, loanwords in Irish would indicate considerable intercourse between the two countries at this time. It will be seen, however, that I am not quite as ready as he was to say that 'by the seventh century the Irish Church has acquired a markedly British stamp,' for I conceive the process as one of interaction, and it is reasonable to believe that, as the Welsh Church came under increasingly heavy pressure from its neighbours, the influence of the Irish Church, based on a country free from outside influences, and where Christianity was now firmly established, would tend to increase. We can even point to some small differences between the two systems, though they are matters of terminology rather than of institutions. For example, the word *sacerdos* and its derivative *sacard* seem to replace *presbyter* and *cruimther* in the meaning of 'priest' in Ireland at quite an early date, while in the British Church its usual meaning was 'bishop'; I cannot offer any explanation of this. And it is also strange that there is no trace of the *paruchia*, which is what we might call the sphere of influence of a bishop or an abbot, in early British sources, or in any of the neo-British languages. It is, admittedly, an imprecise word; Bieler translates it as 'parish' in his edition of the so-called 'First Synod of St Patrick' but adds 'i.e. diocese' in the notes to the passage where the domain of a bishop is referred to.[25] That it was looked on as a fairly small area by the eighth century is clear from the usage of the Würzburg glossator, who added to the passage in Ephesians i.20 '. . . set him on his own right hand in the heavenly places' the comment *ní far cuairt pairche do-coid;* the editors of *Thesaurus Palaeohibernicus* translate this as 'not on a diocesan visitation hath he gone,' but, of course, the meaning is much more like 'it's not on any parish visit he has gone.' However, a solution to this problem may lie in the observation recently made by Dr Kathleen Hughes who points out that, in Latin documents which may well be ascribed to the sixth century, the terms *paruchia* and *plebs* appear to be interchangeable, and she suggests that both denote the land inhabited by a particular group of people, 'possibly the *sept* or even the *túath*.'[26] The un-Irish and imprecise term *sept* can be ignored; the possibility that the sphere of influence of the bishop or abbot was the *túath* – what Binchy would call the 'tribe' – is very great, and it will account for the later development of the word *plebs* into the meaning of 'parish,' as in W. *plwyf*, Br. *plou*. Later, of course, *paruchia* takes on a greatly extended meaning in Ireland; Cogitosus, writing in the 630s, says that the *paruchia* of Brigit 'has spread throughout the whole Irish island,' and the *Liber Angeli* allots all Ireland to Patrick as his *paruchia*. But this is the language of pious hyperbole, and means no more than did John Wesley's intention to take the whole world for his parish. The Würzburg glossator's *cúairt phairche*, and the secondary meanings of modern English 'parochial,' give us a better idea of the narrow limits of the *paruchia* or *plebs* of the sixth-century church in Britain or Ireland, and we may note that the passage from *Liber Angeli* preserves, behind its highflown language, the distinction between *terminus* and *paruchia*.[27] The *terminus* (Ir. *termonn*, but W. *llann*) was the land held by the bishop or abbot, contrasted with the *paruchia* (Ir. *pairche*, but British *plebs*, W. *plwyf*) which was his sphere of influence, probably originally identical with a *plebs* or *túath*. The organization was the same; only the words are different.

I have had no new or startling discoveries to put before you in this paper. That Christianity came to Ireland from Britain, that the process must have begun long before the traditional date assigned to St Patrick, that from his time onward the British and Welsh churches had a common language and common institutions – none of these things is new; all that I have been able to offer on my own behalf is a certain amount of evidence which seems to show that by the sixth century Ireland was able to repay some of her debts to the British Church, and that the study of sub-Roman Christianity in Britain must take account of relations with Ireland in the sixth century.

Notes

1. Sommerfelt, A., 'External versus internal factors in the development of language', *Norsk Tidsskrift for Sprogvidenskap* 19 (1960), 304
2. Hanson, R. P. C., *St Patrick, a British missionary bishop*, 15
3. Bieler, L., *Epistolae S. Patricii* ii, 139
4. *Op. cit.* ii, 128
5. Mac Cana, P. 'W. *dyfod*, *mynd*, Br. *dont*, *mont*, 'bring', *Ériu* 20 (1966) 215
6. MacNeill, E., 'The Beginnings of Latin Culture in Ireland', *Studies* 20 (1931), 39ff.
7. O'Rahilly, T. F. *The Two Patricks* (Dublin, 1942)
8. *Anecdota from Irish Manuscripts* iv 19 §211
9. See *Celtica* 4 (1958), pp. 288 ff.
10. Binchy, D. A., 'Patrick and his biographers', *Studia Hibernica* 2 (1962), 165–6
11. Carney, J., *Studies in Irish Literature and History* (Dublin, 1955) 1362
12. de Búrca, S., 'The Patricks: a linguistic interpretation', *Lochlann* 3 (1965) 1278ff.
13. *Op. cit.*, 73
14. Watkins, T. A., 'Points of Similarity between Old Welsh & Old Irish Orthography', *Bulletin of the Board of Celtic Studies of the University of Wales* 21 (1964–6), 135–41
15. Vendryes, J., *Lexique étymologique de l'irlandais ancien*, s.v.
16. *Celtica* 4 (1958), 291
17. Jackson, K. H., 'Final syllables in 'Pádraig' loanwords', *Études Celtiques* 9 (1960–1), 91
18. Quoted by Carney in *The Poems of Blathmac* (Irish Texts Society, vol. 47, Dublin, 1964), 162
19. Binchy, D. A., 'Some Celtic legal terms', *Celtica* 3 (1956) 221–8
20. Thurneysen, R. *Grammar of Old Irish*, (Dublin, 1946), 249
21. Binchy, D. A. *Críth Gablach* (Dublin, 1941) ll 434–5
22. See *Contributions to Irish Lexicography* (RIA) s.vv.
23. *Book of Leinster* (ed. Best, Bergin and O'Brien) 5998–6000; *Annals of Ulster*, s.a. 525, 535
24. *The Two Patricks*, 41
25. Bieler, L., *The Irish penitentials* (Dublin, 1963), 58, 240
26. Hughes, K., *The Church in early Irish society* (London, 1966), 50
27. *Ibid.*, *op. cit.*, 276

Eccles in English Place-Names

Kenneth Cameron

In 1922 Ekwall wrote 'Names such as Eccles, Eccleston, in my opinion indicate that there were British churches in the places so called.'[1] He derived Eccles[2] from Brit **Eclēs* 'a church,' compared this form with Old Welsh *eccluys*, Welsh *eglwys*, Old Cornish *eglos* and Old Irish *eclis*, and took **eclēs* as a loan word from Latin *ecclesia*. Though this etymology was not new, Ekwall noted that there had been different opinions about the origin of the name, but he supported Moorman, who had defended a derivation from a Brit form of Latin *ecclesia*.[3]

No one today doubts that this interpretation is the correct one, though Jackson gives the history of the British loanword from Latin as Vulgar Latin *eclēsia*> PrW **eglẹ̄s*> Welsh *eglwys*, Cornish *eglos*, Old Irish *eclais*=[egliʃ], where Vulgar Latin -*cl*- has given PrW -*gl*- by lenition. Jackson also points out that the Brit word does not come directly from Latin *ecclēsia*, and that Ekwall's British form **eclēs* should read Brit **eclēsia* or PrW **eglẹ̄s*.[4]

Commenting on the significance of the place-names Eccles, Eccles-, Ekwall suggested that we may suppose they denoted places of some importance or structures of a more lasting kind than ordinary British villages.[5] Jackson has put it a different way, for he says that the name Eccles implies the existence of some sort of British population-centre with organized worship.[6]

With our present state of knowledge, I do not see that we can improve on this interpretation. No British church-site has as yet been identified on the ground at any of the places whose names contain **eglẹ̄s*, but sometime the archaeological evidence may well be available.

So far, six names in Eccles have been noted:

La Eccles (w. of Manchester), *Eccles* a. 1185, c. 1200, 1253 (La 37–38).

Db Eccles Ho (w. of Chapel en le Frith), *Eccles* Hy 3, *Ecles* 1285 (Db 62).
Eccles Ho (s. of Hope), *Ekelis* 1306, *Ekles* 1359 (Db 120).

Nf Eccles (s.w. of Attleborough), *Eccles* 1086, 1212 (DEPN s.n.).
Eccles (formerly on coast near Hickling), *Heccles* 1086, *Eccles* 1086, 1254 (DEPN s.n.).

K Eccles (near Aylesford, *of æcclesse* c. 975, *Aiglessa* 1086, *Ecclesse* 1166, *Eccles* 1208 (KPN 305).

There can be little doubt that each of these names is in fact to be derived from **eglẹ̄s* 'a church,' which would appear in PrOE as **eclēs*. In the borrowing of the Brit name sound substitution has taken place, for OE had no single medial

-*g*- of its own, except when it followed a nasal, and so -*c*- was substituted for it. A shift of stress from the second part of the name to the first has also taken place, so that an early form must have been **Écles*, hence the modern name.

Eccles, however, occurs too as the first component of some compound English place-names. But, it is by no means certain that the source of this is always PrW **eglēs*. Ekwall has argued that this is in fact very doubtful when the final element denotes a stream, as in Ecchinswell (Ha), Ecclesbourne (Db), and *Ecelesford*, the older name of Ashford (Mx), itself a ford across a river called *eclesbroc* in 962, as well as in several lost names.[7] He would prefer to take *Eccles* – here as an old river-name, though its etymology is by no means clear. His argument, however, demands respect, and it is better at this stage to omit these river-names from our list. This leaves us with fourteen compound place-names, which seem certain examples of OE **Ecles* (<PrW **eglẹ̄s*), with an OE word as the second element. The commonest of these are OE *tūn* and *halh*, dative singular *hale*, each of which occurs four times.

OE *tūn* 'a homestead, village' is found in

La Eccleston (w. of St Helens), *Ecclistona* 1190, *Eccliston* a. 1220 (La 108).
Eccleston (w. of Chorley), *Aycleton* 1094, *Ecclestun* c. 1180, *Ekeleston* 1203 (La 131).
Great and Little Eccleston (on the R. Wyre near Poulton), *Eglestun* 1086, *Eccliston* 1212, 1243, *Parua Eccliston* 1261, *Great Ecleston* 1285 (La 161 and 154).

Ch Eccleston (s. of Chester), *Eclestone* 1086, *Eccleston* 1285 (DEPN s.n.).

OE *halh*, dative singular *hale* 'a nook, corner of land, water-meadow' developed a variety of meanings, and it is difficult to determine its exact sense in many place-names. It is, however, the second element in

YW Ecclesall (s.w. of Sheffield), *Eccleshale* 1200–10, 1251, *Ecclessale* 13th, *Ecklishal* 1252 (YW i, 192).
St Eccleshall (s.w. of Stone), *Ecleshelle* 1086, *Eccleshale* 1227, 13th (St 54 and DEPN s.n.).
Wa Exhall (near Alcester), *Eccleshale* 710 (14th), 1253, *Ecleshelle* 1086, *Ecleshale* 1194 (Wa 208).
Exhall (n. of Coventry), *Eccleshale* 1144, *Ecleshale* 1198 (Wa 107–8).

In two examples, the second element is OE *hyll* 'a hill,' and in another it is OE *clif* 'a cliff, bank':

La Eccleshill (near Darwen), *Eccleshull* 1246, *Ekeleshulle* 1276 (La 75–76).
YW Eccleshill (n.w. of Bradford), *Egleshil* 1086, *Eccleshull* c. 1250, 1274 (YW iii, 258–59), and
Du Egglescliffe (s.w. of Stockton), *Egglescliff* 1085, *Ecclescliue*, *Egglescliue* 1197 (NbDu 72).

In addition, OE *feld* 'open country, land free from wood, plain' appears in

YW Ecclesfield (n. of Sheffield), *Eclesfelt* 1086, *Eclesfeld* 1086, 1150–56, *Ecclesfeld* 12th (YW i, 244–45).

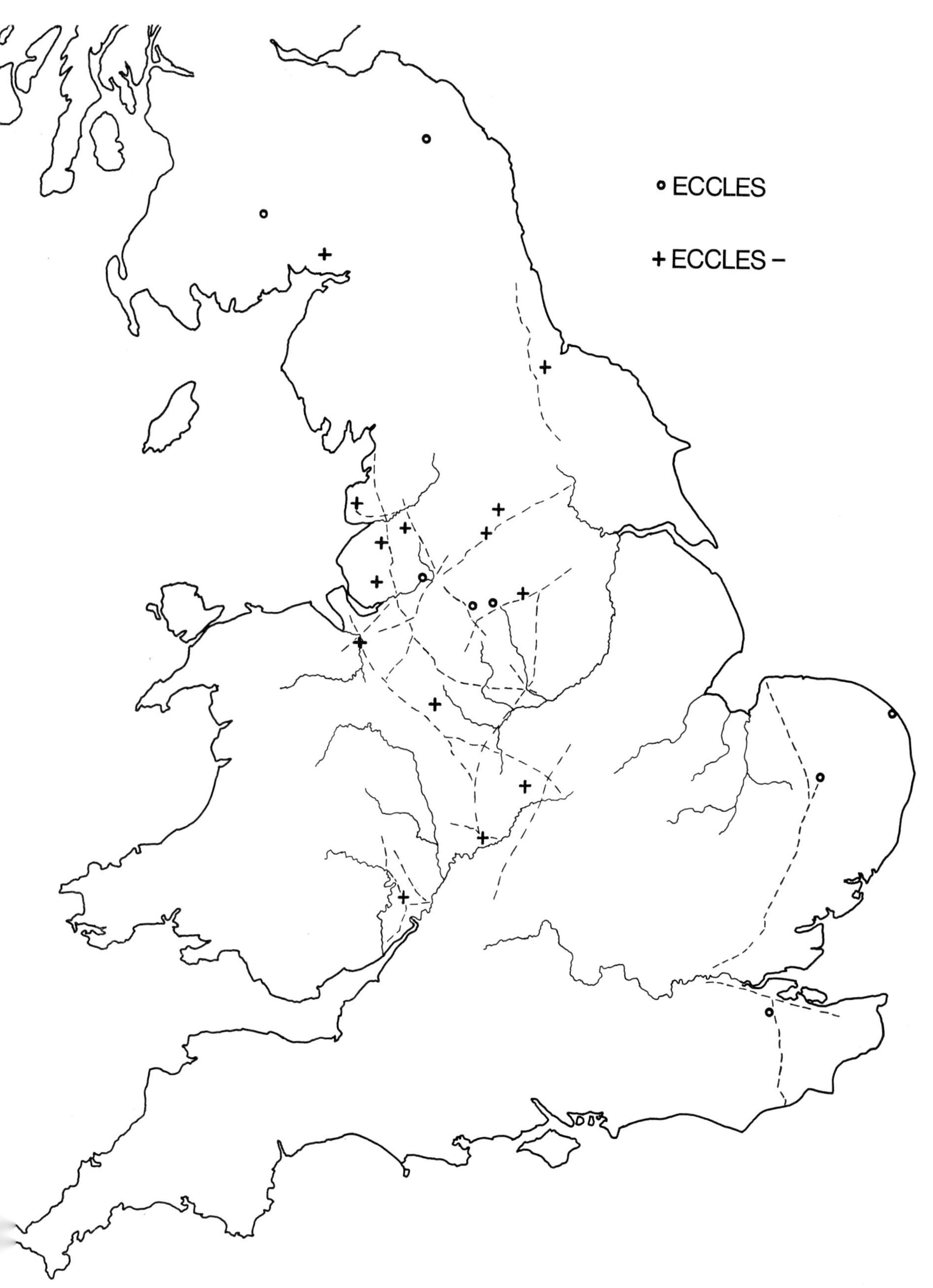

*Distribution map of Eccles (Pr W *eglēs) in Britain, with Roman roads in their vicinity*

OE *lēah* 'a wood,' 'an open place in a wood, glade' in
YW Exley (s. of Bradford, near Southowram), *Ecklisley*, *Ecclisley* 13th, 1247, *Eccleslay* 1277, *Ekelesley* 1286 (YW iii, 91).
and OE (Mercian) *wælle* 'a spring, stream' in
He Eccleswall (s.e. of Ross), *Egleswalle* 1274, *Ecleswelle* 1275 (DEPN s.n.), where the second element may well mean 'a spring,' since Rudhall Brook rises here.

In each of these names Eccles- no doubt denoted a British church, and the name for it was, perhaps, taken over or passed on to the Anglo-Saxons as a place-name. If this is so, we ought to translate Eccleston, for example, as 'the homestead or village at or near *Eccles*,' where *Eccles* denotes 'a British church.' But, it is just possible that in some parts of the country the Brit word **eglẹ̄s* was borrowed, not as a place-name, but as an appellative, though it must be clearly understood that there is no independent evidence that it *was* ever taken over into colloquial use in OE. The only pointer in this direction is the geographical distribution of some of the names themselves, which occur close together, or more widely distributed in a larger area. So, Ecclesall and Ecclesfield are near Sheffield; Eccleshill and Exley are close to Bradford; and the two Derbyshire Eccles are only some eight miles apart. If we count Great and Little Eccleston as originally a single name, there are five examples in Lancashire, which may well go with Eccleston in Cheshire and Eccleshall in Staffordshire, and so provide a group of seven related names. Perhaps the pairs in Norfolk and Warwickshire are also to be associated together. It could be argued that at least in some of these districts we are dealing with PrW **eglẹ̄s* as a localized loan-word in OE. There can, of course be no certainty, but the possibility ought surely to be left open.[8]

Some indication of the geographical distribution of Eccles-names has just been given, and there are only the single examples in Durham, Herefordshire and Kent to be added. They are certainly widely distributed, though with an obvious concentration in the northwest Midlands (including Lancashire south of the R. Wyre), where over half of them occur. There are none in Cumbria, in the east Midlands, in the central south or in the southwest.

In terms of Jackson's British River-Names map,[9] only three are to be found in Area I, though these are all simplex names; the rest are in Areas II and III, with the other three Eccles in Area II. Put another way, all the compound names are situated in areas of Britain not settled by the Anglo-Saxons at an early date, *in the main* from about 600 onwards.

An interesting topographical feature is that all are situated close to rivers or streams, except Eccles (near Hickling) which was on the coast. Some are on hills or on valley slopes, but all are close to water.

But, perhaps the *most* interesting feature I have noted is that many are close to Roman roads, some also to other Roman sites. Eight, Eccles and Eccleshill (both La), Eccles (K), Eccles (Nf, near Attleborough), Eccles (Db, near Hope), Eccleston (Ch), Eccleswall (He) and Exhall (Wa, near Alcester) are all on or close to Roman roads;[10] another five, Eccles (Db, near Chapel en le Frith), Ecclesall, Eccleshill and Exley (all YW) and Eccleston (La, near Chorley) are within about two miles of Roman roads.[11] In addition, Great and Little Eccleston are less than four miles from the probable route of such a road and a similar distance from Skippool, thought to be the site of a Roman harbour on the R. Wyre;[12] Egglescliffe (Du) is about four and a half miles from the road from Stamford Bridge to Durham;[13] Eccleshall (St) is six miles from the road which leads from Penkridge to Whitchurch;[14] and Ecclesfield (YW) is only two miles north of the defensive work known locally as the 'Roman Rig' or 'Roman Ridge.' Only Eccles (Nf, near Hickling), Eccleston (La, near St Helens) and Exhall (Wa, near Coventry) are not apparently near Roman roads. Furthermore, Eccles (Db, near Hope), Eccleston (Ch), Eccleswall (He) and Exhall (Wa, near Alcester) are close to Roman towns or stations, while the sites of Roman buildings have been identified immediately to the north and northeast of Eccles (K).

If one or two of these are considered to be too far from Roman roads for this to be no more than coincidence, we are still left with about three-quarters of the twenty sites of British churches, known to us from place-names, situated within a couple of miles of such roads. Moreover, a quarter are very close to Roman sites. The proportion is strikingly high.

As we have seen, place-names provide us with a group of certainly twenty related names, which denote the sites of British churches. Future research may add to this number, but it is not likely to alter the overall pattern. For example, no additional example has been noted in the considerable material available for Lincolnshire, Leicestershire and Rutland, so that we can be pretty certain that there is not a single Eccles in the east Midlands. Nor has any been discovered in Hampshire or Somerset, for each of which similar unpublished material is available. It would therefore appear that there is also a blank in southwest England, outside Cornwall, which is a special case anyway.

As Kenneth Jackson has said, names in Eccles indicate centres of British Christian worship, each with its own church. We must be thankful that from a study of place-names we have this much to add to what documentary and archaeological evidence can independently provide.

Postscript

After this paper had been read, it was suggested that the Scottish examples of place-names in Eccles, derived from PrW **eglẹ̄s* should be added to complete the picture. These, however, present a difficult etymological problem, for though there are many names in Eccles, it seems highly likely that most are to be derived from Gaelic *eaglais* and do not come direct from PrW **eglẹ̄s*.

Dr W. F. H. Nicolaisen suggests that there may well be only three certain examples of names derived directly from the PrW form.[15] These comprise two simplex Eccles and one compound name:

Ber Eccles, *Eccles* c. 1200, *Ecclys* c. 1220, *Hecles* 1297.

Dum Eccles (near Penpont), *Eklis* 1494.
Ecclefechan (near Hoddom), *Egilfeichane* 1507, *Eglisfechane* 1510, *Egilphechane* 1542, which may mean 'St Fechan's church' or 'little church' (cf. W. J. Watson, *The History of Celtic Place-Names of Scotland*, 168–9).

All three are situated close to a river or stream, like their English counterparts. Further, the two examples in Dumfriesshire are each within one and a half miles of a Roman road,[16] and a similar distance from a Roman fort or camp.

Abbreviations

a.	*ante*
Ber	Berwickshire
Brit	British
c.	*circa*
Ch	Cheshire
Db	Derbyshire and Cameron, K., *The Place-Names of Derbyshire* (EPNS XXVII-XXIX), Cambridge 1959
DEPN	Ekwall, E., *The Concise Oxford Dictionary of English Place-Names*, 4th edition, Oxford 1960
Du	Durham
Dum	Dumfriesshire
EPNS	English Place-Name Society
Ha	Hampshire
He	Herefordshire
K	Kent
KPN	Wallenberg, J. K., *Kentish Place-Names*, Uppsala 1934
La	Lancashire and Ekwall, E. *The Place-Names of Lancashire*, Manchester 1922
Mx	Middlesex
NbDu	Mawer, A., *The Place-Names of Northumberland and Durham*, Cambridge 1920
Nf	Norfolk
OE	Old English
PrOE	Primitive Old English
PrW	Primitive Welsh
s.n.	*sub nomine*
St	Staffordshire and Duignan, W. H., *Notes on Staffordshire Place-Names*, London, 1902
Wa	Warwickshire and Gover, J. E. B., Mawer, A. and Stenton, F. M., *The Place-Names of Warwickshire* (EPNS XIII), Cambridge 1936
YW	West Riding of Yorkshire and Smith, A. H., *The Place-Names of the West Riding of Yorkshire* (EPNS XXX-XXXVII), Cambridge 1961–63

Notes

1. Ekwall, E. *The Place-Names of Lancashire* (Manchester, 1922), 257
2. Ekwall, *op. cit.* 37–38
3. Moorman, F. W. *The Place-Names of the West Riding of Yorkshire* (Leeds, 1910), vii f.
4. Jackson, K. *Language and History in Early Britain*, 412
5. Ekwall, E. 'The Celtic Element' in *Introduction to the Survey of English Place-Names* (EPNS I, i) (Cambridge, 1924), 22–3

Notes

6. Jackson, *op. cit.* 227
7. See. DEPN s.n. Ecchinswell, and Ekwall, E. *English River-Names* (Oxford, 1928), 141
8. Compare Smith, A. H. *English Place-Name Elements* (EPNS XXV-XXVI, Cambridge 1956), i, 145, and *The Place-Names of the West Riding of Yorkshire* (EPNS XXX-XXXVII, Cambridge 1961–3), i, 192
9. Jackson, *op. cit.* 220–3
10. See Margary, I. D. *Roman Roads in Britain*, 2 vols. (London, 1957). The relevant Road Numbers in Margary are 702, 7b, 13, 331, 710a, 6a, 611 and 18a respectively
11. Margary, Road Numbers 71b, 710b, 721, 712, and 70c respectively
12. Margary, Road Number 703
13. Margary, Road Number 80a
14. Margary, Road Number 19
15. I am greatly indebted to Dr Nicolaisen for providing me with all the relevant information
16. Both Margary, Road Number 7f.

The Evidence from North Britain

A. C. Thomas

Introduction

I begin by defining the scope of this study. The term 'Scotland' is scarcely meaningful before the Middle Ages, and I should like to replace it with 'North Britain'. By this, I mean the whole region stretching northward from Hadrian's Wall to the so-called Highland Line, taking in the Scottish Lowlands, the present county of Northumberland, and the former kingdom of Fife. The limits, by coast, are from the Tyne to the Tay on the east, and from the Solway to the Clyde on the west.

The chronological term 'sub-Roman' has never been clearly defined; but, where Christianity is the theme, an obvious division between 'sub-Roman' and 'post-Roman,' as successive periods, does exist. This is the point in time when the monastic missionary church, which had developed in south Wales and Ireland during the sixth century, appeared in North Britain. In the eastern part of North Britain, the return of the Bernician prince Oswald from exile *inter Scottos*, and the foundation of Lindisfarne under Aidan in 634–5, is the relevant event.[1] In the western part, the division is less well-marked; there is now some evidence for Irish secular settlement in the extreme southwest by 500 or so,[2] and Irish monasticism may have followed such settlement a good half-century before the foundation of Lindisfarne. This was however localized in its effect; and we may regard North British Christianity of the fifth, sixth and initial seventh centuries as essentially a sub-Roman movement. It is this movement I wish to examine.

The background to the region is fairly well-known. If we discount the Angles in Northumbria and the odd pockets of Irish in Galloway, North Britain was linguistically a 'P-Celtic' area, the vernacular being what is now called *British*; later in the sixth century, when British separates into regional dialects, this becomes 'Primitive Cumbric.'[3] The two Pictish tongues – one a form of P-Celtic, probably very close to British, the other apparently a non-Indo-European language[4] – are marginally involved in North Britain and will be mentioned again. Culturally, the North British people of sub-Roman times were the descendants of pre-Roman, Iron Age, groups, who had migrated northward late in prehistory.[5] Earlier tribal distinctions, now becoming increasingly apparent with further archaeological enquiry, and also distinctions in the degree of *romanitas* attained in differing parts of the region, must be duly considered, even after 400 A.D.; but the general cultural uniformity still remains.

The problems which this study must seek to formulate and answer are clear-cut ones. Granted that Christianity came first to North Britain in Roman times, did it survive anywhere in the sub-Roman period? If it survived, did it affect an increasing area, or number of communities, and how could this ever be demonstrated? Was Christianity in sub-Roman North Britain organized, and if so, in what manner? Prior to the arrival of Irish-based monasticism, was it reinforced from outside, say, from the Church in Gaul? Did the Northumbrians, during their political and territorial expansion in the seventh century, encounter heathen North British, or Christian North British, or both, and what evidence is there on this score? Were any of the Picts Christian, prior to the age of Columcille and the mission based on Iona? These are straightforward questions, and though it has become unfashionable to posit them in so blunt a form, it is time to put them afresh.

Before facing them, however, we must briefly examine the present trend of thought on North British Christianity. This revolves around the earliest and best-known Christian figure of the region, the person popularly called 'Ninian.'[6]

Ninian: the traditional picture

The most determined protagonist of Ninian, since Ailred of Rievaulx compiled his largely unhistorical *Vita Niniani*[7] in the twelfth century, has been Dr W. Douglas Simpson of Aberdeen. Dr Simpson's views on the saint's life, career, and historical status seem to be embodied in two books and four papers, published between 1935 and 1961.[8] These views have gained great currency, especially in educational and religious circles, and in view of their author's eminence and *auctoritas* in so many fields of study, cannot possibly be ignored.

In summary, they run as follows. Ninian was a Romanized Briton who was sent to Rome for a theological education. On his way home, he paused at Tours, where St Martin was then ruling his eccentric pioneer monastery; and the death of Martin in, or about, 397, provides a convenient terminus for this part of Ninian's career. Having returned to Britain, Ninian, who had somehow become a bishop, left the security of his home-town (Carlisle?), and venturing into further Galloway,[9] he built a stone church and founded a monastery at Whithorn. This was not mere whim; it was the direct consequence of, perhaps even an integral part of, Stilicho's reorganization of the northern frontier, designed to impress lasting *romanitas* and the *Pax Romana* on the tribes beyond the Wall. Ninian's church and monastery, the latter a direct imitation of Martin's at Tours, were dedicated to Martin; but they must be seen as just one more facet of the enduring hand of Rome, in this case operating through the medium of late Roman Christianity.

Nor was the work of 'the Apostle of Scotland,' as he has been labelled, limited to his initial foundation. He evangelized what are now the Solway Plain and the Lake District, traces of his work being detectable at Brampton,

Brougham, or anywhere else where churches, or holy wells, can now be shown to have been under the patronage of Ninian or his master Martin. His major endeavour was however reserved for a sterner field. Supported by a handful of disciples, Ninian travelled northeastward across the Lowlands, and utilizing a system of roads and passes which, in earlier centuries, had been employed if not constructed by the Roman legions, he worked his way up the east coast to Aberdeenshire, the Moray Firth, and the far northeast. He need not have stopped at Thurso; as Dr Douglas Simpson wrote in 1935, 'there is in fact no evidence known to me why the Northern islands need not have been impregnated with Christianity from *Candida Casa* even before St Kentigern dispatched his mission of revival to them in the later sixth century.' Again, a trail of dedications, most of them to Ninian but some in pairs involving both Ninian and Martin – and (less explicably) the purely Irish ecclesiastical term *andoit*, *annait*, meaning, roughly, 'an important early church with personal relics' – mark his path; and by the time of Ninian's death, large numbers of the Picts, if not quite the entire Pictish nation, had through his endeavours come to embrace Christ. The work of the Irish monk Columba or Columcille and his fellow-countrymen, though doubtless valuable in ironing out pockets of remnant paganism, or in dealing with subsequent apostasies, must be seen for what it was, a strictly secondary movement. In no way does this Columban episode – Columcille being, as Dr Simpson's biography of this controversial figure puts it, only 'the Apostle of Alba' – detract from the greater, pioneer, evangelization of North Britain's indigenous apostle.

Dr Simpson has, not unnaturally, been obliged to defend certain aspects of this thesis, and some of his articles are really no more than replies to such critical reviews as Wilhelm Levison's[10] or to the revisionism implicit in Professor MacQueen's recent book.[11] Nor, of course, must he be held responsible for the embroideries by less scholarly writers, who find in the stark, vigorous, Simpsonian depiction of the national apostle a suitable hero for the Kirk; and, one might add, a balm to national pride, long vulnerable on the score that Columban monasticism, like the Scottish Gaelic language, was yet another import from Catholic Ireland. But it would not be unfair to point out that Dr Simpson, and with him a very large body of Scottish opinion, shows no sign of retreating from his established central position – the Romano-British background, the connection with Tours and Martin, the evangelical journeyings, and the evidence from dedications.

I have presented Dr Simpson's thesis in bald summary, without interpolated comment. I must now stress that many students of the Early Christian period, inside Scotland as well as outside it, regard this thesis as wholly untenable, and demonstrably wrong in practically every detail.[12] The only points one would concede – that Ninian was British rather than Irish or Gaulish, that he was, as early as Bede's lifetime, believed to have been a bishop, and that he was in some manner connected with a place called *Candida Casa* which is now generally agreed to be the modern Whithorn – are those which rely, not on Dr Simpson's exegesis, but on a short passage written by Bede; they are, moreover, the only points in that passage about which controversy has ceased to arise.

An alternative approach

In one respect alone – the concept of continuity from late Roman Christianity on the Hadrianic frontier to sub-Roman Christianity in North Britain – it is possible, indeed essential, to side with Dr Simpson. A growing body of evidence, the results of increased archaeological activity, and of the Cambridge school of historical criticism led by Mrs Chadwick, is redressing a balance which was starting to dip a little too far on the Celtic-speaking, Atlantic British, side. Professor Jocelyn Toynbee's remark of 1953, 'The so-called Celtic church, surviving continuously in the west and north, was thoroughly Roman in creed and origin; Roman too, initially, in its organization and practice'[13] was, we recall, thought bold by many at the time. Insofar as she refers to sub-Roman times, and insofar as these words exclude later, Mediterranean-inspired developments in Ireland and the Irish colonies, the whole current of subsequent thinking and research has justified her standpoint.

The concept of Christianity in late Roman and sub-Roman North Britain that I want to put forward may appear to lean unduly on the physical, tangible, evidence, and on a series of inferences drawn from the distribution, or nature, of certain physical remains. We must nevertheless realize that, while it is now highly improbable that fresh meaningful historical sources, bearing upon this region at this period, will ever come to light, we have scarcely begun to exhume the corresponding witnesses of human activity in the guise of early North British churches, cemeteries, and related monuments. Dr Simpson's approach from history has given us a picture of sub-Roman Christianity in the north which departs from, rather than conforms to, the general pattern of similar pictures relating to similar barbarian lands on the fringes of the late Empire. The results of careful excavation in the last decade or so – results by no means all, as yet, in print – allow certain inferences which are at variance with the traditional picture; for example, they support the view that monasticism in the accepted sense was not introduced to western Britain until the end of the fifth century, which on any reckoning would be later than Ninian's lifetime. Archaeology, if we use this word in the secondary meaning of 'inferences which are based on the results obtained through the exercise of certain techniques and methods' is, at best, a delicate balance of probabilities; but the same could be said of the unending attempts to infer what Gildas meant about the date of the battle of *Mons Badonicus*, or what Bede had really heard about Ninian and *Candida Casa*. In balancing, then, the probabilities which seem to me to emerge from the study of the physical remains that we shall examine, I have been influenced by one major consideration, and one only; the assumption that the story of sub-Roman Christianity in North Britain cannot be divorced from the imperfectly-known social or political history of the region, and that far greater attention should now be accorded to this background.

Christianity and the northern frontier zone

Whether or not the comments of Origen and Tertullian in the third century[14] can be construed to embrace North Britain, beyond the Wall, as one of the *Britannorum inaccessa Romanis loca*, the record of a bishop of York at the Council of Arles in 314[15] provides some basis for late Roman Christianity in the north. It is a basis which is strengthened by the distribution of physical clues, listed by Professor Toynbee in her 1953 paper, mapped by Dr Frend in 1955[16] and most recently recatalogued, with additions and a useful bibliography, by John Wall.[17] The distribution map itself may be refined. One might first exclude all small portable objects, like the gold openwork rings, the (lost) Corbridge cup, and others whose value and obvious portability reduce their evidential weight to the same level as that of the numerous objects of Roman manufacture found in Ireland,[18] the proceeds of looting and piracy rather than indices of otherwise unrecorded Roman settlers. This weeding-out allows us to concentrate on such fixed remains as mosaic pavements, burials, supposed or acceptable church sites, building-blocks *in situ* with Christian graffiti, and perhaps the far less portable lead tanks of the Wiggonholt type.

The revised distribution appears to indicate two main zones of Christian activity, and the evidence, where dateable, mostly belongs to the fourth century. One zone is of course the extensively Romanized, urban-centred region of south-east England. The other runs northwest from York to the frontier line of Hadrian's Wall, a smaller region sometimes loosely called 'the northern frontier zone.' Here, there is a distinct western emphasis; and on the plausible assumption that fourth-century Christianity involved civilians as well as soldiers, the large and anomalous walled civil settlement at Carlisle must come to mind.[19]

A detailed area map (p. 98) against the physical setting can show, not only the fourth-century tombstone of *Flavius Antigonus Papias*, found in re-use as the lid of a sub-Roman(?) wooden coffin in the Gallows Hill cemetery at Carlisle,[20] but the other stone from Brougham Castle of similar date, to *Tittus* or *Titius M. . . .*[21] There is the lost fragment, probably from a tombstone, from Maryport, where the coin-evidence takes us to the end of the fourth century[22] and where the *Chi-Rho* could well be around 400 A.D.[23]

Despite its size, the settlement at Carlisle seems not to have risen beyond the status of a *vicus*, albeit a walled town, and it could be argued that in spiritual matters the Christians there would have been subject to the bishop at York. Whether this holds good for the troubled times of the later fourth century I do not know; but an argument for a late Roman bishopric of Carlisle, based on the *vicus*, can be adduced if one accepts the existence of Ninian. If we allow Ninian's connection with *Ad Candidam Casam* of Bede (the present Whithorn), our oldest dateable Christian evidence from Whithorn is the inscribed LATINUS

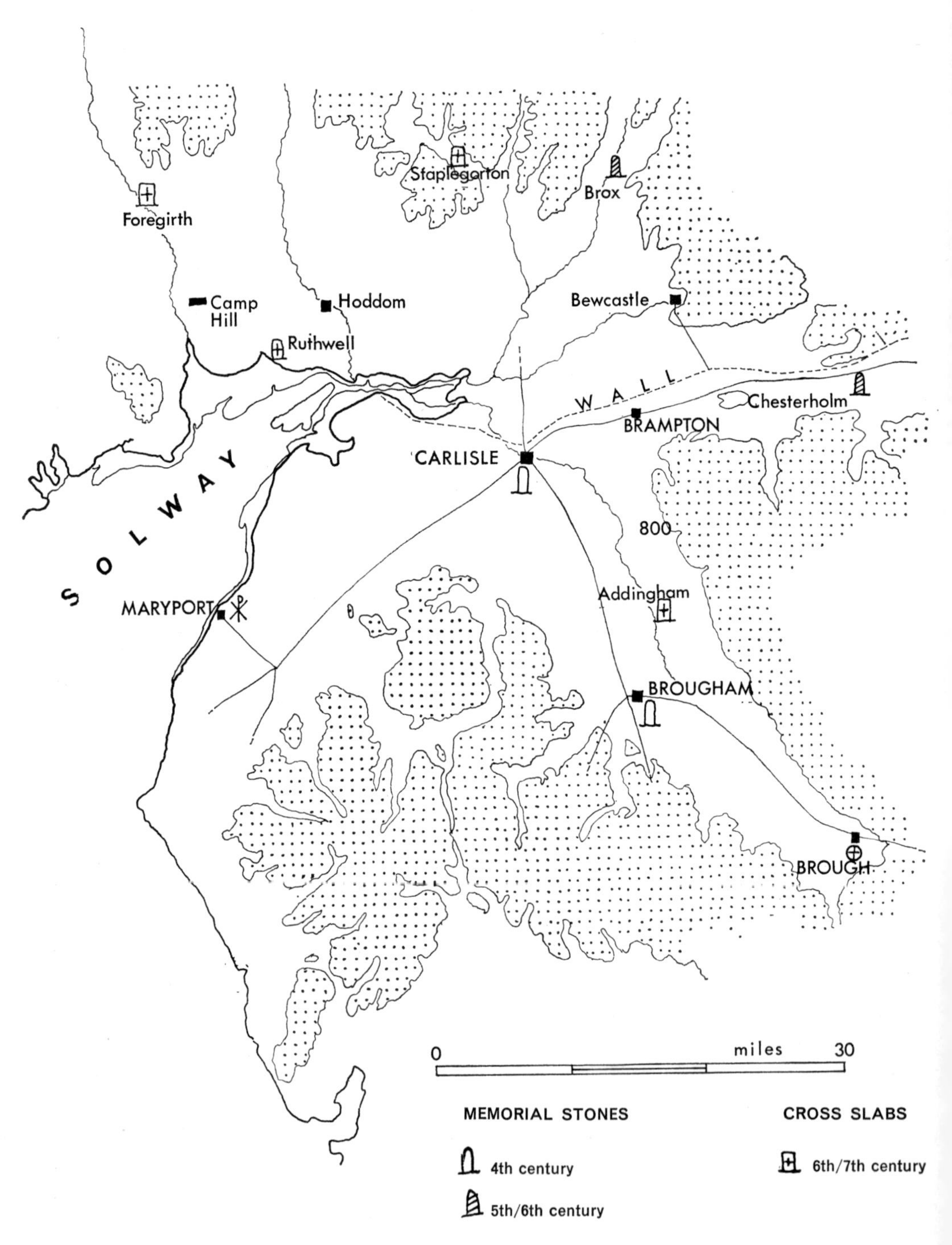

The Carlisle–Solway Area

tombstone, which Dr Radford sees as mid-fifth century[24] and Professor Jackson as nearer 500.[25] Our oldest *potential* evidence is the newly-uncovered inhumation cemetery there, of which more will be said, to which the LATINUS stone may very well have belonged. Neither feature is directly connected with Ninian, but both point to fifth-century Christianity in what may be regarded as Ninian's locality. Rejecting, as we must, the connection with Tours, and chronologically with Martin's death in 397, the only pointer to Ninian's dates is found, independent of Bede's account, in the eighth-century *Miracula* poem with its connection between the saint and a certain King Tuduvallus or Tudwal. I shall offer below a fresh reason for not dismissing such a link between Tudwal (who, it can be argued, may have ruled the Isle of Man) and Ninian not far away at Whithorn. Reckoning back by generations from the *obit* of a descendant, one arrives at the first half of the fifth century for Tudwal, as Radford and others have shown, and as MacQueen, who is inclined to accept this link, has also recently argued.[26]

Now if we allow Ninian to have been the bishop over a community of British Christians centred on Whithorn in the first half of the fifth century, it becomes very difficult to deny a similar spiritual leader to the British Christians of Carlisle. The Carlisle area shows distinct traces of fourth-century Christianity; Carlisle was a large *vicus* inside the Roman frontier, Whithorn a mere native settlement *extra limites;* Carlisle forms the most likely background not only for Ninian but very probably for Patrick as well; and, whatever divergences may arise in dating the Whithorn LATINUS stone, it is patently not as early as those from the Carlisle area. Nor would I suggest for a moment that a church at Whithorn was a successor to any church at Carlisle. The whole point about the anonymous biographer's story[27] of St Cuthbert and Queen Iurminburg visiting Carlisle in 685 is so frequently overlooked that I may be forgiven for stressing it here. It is not so much that the townsfolk, presumably first- or second-generation Anglian settlers who conversed with St Cuthbert and the queen in Old English, were able to show off the town walls and the Roman fountain; their national attitude to such wondrous *enta geweorc* is much better pictured by one of their own poets.[28] It is that the Angles' name for Carlisle, *civitas Luel* in both the Anonymous Life and Bede's, directly renders the British name, which by this time would have broken down from British Latin *Luguvalium* to something like *Ləowel;*[29] this strongly implies continuity of settlement from the fourth century, and there is no reason why Christianity should not have continued at Carlisle well past Ninian's day.

What, then, of Brampton and Brougham and Ninian's missionary work in Cumbria? One cannot have it both ways. If Ninian is to have been bishop of a rustic diocese at Whithorn after 400, Carlisle may have been subject to York or it may have had its own bishop, but surely it cannot have been subject to Whithorn. The concept of an early fifth-century bishop undertaking mission work in a contiguous, and older, diocese must be abandoned. With it, we also abandon the Ninewells at Brampton, the St Martin's church there of the twelfth century, and the St Martin's Oak of the seventeenth century.[30] That there were sub-Roman and late Roman Christians in the Lake District and along the Wall is very probable, but a better instance than Brampton is Brough-under-Stainmore, which has no connections whatsoever with Ninian or Martin; or Chesterholm, with its fifth-century memorial stone of Christian type to *Brigomaglos.*[31] Both Brough and Chesterholm have yielded pottery of, as Eric Birley writes, 'the closing years of the fourth century,'[32] and Brough also produced a (lost) ring with a *Chi-Rho* marked on it, from the river bed.[33]

It is also interesting to note how, in a way analogous to the extension of Christianity into Galloway and Whithorn, traces of fifth- and sixth-century Christian activity occurs north of the Solway and north of the Wall, in the Dumfriesshire plain east of the river Nith, which may have been the diocesan limit of sub-Roman times. The inscribed stone of about 500 from Brox in Liddesdale[34] should be remarked, as should the recently-found cemetery of oriented 'dug graves' inside the site of the hill-fort of Camp Hill, Trohoughton, a typical undeveloped cemetery of this period.[35] The simple, primary, uninscribed cross-slabs or cross-marked boulders from Foregirth, Ruthwell, Staplegorton and (south of Carlisle) Addingham are not earlier than the late sixth century, and are due to Irish influence from further west, but they still testify to sub-Roman, pre-Anglian Christianity here.[36]

Ninian and Whithorn

When we turn to the long, indented coastal plain of Galloway (p. 101), the first thing that strikes us in the present context is the extreme westerly position of Whithorn, nearly 60 miles from Carlisle. Why so far? Why was Whithorn chosen for a bishop's seat? E. A. Thompson has supplied a solution, when he writes[37] 'Bede's statement that he (Ninian) was a bishop distinctly implies . . . that there was a Christian community in southwestern Scotland *before* Ninian was consecrated. Indeed, it is not impossible that this community was sufficiently well organized to send a collective appeal to the appropriate authority (the bishop of York?) for the appointment of a bishop and to enter into consultations on the choice of Ninian. We might go further: Bede does not say and he does not even imply that Ninian was the first bishop of Candida Casa, and it would be impossible to refute the view that he had predecessors there (though few would believe, I fancy, that he had many). However that may be, if our suggestion is rejected and we suppose that Ninian was consecrated bishop of a region in which there was no Christian community already in existence, then we must add that this was an unparalleled innovation which could not easily be accounted for.'

Professor Thompson's ideas can now be coupled with the results of the current excavations below the east end of the priory church at Whithorn. I refer to these results through the kindness of Mr P. R. Ritchie and the courtesy of the Ancient Monuments Inspectorate (Scottish branch).[38] A community of late

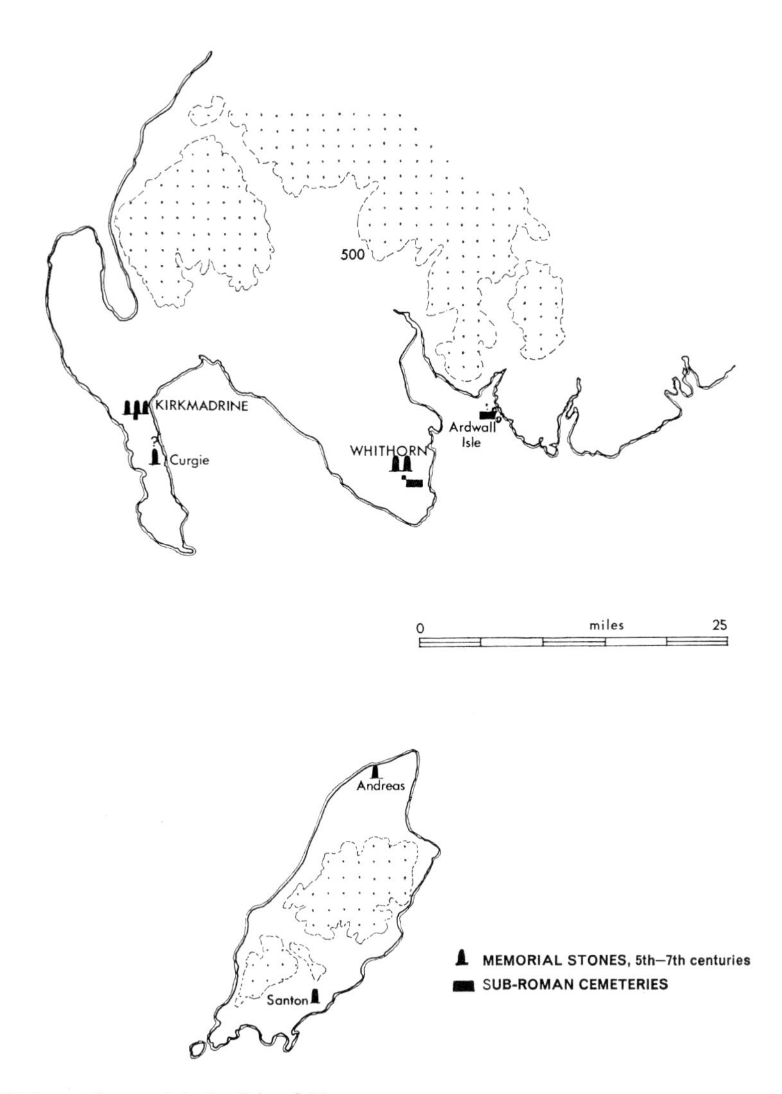

The Whithorn Area, with the Isle of Man

Roman Christians implies a Christian cemetery, and it is wholly possible that Mr Ritchie has found just this. The extended oriented inhumations, crushed by the tremendous overburden, lie in dug graves at a primary level, can hardly be other than Christian, and have disturbed at least one cremation and some sherds of red wheel-made pottery. Is this the remnant of a Roman cemetery, attached to some settlement, and continued in a post-conversion guise (perhaps *before* 400 A.D.) by local late or sub-Roman Christians? Whithorn may well have been the major, if not the sole, Christian community in the area at this time, and this, rather than any other factor, must for the moment explain its choice as the Ninianic *Ursitz*.

Apart from the Whithorn LATINUS tombstone, there are the three at Kirkmadrine, in the Rhinns, the most westerly peninsula. One, which names the *sacerdotes* VIVENTIUS and MAVORIUS, may even slightly ante-date the LATINUS stone.[39] Another, with two names, one of which is FLORENTIUS, is the same period as the LATINUS stone, and a third, with INITIUM ET FINIS, carries us into the sixth century. Kirkmadrine itself shows no signs at all, either from the air or on the ground, of any form of enclosed cemetery of early type, and there remains a suspicion that the original location of these stones

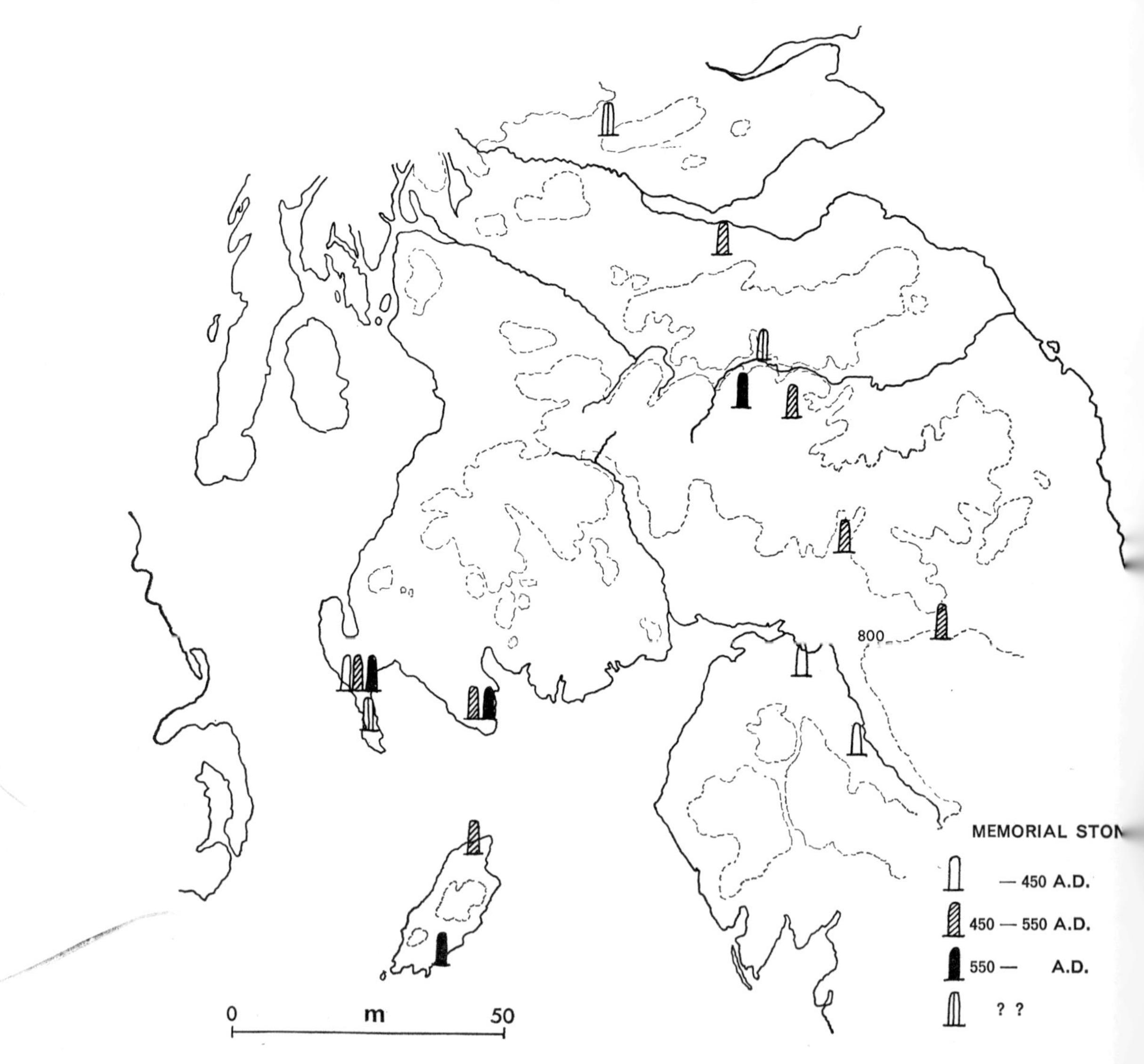

Inscribed memorial stones, North Britain; approximate dates. The lowest category includes lost, dubious, or undated examples

was elsewhere in the neighbourhood[40] – a suspicion strengthened by the quite credible report of a fourth, lost, stone[41] from Curgie, a few miles to the south, found associated with a grave, and seen to bear both the name VENTIDIUS and the information that he was 'a sub-deacon of the church' (DIACONUS?).

Two features of this area should be noted. Within the overall British distribution of sub-Roman memorial stones inscribed in Roman capitals, there is a gap between the North Welsh group, and those in North Britain proper. The type is absent from Ulster, indeed from Ireland, where a different tradition of personal commemoration occurs.[42] Into this wide interval we should insert (p. 102) two stones from the Isle of Man; that from Knock-y-Doonee, Andreas, which commemorates AMBICATUS in both horizontal Roman lettering and (in an Irish parallel form) in ogam,[43] of the late fifth century; and the stone from Santon, a century later, which is the monument (MONOMENTI) of AVITUS or AVITOS.[44] These two stones are witnesses to the existence of a tradition, epigraphically and linguistically linked to the north British mainland, which both antedates and overlaps with the postulated Irish absorption of Man in the sixth century. The nearness of Man to Galloway – a bare eighteen miles from the Point of Ayre to Burrow Head – recalls the reference to King Tudwal in the *Miracula* poem (see above p. 99). Was Christianity in Man in sub-Roman, pre-Irish, times a facet of the diocese of Whithorn?

The second feature is that, at Whithorn and Kirkmadrine, we glimpse briefly that external influence on the Church in sub-Roman Britain which, elsewhere – for instance, in Wales, Cornwall, and southern Ireland – assumes much greater importance. The form of the *Chi-Rho* motif, with the *rho* hook on the uppermost expanded arm of a cross and the enclosing circle derived from the Roman *clipeus*, seen on the three Kirkmadrine stones and the seventh-century LOCI PETRI APUSTOLI pillar at Whithorn,[45] occurs elsewhere on the Atlantic British sea-board. Its immediate source is exotic, possibly *via* the Atlantic coast of Gaul. The British distribution of such primary introductions, with secondary copies, assists in defining a continuing or near-continuing link with the Church in the western Empire, a link which paved the way for the introduction of Mediterranean coenobitic monasticism from the end of the fifth century.[46] The inclusion of western Galloway in this maritime nexus provides a setting, if not an explanation, for the connection between Ninian of Whithorn and Martin of Tours first reported by Bede, even if this was represented only by the acquisition of some major relic in the seventh century.[47] The same remarks apply, of course, to the nature of the Whithorn LOCI PETRI APUSTOLI pillar, whose forked serif lettering and general appearance justify Radford's estimate[48] of a date not earlier than the beginning of the seventh century; and which, though admittedly enigmatic, must also be regarded as reflecting some facet of the cult of relics.

The Tweed basin

The eastern part of our region is marked by two main areas of Christian activity;

the long winding dale of the river Tweed, or 'Greater Tweed-dale' as this, with the surrounding tributary valleys, has been aptly called, and northward across the range of the Lammermuirs, the lands all around the broad lengthy estuary of the river Forth.

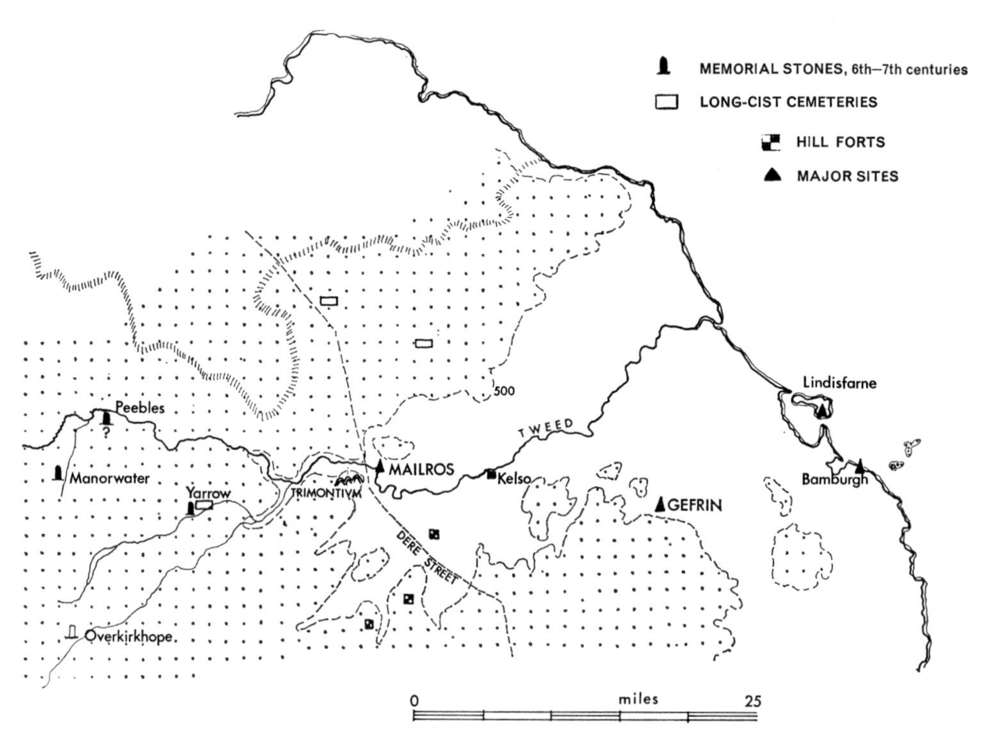

The Central Tweed Basin

Had Christianity penetrated as far north as this before 400, and did it take root there? The Traprain Law treasure, which John Wall has neatly summed up[49] as perhaps 'part of the tableware of a wealthy Roman, or philo-Roman, a travelling official who was also a Christian,' was found in a context which suggests it was both taken as, and treated as, loot. Against this can be set the whole story of Cunedag or Cunedda, a tribal ruler who, on good evidence, can be connected with the area around the Forth; who was somehow induced to migrate, with most of his family and presumably much of his tribe, to north Wales in the early fifth century, as an act of latter-day *foederatio* against the pressure of Irish settlers; and whose immediate ancestors are claimed to have possessed names which can best be explained as versions of Roman ones.[50] The area of northwest Wales with which these migrants are subsequently associated is one of the few in sub-Roman Britain where we can be tolerably sure that there was a flourishing church organization;[51] in later tradition, the sons of Cunedda were regarded as Christians, saints, and founders of churches;[52] and, as Sir John Lloyd long ago commented, if two of these sons were really called *Donatus* and *Marianus*, it is hard to think that they did not come from a Christian background.[53] The problem remains, however; for even if the rulers of the lands around the Forth were Christian in late Roman times, there is no reason to suppose this affected the general populace until later.

In Greater Tweed-dale (p. 104) there are several inscribed tombstones. That from Manorwater belongs to the latter part of the sixth century.[54] A small and very odd incised figure on a stone from Over Kirkhope,[55] if not a late depiction of some Celtic godling, may be an *orans* figure, not necessarily funerary, of the same period. There is a medieval and circumstantial report of a lost stone, found at Peebles in an ancient cemetery by a church, which is said to have borne the words LOCUS SANCTI NICOLAI EPISCOPI.[56] The 'Sancti Nicolai' part strains credulity, and must surely be a misreading, but neither LOCUS nor EPISCOPI are objectionable *per se*, and the fact that the stone could be read at all implies Roman lettering.

The Yarrowkirk stone[57] commemorates two local princes, *Nudus* and *Dumnogenus*, the sons of *Liberalis*. Their names are British, typical of the native revival by the early sixth century, the date of this stone; their father's harks back to Rome. Again this raises the suggestion of a Christian ruling family. In the area, we should also note the suggestive proximity of three features; the triple-peaked Eildon Hills, on the northernmost of which is one of Scotland's largest *oppida*, or tribal hill-towns,[58] hills which gave their name in the form *Trimontium* to the Roman fort of Newstead below them; the intersection of the north–south Roman way of Dere Street and the river Tweed; and the seventh-century monastery of Old Melrose. If the Tweed basin was the home of a distinct people, or tribe, this area must have been the focal point of their territory.

The Forth estuary

When we cross the long ridge of the Lammermuirs, the southern boundary of what later became the Lothians, and enter the lands around the Firth of Forth, we also encounter a part of what has been entitled, all too appositely, 'the problem of the Picts.' The relevance of this problem here is seen in Bede's statement, written before 731.[59] Bede wrote that, so it was said then, the southern Picts, who dwell on this side of the mountains which divide the *australes* from the *septentrionales Picti*, had long before 565 (the supposed date of Columcille's arrival in Iona) forsaken the error of idolatry, and received the faith of truth, when the word was preached to them by Ninian.

In emptying out the bath-water, as it were, of the traditional views on Ninian, one can commit the mistake of emptying out the Pictish baby too. Bede's statement should be regarded as having some kind of basis in fact, as being derived from a reliable source (for example, Trumwine, for a short while before 685 a bishop at Abercorn), and as being abundantly worth further exploration.

Just as the bond of a common religion has hardly ever prevented armed conflict, so religious frontiers need bear no relationship to ethnic, or political, or linguistic boundaries. When Bede wrote that the Clyde had formed the frontier between the British of Strathclyde and (formerly) the Picts, by Bede's day the *Scotti*, on the west,[60] and that the Forth was a similar division between the Picts and, by Bede's day, the Angles, on the east,[61] he must have been repeating traditional information of great age, known to everyone in North Britain. These boundaries are large, natural, obvious ones. North of the Forth lay Pictland, and those who lived there were unalterably Picts, just as Aidan and Finan had been unalterably Irish, and Bede himself immutably English. It is none the less now fairly certain that the more southerly of the Picts, those around Tayside and in Fife, included speakers of P-Celtic, mutually intelligible to the British who dwelt south of the Forth; for one thing, much the same place-name elements are found in both areas. One might have had to travel further northward, over the Tay and even over the Mounth, into the land of the northern Picts, in order to encounter in any density the non-Indo-European language (an inheritance from Scottish prehistory) which is what Bede probably meant by 'Pictish.'[62]

A well-known distribution map, that of the use of the element *pit-*, earlier *pett-*, in the sense of 'farm, steading,' both marks off Pictland from the Lowlands, and defines what is usually taken as the fullest extent of historical Pictland.[63] A similar map, showing the occurrence of a particular type of field-monument associated with supposedly Pictish settlement, the *souterrain* or underground store-house, tells much the same story.[64] Both maps ignore the persistent political division between northern and southern Picts, which goes back to Roman times, was known to Bede, and was physically indicated by the Mounth, the terminal Highland ridge running out to the east coast not far from Aberdeen.

If we look at the other feature securely associated with the historical Picts, the range of incised or decorated stones which display their remarkable art, we observe a different pattern. So-called 'Class I' Pictish stones bear a variety of motifs and designs, incised or pecked-out; and whatever function these stones possessed (almost certainly a funerary one)[65] no serious student would today regard them as other than non-Christian, and presumably pre-Christian, whatever their actual dates. Their distribution is very strongly weighted in favour of Northern Pictland, an area whose conversion to Christianity, on a popular level, is unlikely to have been achieved much before the early 600s;[66] and this is in accord with the most realistic estimate of date, namely that Class I stones begin in the sixth, or possibly the later fifth century.[67] The sparsity of these non-Christian tombstones in southern Pictland – where, on the other hand, the later seventh- and eighth-century 'Class II' stones bearing Christian devices, and with low-relief carving, are most widely found[68] – suggests that, well before the time of Columcille and the Iona mission to the northern Picts, some part of southern Pictland was already, in some degree, Christianized. The part in question is the Tay estuary, and the modern counties of Fife and Clackmannan along the north shore of the Forth.

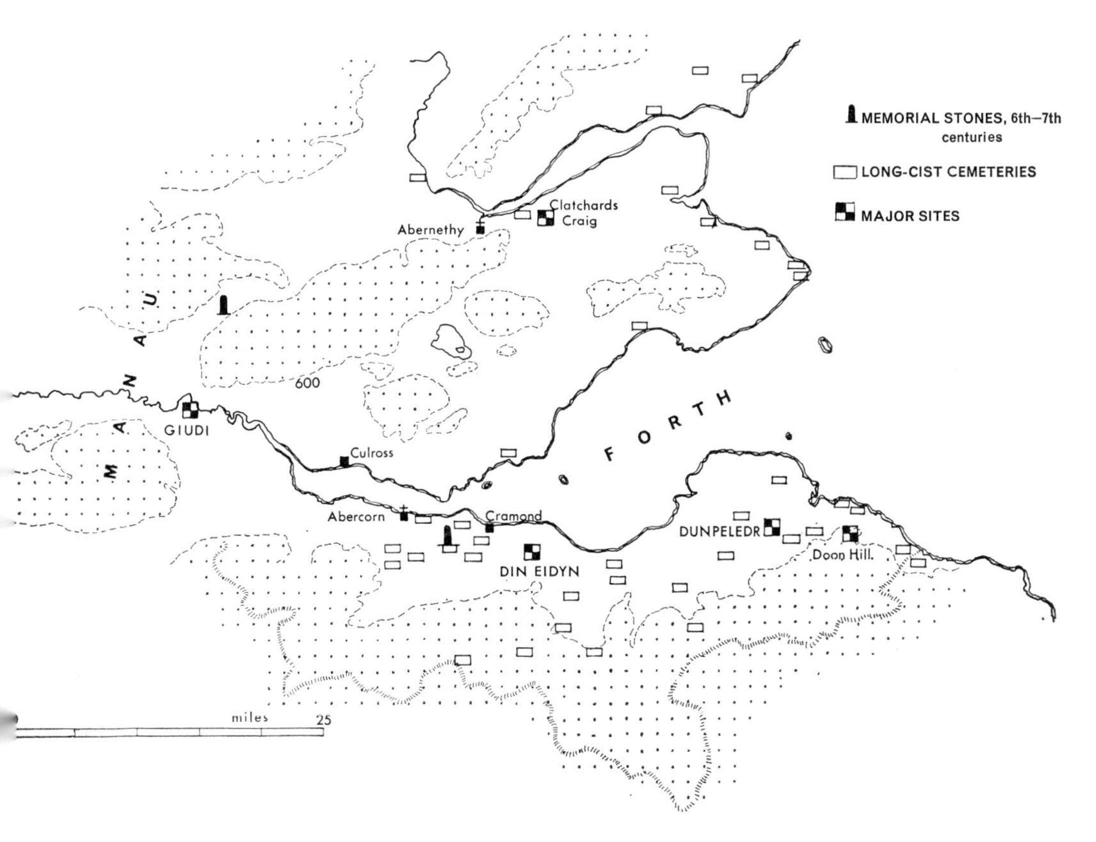

The Lothians and Forth Area

There is a positive counterpart to this negative distributional evidence. The area all around the Forth (above) is characterized by numerous isolated cemeteries of early Christian type, in which the dead were interred in 'long cists,' that is, full-length graves defined by slabs of local stone, set on edge, often roofed with further slabs. These long-cist cemeteries, which can run into hundreds of burials, are exemplified by the excavated one at Parkburn in Midlothian.[69] On the evidence of the Kirkliston cemetery, which holds the inscribed stone known as 'the Catstane,'[70] such cemeteries could go back to the early sixth, and presumably the late fifth centuries. They belong to a wider class of rural 'undeveloped cemeteries' which actually ante-date the construction of small local churches in wood or stone, and which were frequently abandoned in post-Roman times in favour of cemeteries attached to such early churches.[71]

Long-cist cemeteries are by no means universal in North Britain at this period In the Whithorn and Carlisle areas, for example, the 'dug-grave' cemetery where the extended bodies are laid in shallow trenches, seems to have been the appropriate rite.[72] The reasons for such regional divergences are not yet clear, though they may hark back to pre-Christian tribal custom, since we know that the mode of disposal of the dead in the British Iron Age was far from uniform.[73]

It is clear that the 'long cist' province of the Forth area extends north of the Forth; and it can be seen to cover much the same extent of southern Pictland as that in which the pagan Class I Pictish symbol-stones are absent, or sparsely found. Without laying undue weight on medieval tradition, the church sites of Culross, St Andrews, and Abernethy, which occur in this area, are all of considerably antiquity. Abernethy in particular has the distinction of figuring in the 'Pictish Chronicle,'[74] or regnal lists, where its supposed foundation-date is either in the 460s or, more credibly, the 590s; in any case a clear century before the full impact of Christian Northumbria.

The not very strong arguments for the Christian background of Cunedda and his family apart, the Christian evidence around the Forth – the 'Catstane,' the distribution maps, the horizons of such local saints as Serf (Servanus), Kentigern, and Buitte, the reference to Christianity in the *Gododdin* poem[75] – belongs to the sixth, rather than to the fifth century. No doubt some Britons were living in southern Pictland; no doubt some southern Picts, too, both lived and died south of the Forth.[76] It is not inconceivable that Christianity embraced both shores, and that Bede's statement means no more than that some of the southern Picts belonged, before Columba's time, to a church which looked back to Ninian – rather as modern Methodists look back to John Wesley – and which was both older than, and independent of, the Irish monastic mission.

Strathclyde

The fifth, and last, area of North Britain to be discussed is Strathclyde (p. 109), the long broad valley of the river Clyde, with its extensive winding mouth, and the skirts of the (Argyllshire) Highlands to the north. Here again there are faint traces of early, localized, Christianity. Professor Thompson, as a by-product of his discussion of Ninian, makes the point[77] that Patrick's letter to the soldiers of Coroticus can, on one line of internal evidence, be dated to *c.* 455–61. This is, of course, on the assumption that the letter is genuine, which most people accept; that Patrick died in 461, which is open to argument; and that *Coroticus* was a Strathclyde and not a Cardiganshire ruler. What tips the argument for me, at any rate, in favour of a North British *milieu* for Patrick, Coroticus, and the relevant *epistola*, is the likelihood that *Banna*, or *Banna Venta(?) Berniae(?)*, Patrick's birth-place, could on the Rudge Cup evidence[78] be around the western end of Hadrian's Wall; that no other locality suits all the requirements so well; and that the late Roman Christianity of Carlisle offers the best background for Patrick, as it does for Ninian. A phrase like *socii Scottorum atque Pictorum*

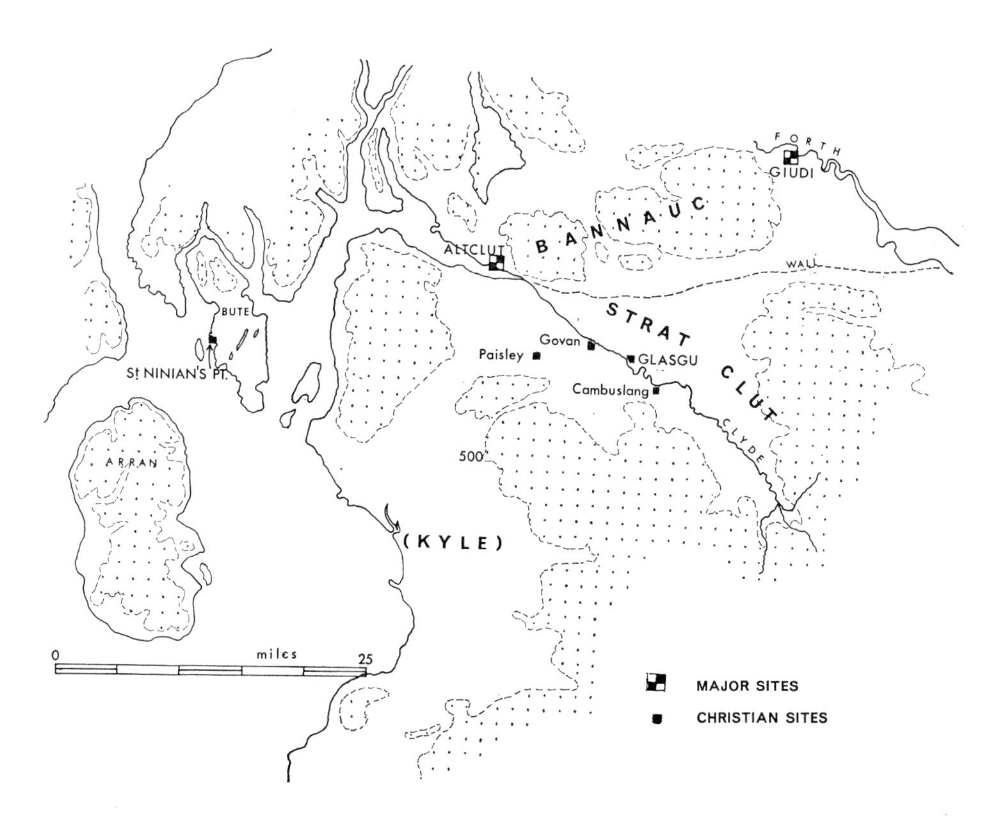

The Strathclyde Area

apostatarumque would come spontaneously to the mind of a North Briton of Romanized upbringing; the label *Picti*, surely in origin a military nick-name, must have been a commonplace for several centuries along the Wall. Would a native of the Midlands, or the Severn shore, think in terms of *Scotti et Picti?* As for Coroticus, the title to the *Epistola* (added apparently by Muirchu)[79] which glosses *Corotici* as *regis Aloo*, points to Ail Cluade, Bede's Alcluith, the Rock of the Clyde or Dumbarton Rock, as W. J. Watson and others have shown.[80] This is witness to no more than a belief in seventh-century Ireland that Coroticus was a Strathclyde king, but it is a valuable clue, and there is no corresponding sign-post to the Welsh identification.

The parallel to Cunedda and his family in the Forth area is only partial; the most that can be inferred here is that, about the middle of the fifth century, the tribal monarch of Strathclyde and his *milites* – a free war-band, or hired levies – were nominally Christian. Patrick does not mention Ninian; he does not refer explicitly to any conversion.

Equally important, in my opinion, is a curious passage in Jocelyn's Life of Kentigern,[81] and this despite the very much later date of its compilation. It is the reference to the *cemiterium quoddam a Sancto Niniano consecratum*, to which the old man *Fregus* (read 'Fergus') is drawn for burial in a wagon harnessed to two untamed oxen. This cemetery was at *Cathures*, *quae nunc Glasgu vocatur*, and it was at Glasgow that St Kentigern, yielding to the entreaties of the king and clergy and other Christians, albeit few in number, of this region, agreed to establish his see.[82]

The cemetery is an important, and underrated, element in this story. The fact that Jocelyn failed to understand whatever story (bereft of the stock miracle of the untamed animals) he used here suggests that it is one of several aspects which may really have survived from seventh-century tradition,[83] and now adduced to explain the predominance of Glasgow. For despite its allegedly Ninianic consecration, no one had yet lain in this cemetery; Fergus' was the first burial, and was followed by very many others. Great reverence was paid to the tomb of Fergus, Jocelyn tells us. An explanation of all this might be the re-use, after a prolonged lapse, of a sub-Roman undeveloped cemetery, still recognizable as such; *e.g.*, by its enclosing bank, or shape. The Fergus story may then be the aetiology of some prominent shrine, or insular version of *cella memoriae*, visible within the cemetery. Such phenomena would still be intelligible by the seventh century, but would mean little or nothing to Jocelyn and his circle five centuries afterwards.

If the 'Ninian' tradition goes back to some such time as the seventh century, its validity is the same as that of Bede's comments about the early conversion of the southern Picts; a record of belief that Christianity had been established in Strathclyde, strongly enough to warrant the canonical consecration of a local cemetery, before the time of Kentigern. Now Kentigern, whose obit under the name of *Conthigirn* (*i*) is given in the *Annales Cambriae* as 612 A.D. has sixth-century connections, for example with St Servanus in the Forth area, from which Kentigern appears to have come; and though we need not go so far as to suppose that Ninian went to Strathclyde in person, any Christian activity in Strathclyde prior to Kentigern's time might well have lain within the sphere of the Whithorn episcopacy.

Strathclyde has produced no inscribed stones, though the immense spread of Glasgow has probably swallowed up many potential sites. The known ones include Govan, which is connected with a saint Constantine – possibly the one whose *conversio ad Dominum* is mentioned in the *Annales Cambriae* under 589.[84] In the medieval Life of the Welsh saint, Cadoc, a passage which may be interpolated describes a visit to Scotland and the foundation of a church which is generally identified as Cambuslang, on the south bank of the Clyde upstream from Glasgow.[85] These are British, not Irish, figures, consistent with a sixth century British church in the area, and one might add the place-name Paisley which, according to Watson,[86] may come ultimately from *basilica*, either at a late stage through Irish or Gaelic, but just conceivably through British. As in the Whithorn area, there is a 'dug-grave' cemetery; some of the burials lie north–south, and these, perhaps pre-Christian, are overlain by others oriented in

Christian style, which themselves antedate both an enclosing wall and a small stone chapel of late seventh- or early eighth-century character. This is the cemetery at St Ninian's Point on Bute,[87] in the mouth of the Clyde. The ascription to Ninian is no doubt medieval, but the cemetery would appear to go back to sub-Roman times.

Discussion

We have looked at the evidence for sub-Roman Christianity in five areas; Carlisle with the Solway plain, Whithorn and Galloway, the Tweed basin, the lands around the Forth, and Strathclyde. Some tentative conclusions emerge at once. In the Carlisle area, Christianity was present in the fourth century, and may have continued unbroken through the fifth and sixth as well. In western Galloway, it appeared by the middle of, if not the beginning of, the fifth century, and has of course lasted there until today. In the Tweed basin, one cannot detect Christianity before about 500, with the Yarrowkirk stone. In both the Forth area, and Strathclyde, there are hints of very local Christianity at the ruling-family level at the end of the Roman period proper, but in both areas, the evidence really belongs to the sixth century.

There is thus a clear spread from south to north, as one might expect. But before hailing this as vindication of the idea that Ninian, and his church, constituted first and foremost a missionary movement, we should consider the following points. The evidence we possess is, outside Carlisle and Galloway, extremely slender; and in the three northern areas, in each case the clues are distributionally centred on the seats of power in sub-Roman times. From Hadrian's Wall to the 'Forth–Clyde' line is a bare 70 miles; Christianity did not apparently travel fast or far during the fifth century, the age of Ninian himself. Neither the rate of progress nor the intensity of evangelization will stand comparison with what seems to have happened in Ireland, or the Irish mainland colonies, in the sixth and seventh centuries; or, closer at hand, in seventh-century Northumbria.

I would be loth to deny that by precept, by prayer, by force of character, and by such methods as those dramatically employed in the pagan Gaulish countryside by Martin of Tours,[88] the man we know as Ninian, and others associated with him, did enlarge the existing Christian flocks of their day. To that extent, and to that extent only, the term 'missionary' is justified; as it is justified, should one care to apply it, in the case of Martin. I am emphatically sure that the idea of a grand missionary tour up the east coast, into Pictland, Caithness, and the northern Isles is unsupportable on present evidence; and that the evidence adduced refers, not to sub-Roman times, but to a largely fortuitous scatter of medieval dedications and rural folk-lore.

Can any pattern, then, be seen in the evidence so far examined? I believe so; and the explanation resides in the nature of the distinct areas in which the clues are found. The church in sub-Roman northern Britain was a diocesan church, and what we have been looking at are the remains of sub-Roman dioceses. It is impossible to do more than sketch the physical extent of these dioceses, if indeed they possessed any clear-cut boundaries; but the coincidence of these areas with the individual kingdoms of the North British leads me to suppose that we are dealing with territorial, tribal, bishoprics.

I make no apology for returning to the mid-second century A.D., and the *Geography* of Ptolemy as it applied to the British Isles. Pre-Roman tribal groups did on occasions survive in a modified form into the sub-Roman era; one thinks of the *Dumnonii* and the *Demetae*, peoples who outlasted the Roman system of *civitates* and in a sense are yet with us in the names of *Devon* and *Dyfed*. In North Britain, as I have used this term, we need to look at the history of five peoples or tribes mentioned by Ptolemy (below).

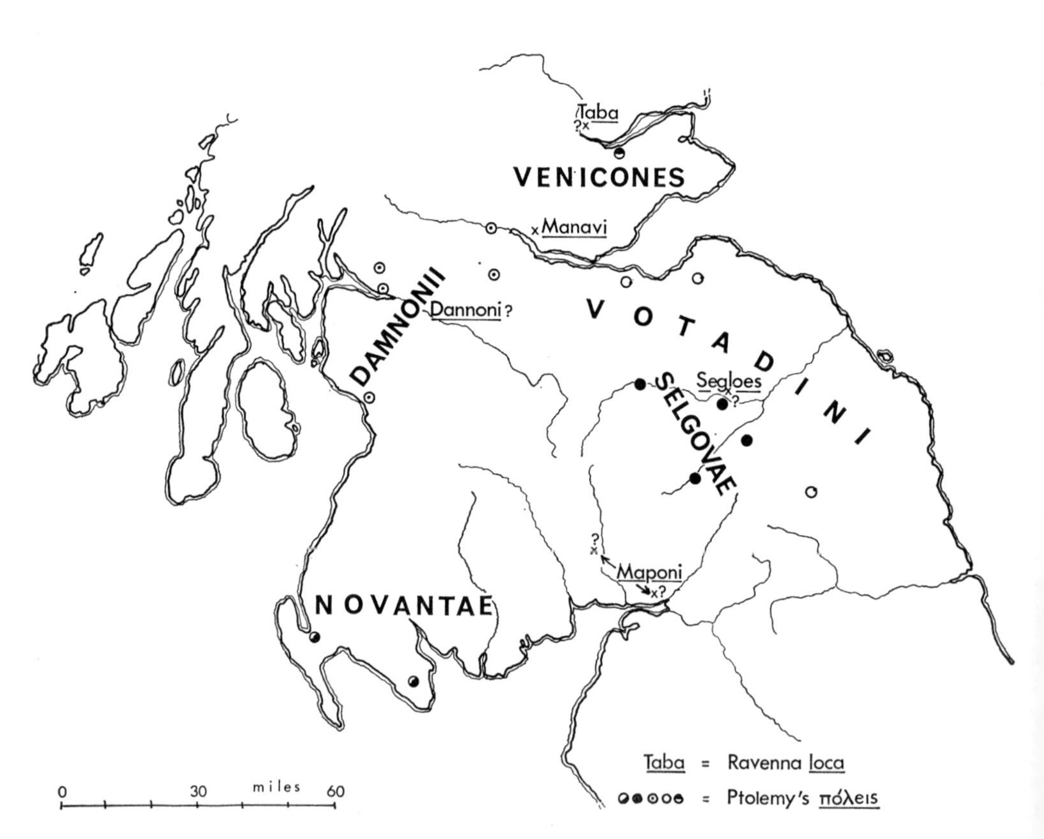

The native tribes of North Britain in the early Roman period: tentative reconstruction from Ptolemy's evidence, after Crawford, Richmond and others

In Galloway, the *Novantae*[89] are assigned the *poleis*, whatever this term implies, of *Rerigonium* and *Loukopibia*. The former is agreed to be on Loch Ryan, by Stranraer. The latter commences with an alleged adjective **leucos*,

**loucos*, 'white.' That it should have anything to do with Whithorn is a linguistic chestnut so old that I hesitate to mention it here; but before we exhaust our mirth we might recall (a) that we do not know the native British name for Whithorn, and can scarcely suppose that the local North British used the Latin name *Candida Casa* : (b) that the name 'Rosnat,' derived from external sources of much later date, cannot now safely be reckoned to fill this gap;[90] and (c) that Bede, whose obvious interest in philology has never been properly explored, appears to have been able to translate straightforward British or Primitive Irish names into Latin, and would also have known the cognate Greek adjective *leukos*.

The emphasis of the *Novantae*, on Ptolemy's evidence, lay well to the west, in Wigtownshire rather than Kirkcudbright; and this may partially explain the choice of Whithorn as a centre.

Whether or not there really were two fifth-century dioceses, one in western Galloway, the other centred on Carlisle, with the Dumfries Nith as the most likely boundary, one imagines that by the sixth century they could have jointly provided the religious hierarchy of the sub- and post-Roman kingdom of *Rheged*. H. M. Chadwick's contention[91] that this stretched as far south as Rochdale is perhaps open to doubt, but Rheged is agreed to have contained Carlisle, and we can allow that it ran as far west as Dunragit in Wigtownshire.[92]

The British kingdom of Strathclyde, whose own intra-national[93] name appears to be lost, but whose inhabitants called themselves *Cumbri*,[94] is the successor to Ptolemy's *Damnonii*. Not all their *poleis* are identifiable, even if one follows Sir Ian Richmond's idea that most Ptolemaic names are those of Roman, not native, sites,[95] but they should stretch across Strathclyde from the Ayrshire coast to the southern flank of Pictland. W. J. Watson considered that Dumbarton Rock, the sub-Roman citadel of *Ail Cluade*, is represented by Ptolemy's *Alauna*.[96]

Greater Tweed-dale was the home of the *Selgovae*, 'the Hunters,' and their principal *polis*, the great tribal oppidum on Eildon Hill North, may have been known by the British cognate, and similar, form of the Roman *Trimontium*, Newstead. The dramatic triple peaks of the Eildons cannot have failed to possess great religious significance to the pagan British, and a further emphasis is given if we add to this locality, where Dere Street crosses the Tweed, the tribal meeting-place of *Locus Selgovensis*, which appears contracted to *Segloes* in the Ravennas list.[97] We might envisage these *loca*, permitted and recognized by the Romans, as the scenes of massive commercial and religious gatherings, on the lines of the Irish *oenach*.

The reference to an otherwise unknown ruling family on the Yarrowkirk stone shows that, whatever sub-Roman principality lay here, it was distinct from, if subject to, its greater northern neighbour in the Forth area. Can we guess that this little state, whose coastal lands would have been the first victims of the Anglian settlement, was the lost British **Berneich* or **Bernaccia*[98] which, in the seventh century, continued in a fresh guise as the Bernicia of the Northumbrians?

Ptolemy's *Votadini* were spread over a wide region, from the Forth down to Redesdale, perhaps earlier down to the Tyne or even the Tees; and the archaeology of native sites from the Lothians to Northumberland confirms this general cultural unity. But by sub-Roman times, when the tribal name re-appears as the *Gododdin* of the great British poem, and in the area-name of Manau *Guotodin*, this kingdom has shrunk to its northern domain. The potential sub-Roman citadels – North Berwick Law, Traprain Law, Edinburgh Castle, Stirling Castle (all, like Dumbarton Rock, isolated mounds of impressive natural strength) – are strung out along the Forth. In some way incorporated in the west of the kingdom was the district *Manau*, apparently around Stirling, where the Ravennas *Locus Manavi (i)*, whose name survives in the modern Clackmannan, 'the stone of Manu,'[99] may have been near the crossing of the Forth. By the period of the *Gododdin* poem, the end of the sixth century, *Din Eidyn*, the Castle Rock of Edinburgh, appears to have been the counterpart of *Ail Cluade* over to the west.

Ptolemy's *Venicones*, in the present Fife, with their *polis* of *Orrea*, 'The Granary,' at Carpow on the Tay, may have included Celtic speakers, even if the tribal name is not certainly Celtic; but their land belonged to a *regio* of the southern Picts. Are these people, any Christians amongst whom are best explained as participants in a diocese of the Forth, the Picts of the *Niuduera regio* whom Cuthbert visited? The place-name cannot any longer be thought to belong to Galloway, or to be connected with that of the river Nith.[100] Hunter Blair's suggestion[101] that it derives, *via* a linguistic hurdle, from the same source as Bede's *Giudi*, deserves consideration.

The pattern (p. 115) is thus a simple one. A diocese at Carlisle, and its offshoot in western Galloway, may have combined to serve Rheged. By the sixth century, three more dioceses had come into existence; those of Berneich in the Tweed basin, of the people of Gododdin and the Picts of Fife in the Forth area, and of the British kingdom in Strathclyde (where Kentigern may indeed be the name of the first bishop). I advance this hypothesis the more firmly, now that we have the benefit of Dr Kathleen Hughes's fine study of the church in Ireland at the same period.[102] In facing a topic which most previous students have evaded, the question of the territorial diocese in Patrician, post-Patrician, and monastic times, she has concluded that such did exist, attached to the numerous Irish petty kingdoms, alongside and independent of the greater monastic *paruchiae*, and served by what she describes as 'tribal bishops.' Were Ninian, Kentigern, the *sacerdotes* on the Kirkmadrine stone, and the mysterious *episcopus* of the lost Peebles inscription, then tribal bishops of sub-Roman North Britain? I believe, on the present evidence, that this is the explanation most in accord with what we are slowly learning about the early Church in these Isles; and I do not see that this detracts from the individual status of these dimly-perceived figures.

One final question poses itself before we conclude; did anything of this

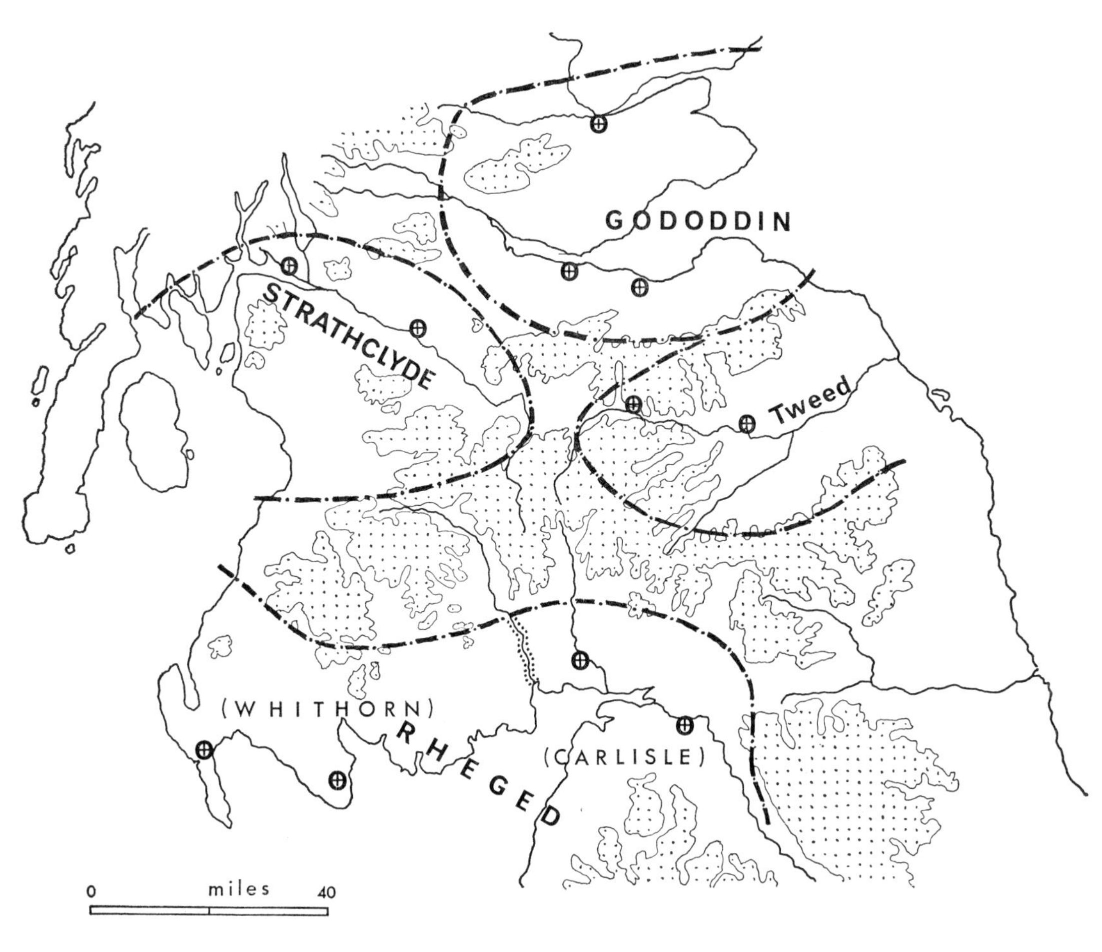

Sub-Roman territorial dioceses in North Britain; a very tentative reconstruction (boundaries only approximate). For the individual sites, see pp. 98, 101, 104, 107 *and* 109

survive into the post-635 church of Northumbria? There is one aspect of early Northumbrian place-names, in their religious context, which has escaped attention. Most of the seventh-century monasteries and major churches have names of Old English type, given them by the Northumbrian Angles.[103] The British *Metcaut* became *Lindisfaranensis ecclesia*, whatever the true etymology of the latter may be. Other instances are of course (using Bede's participial forms) *In Gyruum*, Jarrow; *Hagustald-ea*, Hexham; *Streanaeshalch*, Whitby; *Laestinga-eu*, Lastingham; *In Getlingum*, Gilling, and *In Dera Wudu*, Beverley. Even those embodying British river-names, like *Tinemuda*, Tynemouth, and *Uuiraemuda*, Monkwearmouth, or an older British element in an inversion-compound, like *Coludesburh*, Coldingham, belong to this group.

The exceptions, leaving for the moment Whithorn aside, are *Luel*, the double monastery headed, before 685, by the sister of Queen Iurminburg; *Mailros*,

Old Melrose, a monastery of Irish type founded from Lindisfarne not long after 635; and *Aebbercurnig*, Abercorn, raised to a temporary see in 681, but likely to have been founded following the Anglian capture of Edinburgh about 638, and from its physical form almost certainly before 664.[104] Whithorn, *Ad Candidam Casam*, is not quite on a par with *Ad Caprae Caput*, Gateshead, which Mawer suggested may have been named from a false etymology suggested by a similar-sounding British name. Had the British name of Whithorn commenced, like *Loukopibia* of Ptolemy's survey, with an adjective whose similarity to the Greek *leukos* would have struck anyone at Bede's level of education, we could expect *Candida Casa* to be a supposedly direct translation. I frankly cannot see how else the name arose.

What can this mean? Whithorn must have been an extant church when the Northumbrians encountered it, even if, as I have elsewhere argued at length,[105] it had since Ninian's time assumed monastic form under the influence of the Irish colony in Galloway. At *Luel*, Carlisle, it is equally probable that a church had continued to exist since late Roman times. I would suggest that both *Mailros* and *Aebbercurnig* had in some fashion been the mother-churches of the tribal dioceses of the Tweed and Forth regions respectively, and that, as at Carlisle and Whithorn, there was never any question of attaching fresh, Anglian, names to them. The position of Old Melrose in particular must lie close to the seat of sub-Roman power in the Tweed, and Abercorn is not far from Edinburgh. By an extension of this argument, it could be supposed that other non-Anglian church names cited by Bede, or other seventh- and eighth-century sources, for instance *Campodonum*, Dewsbury, indicate sub-Roman churches continuing into Christian Northumbrian, or Christian Mercian, times, and I consider this a distinct probability.

At this point we can go no further. Some wholly archaeological lines of enquiry, for example the degree of continuity between late Roman Christian, or for that matter Roman *pagan* burial practices, and those detectable in sub-Roman North Britain, are already producing interesting results. Field-work has still to be undertaken in certain blank areas, like the long coastal plain of Ayrshire, the former Kyle, about whose Christian past we know virtually nothing. The picture of a diocesan, if loosely organized, church in the north in sub-Roman times to which the present study has led us departs in considerable measure from the usual view of Ninian and the earliest days of Scottish Christianity; and in putting this picture I hope I have not seemed over-critical of older, 'traditional,' ideas, and of those who still hold to them. As an old friend has recently written, 'Perhaps in every archaeologist there is a little failed historian whimpering to be let out.'[106] The converse, it might be argued, is just as true; but all the lines of evidence, whether archaeological or historical, seem to me to converge towards a view of early Northern Christianity which is at least in accord with our present, wider, thinking on the nature of the Church in the later western Empire.

Notes

1. Bede, *HE*, iii, 1–4; ed. Plummer, C. *Venerabilis Baedae Opera Historica* (Oxford, 1896, 2 vols.)
2. Thomas, C., 'Ardwall Isle: the excavation of an Early Christian site of Irish type,' *TDGNHAS*, 43 (1966), 84–116, esp. 112–6; fuller account with maps in final report on same site, *Med Arch* 11 (1967), forthcoming
3. Jackson, K. H., *LHEB*, 4–6; the definitions now in general use are Jackson's
4. Jackson, K. H., 'The Pictish Language,' in *Problem*, chap. 6
5. Cf. *RNNB* and *IANB*
6. Bede (*HE*, iii, 4) calls him *Nynia* (abl.); Plummer, *op. cit.*, II, 128, regarded this as from a nom. *Nynias*, equating the name with 'Nennius.' The 8th-cent. *Miracula* poem (now ed. MacQueen, W., *TDGNHAS* 38 (1959–60)) gives a gen. *Nynie* (=*Nyniae*), supporting a nom. *Nynia*. A. O. Anderson ('Ninian and the Southern Picts,' *Scot Hist Rev*, 27 (1948), 45)) postulates a lost (Brit.) masc. termination (**-os*) to surmount the hurdle of the extant fem. ending in *-a*; **Ninia-vos*, **Ninia-sos*, etc., with penultimate stress. 'Ninian(-us)' presumably arose from some such misreading as of *Niniauus*
7. Ed. Forbes, A. P. (Bishop of Brechin), *The Historians of Scotland, V: St Ninian and St Kentigern* (Edinburgh, 1874); the text, which requires critically re-editing, 137–57, the translation, 3–26
8. *The Celtic Church in Scotland* (Aberdeen, 1935); *St Ninian and the Origins of the Christian Church in Scotland* (Edinburgh, 1940); 'New Light on St Ninian,' AA 23 (1945), 78ff.; 'The Ninianic Controversy,' *TDGNHAS* 27 (1950), 155ff.; 'Brocavum, Ninekirks and Brougham: A Study in Continuity,' *TCWAAS* 58 (1959), 68–87; 'More thoughts on the Celtic Church,' *Scottish Gaelic Studies*, 10, i (Aberdeen, 1963), 1–15
9. 'Galloway'=Scotland's two southwestern counties, Wigtownshire and the Stewartry of Kirkcudbright
10. Of *St Ninian and the Origins, etc.*; *Antiquity* 14 (1940), 442–3
11. MacQueen, J., *St Nynia; a study of literary and linguistic evidence* (Edinburgh, 1961)—cited *St Nynia*
12. The following list, which omits critical reviews, is a (by no means exhaustive) list of the major erosions of Dr Simpson's thesis. On the dedication evidence, Grosjean, P. in *Anal. Boll.* 76 (1958), 357ff., and Chadwick, O. in *SEBH* (*vide* note *infra*), chap. 7. On the unproven connection with Martin, and Tours, Chadwick, N. K., in *TDGNHAS* 27 (1949), 9–53, and MacQueen, *St Nynia*, *passim*. On the improbability of Ninian as a peripatetic episcopal missionary, Thompson, E. A. *Scot Hist Rev* 37 (1958), 17ff. On the lack of the claimed connection between the Whithorn memorial stones and early Pictish art, Thomas, C. in *Arch J* 120 (1964), 31–97, *passim*. On the absence of any physical trace of a Ninianic monastery at the modern Whithorn, Thomas, C. in *TDGNHAS* 38 (1960), 71–82, and 42 (1966), 104–116. On Dr Simpson's handling of sources, Wilhelm Levison's review (*op. cit., supra*), Anderson, A. O. in *Scot Hist Rev* 27 (1948), 25–47, and Bullough, D. in *Scot Hist Rev* 43 (1964), 111ff., and 44 (1965), 17ff., *passim*. On the relegation of Columcille and Iona mission to a secondary role, a whole series of works, commencing perhaps with Duke, J. A. *The Columban Church* (Edinburgh, 1957)
13. Her 'Christianity in Roman Britain,' *JBAA* 16 (1953), 1–24 cited here *Toynbee* 1953 – at 24
14. *Toynbee* 1953, 1–2, with references to sources
15. *Toynbee* 1953, 4 (*Eborius de civitate Eboracensi*)

Notes

16. Frend, W. H. C., 'Religion in Roman Britain in the Fourth Century,' *JBAA* 18 (1955), 1–18, with map, pl. I
17. Wall, J., 'Christian Evidences in the Roman Period; the Northern Counties' (Part I: *Arch Ael* 43 (1965), 201–225, and Part II: *Arch Ael* 44 (1966), 147–164 – cited as *Wall* 1965, *Wall* 1966, respectively)
18. O Riordain, S. P., 'Roman Material in Ireland,' *PRIA* 51, C 3 (1947), 35–82; a reappraisal of this field is promised by Dr R. H. M. Dolley (Belfast)
19. Salway, P., *The Frontier People of Roman Britain* (Cambridge, 1965), 41–45; see also Shaw, R. C., in *TCWAAS* 24 (1924), 94ff.
20. Salway, *op. cit.*, 216–7: *RIB* no. 955
21. *CW* 32 (1932), 133–4; *Wall* 1965, 204–5 and fig. 1; now *RIB* no. 787. Dr Salway informs me that he rightly omits this as not being absolutely certainly a civilian
22. Salway, *op. cit.*, 102–6: Collingwood, R. G., in *CW* 36 (1936), 85ff., at 99; and Jarrett's report (*infra*) of post-369 pottery
23. Reappraised by Jarrett, M., in *TCWAAS* 54 (1954), 269ff., and figured also in *Wall* 1965, 213, fig. 3
24. Radford, C. A. R., 'Excavations at Whithorn: Final Report,' *TDGNHAS* 34 (1956), 131–194, at 175
25. *LHEB*, 191
26. MacQueen (*St Nynia*, 8–12) gives the references; one cannot refine the *floruit* closer than the first half of the 5th century
27. *Vita Sancti Cuthberti auctore anonymo*, cap. viii, whence *Vita Sancti Cuthberti auctore Beda* ('Prose Life'), cap. xxvii; both in Colgrave, B. ed., *Two Lives of St Cuthbert* (Cambridge, 1940), 122 and 242 respectively
28. 'The Ruin': see Gordon, R. K., *Anglo-Saxon Poetry* (London, 1954), 84
29. Jackson, K. H., 'On some Romano-British place-names,' *JRS* 38 (1948), 54–8; and *LHEB*, 688. Professor Jackson points out to me that Bede's *Lugubalium ciuitatem* is a piece of Bedan pendantry that must derive from a *written* source (cf. also Bede, *HE*, iv, 29)
30. Cf. Collingwood, R. G., in *TCWAAS* 25 (1925), 9ff.
31. *Wall* 1965, 206–7, and refs.; for the date, Jackson, *LHEB*, 192 n. 2, 448, 648 (about A.D. 500 or so)
32. Birley, E., 'Roman Pottery from Brough under Stainmore,' *TCWAAS* 46 (1946), 294ff.
33. *Wall* 1965, 223–4
34. *PSAS* 70 (1935), 33ff.; late 5th or early 6th, *LHEB*, 290
35. Simpson, D. D. A. and Scott-Elliot, J., 'Excavations at Camp Hill, Trohoughton, Dumfries,' *TDGNHAS* 41 (1964), 125–34
36. Foregirth; Truckell, A. E., in *TDGNHAS* 42 (1965), 150, fig. 2. Ruthwell; Radford, C. A. R., in *TDGNHAS* 28 (1950), 158, fig. 14. Staplegorton; Radford, C. A. R., in *TDGNHAS* 33 (1955), 179, fig. 1. Addingham; Bailey, R., in *TCWAAS* 60 (1960), 37–41
37. Thompson, E. A., 'The Origins of Christianity in Scotland,' *Scot Hist Rev* 37 (1958), 17–22, at 19
38. Cf. Cruden, S. E., 'Excavations at Whithorn and Iona,' in *The Scotsman* (Edinburgh), 'Week-end Magazine' section, 4 May 1963
39. Macalister, R. A. S., *CIIC*, nos. 516–8; for the dating, *LHEB*, *sub ind.*, 751–2 (to Macalister's numbers)
40. The Kirkmadrine stones were not found *in situ*: cf. *PSAS* 51 (1917), 199ff.
41. See *TDGNHAS* 36 (1958), 184ff; originally, Todd, W. *The Clerical History of the Parish of Kirkmaiden* (1860), intro.

Notes

42. Cf. *CIIC*, introduction; see also the useful paper by Bu'lock, J., *Arch Camb* (1956), 133–41
43. *CIIC* no. 500; for date and linguistic importance, *LHEB*, *passim*.
44. *CIIC* no. 505
45. *CIIC* no. 519; best discussion now Radford's, in *TDGNHAS* 34 (1956), 174–8
46. The 'primary' examples occur in Cornwall, co. Kerry, and northwest Wales. If, as I now suspect, my class 'E' imported ware (*Med Arch* 3 (1959), 96–99) derives, not from the Rhineland as then thought, but from the Saintes-Bordeaux area, the British distribution of class 'E' (*op. cit.*, map, fig. 46(b), with some dozen additions since 1959) may be directly relevant. See now *Cornish Archaeology* 6 (1967)
47. See Chadwick, Mrs N. K., 'St Ninian; a preliminary study of sources,' *TDGNHAS* 27 (1949), 9–53, including the (doubtful?) idea, *ibid.*, 47, that the 'Martin' connection could be as late as Pecthelm's time (*c.* 720 – Bede, *Hist Eccles*, iii, 4, allowing with MacQueen, *St Nynia* 25–26, that Bede's *iam nunc* means 'within the last decade, last few years or so')
48. In *TDGNHAS* 34 (1956), 178
49. *Wall* 1966, 150
50. But on this much-stressed claim, see Jackson, K. H., 'The Britons in Southern Scotland,' *Antiquity* 29 (1955), 79–80
51. *E.g.*, from the occurrence of terms like *sacerdos* and *presbyter* on 5th and 6th century inscribed memorial stones; for the general area, see Alcock, L., 'Wales in the 5th to 7th centuries A.D.; the archaeological evidence,' and Foster, I. Ll., 'The Emergence of Wales,' chaps. vii and viii of *Prehistoric and Early Wales*, ed. Foster and Daniel (London, 1965)
52. Cf. Bowen, E. G., *The Settlements of the Celtic Saints in Wales* (Cardiff, 1954), 70–74 and fig. 18
53. Lloyd, Sir J. E., *A History of Wales* (1911) vol. I, 119
54. *CIIC* no. 511 (Macalister's *Chi-Rho* on this stone is wishful thinking; cf. *PSAS* 70 (1936), 35ff.)
55. Roy. Comm. Anc. Mon. (Scotland), *Selkirk Inventory*, frontispiece
56. Reported by Mr Gordon Maxwell (lecture to Soc. of Antiquaries of Scotland, 1966); *Peebles-shire Inventory*, 2, 203–4
57. *Selkirk Inventory*, no. 174
58. Feachem, R. W. in *IANB*, 79–81 and fig. 15
59. *HE*, iii, 4; the best translation and discussion is MacQueen's, *St Nynia*, Iff.
60. *HE*, i, 1; i, 12
61. *Ibid.*, i, 12
62. *Ibid.*, i, 1; I suspect the four languages, English, British (P-Celtic), , 'Scottish' or Primitive Irish, and Pictish, are listed in (to Bede) order of decreasing intelligibility
63. Jackson, in *Problem*, map 6. This does not imply that **pett*, *pit*, was unknown south of the Forth; merely that another word, **treb*(*-os*), *tref-*, was employed in the same semantic role, as also in Wales and Cornwall. Cf. Watson, W. J., *The History of the Celtic Place-Names of Scotland* (1926 – cited *Watson* 1926), who reminds us (*ibid.*, 357–65) that of course *tref-* names overlap into southern Pictland
64. Mapped by Stevenson, R. B. K., *IANB*, 33, fig. 6
65. Thomas, C., 'The Interpretation of the Pictish Symbols,' *Arch. J.* 120 (1964), 31–97 *passim*
66. The date of Columcille's first visit to (?) Inverness is unknown, but must lie between 563 and 597. The *Life* by Adamnan makes no suggestion of immediate, wholesale, conversion

Notes

67. Thomas, *op. cit., supra;* the early dating also has Radford's support
68. Stevenson, R. B. K., *Problem*, map 3, 100
69. Henshall, 'The Long Cist cemetery at Parkburn, Lasswade, Midlothian,' *PSAS* 89 (1958), 252–83
70. See catalogue of such cemeteries, with references, in Dr Henshall's paper (*op. cit., supra*)
71. The idea of the 'undeveloped cemetery' is elaborated in my *Christian Antiquities of Camborne* (Warne, 1967), 48ff.
72. *E.g.*, as at Whithorn, Ardwall Isle, and Trohoughton
73. Cf. (partial discussion), Radford, C. A. R., 'The Tribes of Southern Britain,' *PPS* 20 (1954), 1–26, with distributions
74. Chadwick, H. M. *Early Scotland* (Cambridge, 1949), chaps. i and ii, discusses this: but see review of this book by Anderson, A. O., *Scot Hist Rev* 29 (1950), 79–87, and for Abernethy, see also Anderson, M. O., in *Scot Hist Rev* 28 (1949), 35ff., and 29 (1950), 13–22
75. Jackson, *op. cit.* n. 50 *supra*, discusses this
76. Cf. the Class I Pictish stones from Edinburgh (Allen, J. R. and Anderson, J. *The Early Christian Monuments of Scotland* (Edinburgh, 1903), fig. 438, 421) and possibly Borthwick (Feachem, R. W., *PSAS* 84 (1949–50), 206)
77. In *Scot Hist Rev* 37 (1958), 20–21
78. Richmond, I. A., 'The Rudge Cup: II, The Inscription,' *Arch Ael* 12 (1935), 334–42
79. In Bieler's edition (Bieler, L. *Libri Epistolarum Sancti Patricii Episcopi* (Dublin, 1952), I, 91), note under *Inscriptio deest:* on this see also Binchy, D. A., *Studia Hibernica* 2 (1962), 108
80. *Watson*, 1926, 33
81. ed. Forbes (as n. 7 *supra*) – text (cap. ix), 178–9, transl., 54–6
82. Cap. xi (Forbes' edition, 181–2)
83. Cf. Jackson, K. H. ('The Sources for the Life of St Kentigern,' in *SEBC* chap. vi), who is prepared to admit a residue of oral tradition descending from post-Roman Strathclyde, if not (*ibid.*, 343–50) to agree with MacQueen's suggestion that the prototype *Vita* was a 7th-century Glasgow composition
84. There are too many Constantines in post-Roman Britain to warrant the usual identification of this man with the Dumnonian king abused by Gildas
85. Cf. Wade-Evans, ed., *Vitae Sanctorum Britanniae et Genealogiae* (Cardiff, 1944), text and trans; 24–141. The 'Scottish' episode, caps. 26 and 36, can be removed without affecting the narrative
86. *Watson*, 1926, 194
87. Aitken, W. G., in *Trans Bute Hist Soc*, 14 (1955), 62ff.
88. See the *Life* by Sulpicius Severus, ed. and trans. Hoare, F. R., *The Western Fathers* (London, 1954), 3–45, notably caps. xi–xv
89. I give these names in their Latin forms, rather than Ptolemy's Greek versions. For this whole subject, see Richmond, I. A., 'Ancient Geographical Sources for Britain north of Cheviot' (chap. vi) and 'The Sources' (app. to chap. vi), both in *RNNB;* Jackson, in *Problem*, chap. vi, *passim; Watson* 1926, chaps. i & ii; O.S. *Map of Roman Britain* (London, 1956), fig. 1, and p. 20 of intro.; and, for the Ravennas *Cosmography*, Richmond, I. A., and Crawford, O. G. S., 'The British Section of the Ravenna Cosmography,' *Arch.* 93 (1949), 1–50, with Sir Ifor Williams' valuable linguistic notes on the actual names
90. Since P. A. Wilson's discussion, 'St Ninian and Candida Casa: Literary Evidence from Ireland,' *TDGNHAS* 41 (1964), 156–85

Notes

91. In *Early Scotland*, 144
92. *Watson* 1926, 156: for this site, see *TDGNHAS* 29 (1951), 155ff.
93. 'Intra-national' names: = the tribal or national names by which given peoples call themselves, in their own languages
94. Jackson, *op. cit.*, n. 50 (' . . . a latinization of the native word *Cymry*, meaning "fellow-countrymen" ')
95. Richmond, *op. cit.* n. 89
96. *Watson* 1926, 33; Sir Ifor Williams (op. cit., n. 89) points out that this depends on whether we take the name as *al-auno* or *alau-no*, an unknown factor
97. Richmond, *op. cit.* n. 89, proposes *Selgovensis* – *Selgo(v)e(nsis)s*
98. Jackson, *LHEB* 701–5 ('Appendix; the Name *Bernicia*'), rejects the older derivation from the stem **brigant-* (as in Brigantes)
99. *Watson* 1926, 103ff.
100. Cf. MacQueen, J., 'The Picts in Galloway,' *TDGNHAS* 39 (1961), 127–43
101. See his 'The Bernicians and their Northern Frontier,' in *SEBH*, 165–8; he dislikes Levison's suggestion of 'the nether dwellers,' i.e., the southerly-dwelling Picts (*Antiquity* 14 (1940), 289). He would isolate *niud-* from the suffix *-weras* ('men, folk'), and wonders if the Anonymous Biographer (of Cuthbert) was not attempting to spell a name, gathered by word of mouth from Irish speakers – the Lindisfarne brethren, for instance – given in some form like *mur nGiudan*, 'Firth of Forth' (lit: 'Sea of Giud(i)'), where the *n-* represents the Irish article, and ' . . . where the combination *nG* may have yielded a sound for which the OE alphabet had no exact phonetic equivalent, but which could have been approximately represented by *n*'. I do not know if any Celticist has commented on this idea
102. *The Church in Early Irish Society*, particularly 71–74, 123ff.
103. For these, apart from Ekwall, E., *Dictionary of English Place-Names* (3rd edn.), see Bates, C. J., 'The names of persons and places mentioned in the early Lives of St Cuthbert,' *Arch Ael* XVI (1894), 81ff., and Mawer, A., *The Place-names of Northumberland and Durham* (Cambridge, 1910). *Aebbercurnig* and *Mailros* are discussed by *Watson* 1926
104. Preliminary excavations by the writer, 1963–5: the oval *vallum* and other features place this, with Old Melrose, Coldingham, and various minor Bernician sites, in the category of early, Iona-derived, monasteries, a type likely to have been superseded after the Synod of Whitby by monasteries of a more regular, continental-inspired, kind
105. *Opp. cit.*, n.2 *supra*
106. Piggott, S. in *Journal of the Cork Historical and Antiquarian Society*, 71 (1966), 18

St Patrick and the British Church

L. Bieler

The student of any aspect of St Patrick's life and work is bound to find himself sooner or later at the cross-roads, where his course will be determined by his evaluation of evidence that is either ambiguous or contradictory, and where his decision often involves the weighing of the imponderable. The present study is no exception.

Our subject must be studied with particular reference to three phases of Patrick's life: his early years until his Irish captivity; his vocation and ecclesiastical formation; his mission.

That Patrick was a native of Britain is known on the best – some would say, the only – authority, viz himself. Twice in his Confession (23 and 43) he refers to his *parentes* as living there, and in the second place he calls Britain his native country (*patria*); in his letter against Coroticus (2) he denies the soldiers of that ruler the title of *ciues mei*, which *per se* they could claim, because of their savage attack on his Irish converts. It is in Britain that he went to school (with little application and poor results), and that he led that worldly life on which, in later years, he looked back with such bitter remorse; it is there, that, returned from Irish servitude, he found his vocation.

Patrick came from a Christian family. Both his father Calpornius and his grandfather Potitus had taken holy orders,[1] if only, as was first surmized by Bury[2] and recently argued in detail by Professor Hanson,[3] in order to escape the financial burden of their decurionate, and in this way to save the family estate for the next generation. About the religious atmosphere in Patrick's home we know nothing. Patrick does not even tell us how his family reacted to his missionary vocation.[4] The society in which young Patrick moved would, on his own testimony, seem to have been as worldly in spirit, though Christian in name, as was British Christian society in the time of Gildas. When Patrick interprets his captivity as a punishment for his un-Christian life he includes himself in the many thousand people whose fate he shared, and who had deserved no better than had he: 'we turned away from God, and did not keep His commandments, and did not obey our clergy,[5] who used to remind us of our salvation.'[6] It might, of course, be argued that this was the attitude of the younger generation, of those who were taken captive because of their fitness to work as slaves. It is unlikely, however, that indifference to the demands of a Christian life would have been so rampant among the young had their elders raised serious objections. At the same time Patrick – indirectly – pays a tribute to the British clergy of the time, or at least to some of its members: they did their pastoral duty and untiringly (note the use of the imperfect, *admonebant*) reminded their flock of their eternal destination. If their words fell on deaf ears the fault was not theirs.

It is unfortunate for the historian that Patrick does not give a more detailed picture of Christian life and ecclesiastical conditions in the Britain of his early days to enliven the vague generalizations of contemporary continental writers, but here as throughout his Confession he is concerned merely with events and situations bearing on his spiritual life and his apostolate.

The second phase extends from Patrick's arrival at home after six years of slavery in Ireland until his return to that country as a missionary bishop. His family welcomed him back and urged him never to go away again. The Patrick who had come home, however, was a different person from the boy who had been captured by Irish raiders. During his years of servitude he had found 'the living God'; and there grew in him a desire to bring to his former masters the faith which he had begun fully to realize when serving them as a slave. The awareness of a vocation to the Irish apostolate first took shape in a dream in which he heard the voice of the Irish calling him back, and then in two experiences which one is inclined to describe as mystical prayer: 'And another night – whether within me, or beside me, I know not, God knoweth – they called me most unmistakably with words which I heard but could not understand, except that at the end of the prayer He spoke thus: "He that has laid down His life for thee, it is He that speaketh in thee"; and so I awoke full of joy. And again I saw Him praying in me, and I was[7] as it were within my body, and I heard Him above me, that is, over the inward man, and there He prayed mightily with groanings. And all the time I was astonished, and wondered, and thought with myself who it could be that prayed in me. But at the end of the prayer He spoke, saying that He was the Spirit, and so I woke up.'[8]

Apart from the all-important point that the substance of his dream was confirmed by the Spirit, Patrick is again rather less explicit than we might wish. There is, for example, not a word about the external forms of his new religious fervour. Did he continue those prolonged prayers which he used to say by day and night in the solitude of woods and mountain when a shepherd in Ireland?[9] He does not mention any person with whom he discussed what even before his compelling dream must have caused him much searching of heart – unless it was Victoricus, who in that dream 'came to him as from Ireland with innumerable letters, and gave him one of them.'[10] After that dream, and above all after the two experiences which followed, did Patrick seek spiritual guidance? Perhaps he was not the man to do so; but his silence does not exclude the possibility that he did.

As is well known, Patrick's account goes on immediately from the second of his mystical experiences to a crisis in his life during which once more his vocation was confirmed by a divine voice.[11] This is the essence of Patrick's argument, and the theme of his Confession from beginning to end: he did not go to Ireland of his own will, but in answer to a divine call, in obedience to the Spirit, knowing himself to be chosen by God in spite of his all too obvious human shortcomings. In this context the details of his ecclesiastical training are of no importance and therefore are passed over, with one exception: that on the eve of his elevation to the diaconate he confided to a close friend (*amicissimo meo*), who must have been an ecclesiastic of some importance, a sin of his boyhood which troubled his mind on that occasion (*propter anxietatem maesto animo*).[12] The reason why Patrick records this detail is, of course, that it was the revealing of that sin by his friend that sparked off the crisis which called again for divine intervention.

The crucial events in Patrick's life to which he alludes in this section of the Confession pose also a crucial problem to Patrician scholars, and their conflicting views have by now become firmly entrenched positions. The problem is essentially one of places and times. One thing only is certain – that the *defensio* mentioned in 32 took place in Britain, and at a time when Patrick was out of the country: *quod ego non interfui nec in Brittanniis eram*. Where, then, did Patrick stay? The only plausible alternatives are Gaul and Ireland; and our choice hinges on the question of times and of the general historical background. If at the time of the *defensio* Patrick was in Ireland, he must have been on trial for the conduct of his mission, and such a trial would not have taken place until that mission had gone on for a certain number of years; if, on the other hand, he was staying in Gaul, this must have been before his mission to Ireland started because the missionary tells us in so many words that he longed to visit his brethren in Gaul but was bound by the Spirit not to abandon his Irish flock.[13] In that event Gaul was almost certainly the country where Patrick trained for the priesthood, and this is exactly what Muirchú tells us on independent authority.[14] Muirchú's source, as is well known, makes Patrick a disciple of St Germanus of Auxerre, and the immediate successor to Ireland's shortlived first bishop, Palladius.[15] Muirchú's story of the successive missions of Palladius and Patrick would then cover the same period (though not the same events within it) as does Patrick's account of his crisis.

The second alternative is, in my opinion, by far the more probable one. A first argument can be derived from the general structure of the Confession. After Patrick's self-introduction and the brief account of his captivity at the age of sixteen and its effect on him (1–2) there follows a section which is mainly an avowal of his obligation of thanksgiving to God on the one hand and of his hesitation in the past of doing so on the other (3–15). Then comes the story of Patrick's captivity, his escape and return home, and his vocation (16–25). Next comes the section here under discussion (26–33, with the praise of God, 34, as a peroration). Chapter 35 clearly marks a new beginning; Patrick now goes on to an account of his missionary work in Ireland, which ends with 60, to be followed by the concluding chapters 61 and 62. The place of the 'crisis'-section before the mission report would *prima facie* indicate that the crisis was prior in time. This is confirmed by Patrick's choice of certain expressions – *defensio*, *pulsare*, *reprobatus sum* – which, to my mind, would be very strange if the events so described fell in Patrick's episcopate.[16] If the occasion on which Patrick's sin was made known is termed *defensio* it cannot have been a synod convened for the purpose of censuring, let alone deposing, him; granted even that a counsel for the defence had been provided, Patrick could not well have referred to that synod as *defensionem illam*.[17] The only plausible meaning of *pulsare* in this context is the metaphorical use (known from classical antiquity) of 'to knock' meaning 'to solicit,' which is appropriate at the 'screening' of a candidate but hardly so at the trial of a person facing ecclesiastical censure or deposition.[18] Finally, Patrick was rejected (*reprobatus*), and not deposed.

I take it, then, that Patrick, while residing at Auxerre, became a candidate for the head of the Irish mission, but was rejected by a 'board meeting' – to use a modern equivalent – that was held in Britain. There is only one known event that meets the case; *i.e.*, the delegation of Germanus and Lupus to Britain against the Neo-Pelagians in 429.[19] It must have been in the course of this mission that the creation of an Irish episcopate was contemplated, and that Auxerre's candidate, Patrick, was passed over in favour of Palladius, whom he succeeded after his premature death. The *volte-face* of Patrick's principal champion[20] might be explained by the opposition of British bishops, whom, in the circumstances, the Gallic delegation did not wish to antagonize.[21] Opposition from the very beginning would explain the hostility of British bishops to Patrick throughout his missionary period, and especially, if the late Père Grosjean was right,[22] over the Coroticus affair. I wonder are the opponents of Patrick's vocation who say behind his back: 'Why does this fellow throw himself into danger among enemies who have no knowledge of God?'[23] members of the British clergy rather than (as I have hitherto assumed) some of Patrick's *seniores* at Auxerre. Patrick, intending to study for the priesthood as a prospective missionary, would naturally approach first the ecclesiastical authorities of his own country; having been refused by them because of his sinful youth and his lack of learning, he might have decided to leave Britain for Gaul.[24]

The British church would seem to have retained a critical, not to say hostile, attitude to Patrick until the end of his life. If my reconstruction of Patrick's temporary rejection and ultimate consecration is accepted, this would be quite understandable. Auxerre had withdrawn its candidate when the British objected that they considered him both unqualified and unworthy, and a prominent member of the Auxerre community had even gone out of his way to prove their change of mind. Palladius had been consecrated bishop for Ireland; when, however, he died unexpectedly, the rejected candidate, Patrick, was made his successor. However justified this decision may have been in the circumstances, to the British bishops it must have appeared in a different light, and they did not take kindly to their new colleague. Patrick felt that they despised him,[25] that to them he was a stranger whose words carried no weight,[26] that they even misconstrued his motives.[27] This 'harping' on his unworthiness must have grieved the successful bishop more than did the objections to his 'rusticity,' which he admits as a fact,[28] although he knew that it did not disqualify him in the eyes of God.[29] These latter objections, he says, were made in good faith (*non ut causa malitiae, sed non sapiebat illis*); for the former he can find no excuse. There is, however, no evidence to show that he bore the British church any hostility. Canon 33 of the 'Synod of Patrick,' which I still regard as, basically, a document relating to Patrick's mission, insists merely on the normal demand that a cleric coming to Ireland 'from the Britons' should have a letter of introduction. This canon would also prove that, personal differences apart, the church of Britain took some share in the evangelization of the neighbouring island.

When, after the raid of Coroticus, Patrick demanded, perhaps a little rashly,[30] the excommunication of the raiders, their sympathizers at home, and the ruler himself,[31] it can easily be imagined that the hard feelings against him were revived in the hearts of many, clergy and laity alike, who were prepared to make considerable allowances in the case of a man on whom they must have looked as the defender of Roman Britain, or of whatever was left of it, against the incursions of barbarians.[32] It might well be, as Père Grosjean thought, that it was renewed criticism of Patrick as a British reaction to his Letter that wrung his Confession from him.[33]

In surveying the British attitude to Patrick's conduct of his mission the events behind chs. 26 to 33 of the Confession can, on my premises, have no place. I have already stated the reasons for my different interpretation of the evidence. This is, perhaps, the place for saying something concerning those passages in Patrick's account which are often quoted as evidence of accusations brought against Patrick by a British synod after he had been a missionary bishop in Ireland for some considerable time. We need not dwell on statements which will inevitably be interpreted according to an opinion formed already on other grounds. For example, the *seniores* who rebuke Patrick for his refusal of penitential offerings[34] clearly belong to the 'mother-church' or 'basis' of Patrick's mission; but whether this church is to be sought in Gaul or in Britain depends on considerations that have nothing to do with the passage in question. Similarly, the *dominicati rethorici*[35] ('learned ecclesiastics' according to the convincing interpretation of Professors Karl Mras[36] and Christine Mohrmann[37]) whom Patrick challenges, might have existed in either country – though a reference to Britain now seems to me more probable.

There are, as far as I can see, only two short phrases which might be interpreted as evidence to show that Patrick in his capacity as a missionary bishop was officially censured by the leaders of the British church. In *Conf.* 26 he says: 'My sins were brought up against my laborious episcopate.' I have never been able to understand why Patrick could not have written these words in retrospect, after many years of missionary experience; besides, it needed little imagination to anticipate the difficulties and dangers of such a mission, and Patrick, of all people, would have no illusions.[38] The other phrase describes Patrick's emerging from the crisis through which he had gone: *fides mea probata est coram Deo et hominibus.*[39] In their context these words are most naturally taken to mean 'my trust was proved right before God and men.' However, the Annals of Ulster under the year 441 have the following entry: *Leo ordinatus xl.ii. Romane eclesie episcopus et probatus est in fide catolica Patricius episcopus* (cf. Annals of Innisfallen under the same year: *Probatio sancti Patricii in fide catholica*). Some scholars have interpreted these entries as references to some sort of papal approbation, and Dr Morris sees in this *probatio* the solution of Patrick's 'crisis.'[40] My first objection is the lack of evidence of *probatio* as a canonical term, a fact for which I have the word of so eminent a canonist as Professor Stephan Kuttner of Yale. My second objection is the nature of the alleged *probatio*: an approval of Patrick's orthodoxy, which as far as we know, was never in question.[41] My third objection is that the phrase of the Confession on which the Annals of Ulster entry has evidently been modelled means nothing of the sort in its context. The *probatio* of Bishop Patrick by Pope Leo almost certainly has its origin in a misinterpretation of Patrick's words.[42]

To sum up my view of the subject: the British church would appear to have opposed Patrick's career at all stages. Its authorities refused him as a candidate for the priesthood when he wished to prepare himself for a future mission to Ireland and thus forced him to train abroad; British bishops opposed his appointment as head of the Irish mission in or about 429; they must have resented his consecration as successor to Palladius in the early 430s; they turned acidly against him after his excommunication of their protector Coroticus. There is no unequivocal evidence to show that Patrick's mission had been sponsored by the church of Britain or that the ecclesiastical authorities of that country were in a position to take, or, for that matter, ever did take, disciplinary action against him.

The student of a period so badly documented as is British ecclesiastical history during the second half of the fifth century must, of course, beware of concluding anything *ex silentio*. Otherwise, the absence of any British record concerning either the appointment or the censuring of Patrick by a British synod (if such was the case) would be an argument against a British basis of Patrick's mission and, by implication, in favour of a Gallic one. My concluding suggestion is not put forward as an argument. The fact that Bede does not make a single mention of Patrick – although he records, from Prosper, the mission of Palladius (*HE* i. 13) – has always been felt to be rather strange. It would be all the stranger if Patrick had been an emissary of the church of Britain.

Notes

1. *Confession* 1
2. Bury, J. B. *The Life of St Patrick and his Place in History* (London, 1905), 19f.
3. Hanson, R. P. C. *St Patrick, a British Missionary Bishop* (Nottingham, 1966), 16–18. I do not believe, however, that these considerations allow us to determine more accurately the date of Patrick's birth. His words *patrem habui Calpornium diaconum* need not imply that Calpornius was already a deacon when Patrick was born
4. Dr. J. Morris 'Dark Age Dates', in *Britain and Rome : Essays presented to Eric Birley* (1966) 150; 'The Dates of the Celtic Saints', *JTS*, xvii (1966), 360, 363, interprets *Conf.* 37 *et munera multa mihi offerebantur cum fletu et lacrimis* as meaning that Patrick's people tried to persuade him to stay at home and take over the municipal office (*munera*) that would go with the family estate. There are, however, several objections to taking *munera* here in the technical meaning of that term. Firstly, the plural *munera* would be strange because, for all that we know, only one *munus*, the decurionate, could be meant, and this, as has been said, was hardly an inducement for Patrick to stay. Secondly, the words *cum fletu et lacrimis* distinctly suggest that the offerers were penitents, cf. *peniteat in fletu et lacrimis*, Vinnian 12; 29; *cum fletu et lamentatione . . . paenitentia* Synod. II s. Patricii c.3. Patrick's refusal of *munera* here is almost certainly of the same kind as his refusal of *munuscula* offered by pious women in *Conf.* 49
5. Professor Hanson, *op. cit.*, p. 16, translates 'bishops.' In the Latin of the times, *sacerdos* can mean either 'presbyter' or 'bishop'; and in *Epist.* 6, where Patrick speaks of Coroticus as one who despises God and his *sacerdotes*, who have power to bind in heaven what they bind on earth, he apparently thinks of bishops (more particularly of himself) in the first place. His remark in *Conf.* 1, however, refers to a single district where there would have been no more than one bishop; hence the plural *sacerdotes* would seem to be used with a more general meaning
6. *Conf.* 1. The Translation of Patrick's writings used in this paper is basically mine: *The Works of St Patrick* (London, 1953=*Ancient Christian Writers* 17)
7. All surviving MSS (contrary to a statement by Dr Morris, *JTS*, xvii, 360 n.1) read *et eram quasi intra corpus meum;* and, poor sense that it may seem to make (Morris, *ibid.*), I still hesitate to accept in its place the *erat* of *v*, which need not be more than a guess by the Bollandist editor of the Vedastinus, Daniel Papebroch
8. *Conf.* 24–25
9. *Ibid.*, 16
10. *Ibid.*, 23
11. *Ibid.*, 26–33
12. *Ibid.*, 32
13. *Ibid.*, 43
14. *Vita s. Patricii* I, 6(5)–10(9). Acceptance of Muirchú's account is, of course, quite independent of one's interpretation of *Conf.* 26–33. For example, Morris (*Dark Age Dates*, 180 n. 47; *JTS*, xvii, 366) believes that Muirchú follows a genuine historical source, although he interprets *Conf.* 26–33 in the sense that Patrick's episcopate was censured by a British synod
15. There probably were Irish Christians in southwest Britain, and they might well have been given into Palladius' care (so Morris, *JTS*, xvii, 356f.); however, his mission must have been primarily to Ireland, because Prosper (*Contra Collatorem* 21, 2) speaks of the Christianization of a *barbarian island*
16. See my article, 'Patriciology', *Seanchas Ardmhacha* 1961–2, 25–61
17. He might, conceivably, have spoken of *defensio mea* were it not that the person who, according to this theory, was expected to plead for him did exactly the opposite

Notes

18. By a lapse of memory, Morris (*JTS*, xvii, 362 n. 3) quotes White's 'put me to shame' and my 'let me down' as translations of *pulsaret pro me;* they render, of course, *me dehonestaret*
19. See Prosper, *Chronicle* s.a. 429; Constantius, *Vita Germani* C.12ff.
20. Not, I am sure, Germanus. Patrick would hardly have styled a former superior *amicissimus meus* (*Conf.* 27; 32)
21. The official character of the mission of Palladius (A.D. 431) and the presumptive reasons behind it (cf. Morris, *l.c.* 356f.) should not be read into the events of 429. There is no reason for supposing that Ireland had entered into the considerations of Palladius at that time; it might well have done so on receiving a report from Germanus and Lupus returning from Britain
22. See below, p. 127
23. *Conf.* 46
24. This interpretation is suggested also by the words which precede and follow the passage quoted: *Vnde autem debueram sine cessatione Deo gratias agere, qui saepe indulsit insipientiae meae neglegentiae meae . . ., qui adiutor datus sum et non cito adquieui secundum quod mihi ostensum fuerat* (cf. 23) *et sicut spiritus suggerebat* (cf. 24–25), . . . *quia multi hanc legationem* (his vocation, not his actual mission, as is clear from Patrick's fuller quotation of Eph. vi. 20 in *Conf.* 56, *Epist.* 5) *prohibebant;* and, resuming the initial idea at the end of the chapter, *nunc mihi sapit quod ante debueram*
25. *Epist.* 1; 12
26. *Ibid.*, 11: 'If my own people do not know me, a prophet hath no honour in his own country. Perhaps we are not of the same fold, and have not one and the same God as father'
27. *Ibid.*, 10: 'Did I come to Ireland without God, or according to the flesh?' Cf. Grosjean, P., *Anal Boll*, 63 (1945), 103 n. 1
28. *Conf.* 46
29. *Ibid.*, 9–13
30. See Grosjean, P., *Anal Boll*, 76 (1958), 364
31. Cf. *Epist.* 2; 7; 21
32. Cf. Grosjean, P., *Anal Boll*, 63 (1945), 103f.
33. *Ibid.*, 105–11
34. *Conf.* 37
35. *Ibid.*, 13
36. *Anzeiger für die Altertumswissenschaft* (1953), 109f.
37. *The Latin of St Patrick*, 29ff.
38. See my article, 'Patriciology', op. cit., 21
39. *Conf.* 30
40. 'Dark Age Dates', 163, 180 n. 47; *JTS*, xvii, 364f.
41. Patrick's 'creed,' *Conf.* 4, is not an answer to a charge of heresy
42. This view dispenses, by implication, with Dr Morris's – to my mind far-fetched – interpretation of *Conf.* 43 ('Dark Age Dates', 182 n. 75; *JTS*, xvii, 362, 365)

The Church in Wales

W. H. Davies

I

I would like to begin with a brief examination of the contribution of archaeology, for here, if anywhere, a radical advance in knowledge since the days of Hugh Williams and Sir John Lloyd might well be expected.[1] The first striking fact to emerge from much brilliant work is the light thrown almost exclusively on secular, political and social problems of our period, for with one important exception virtually nothing of any direct importance can be discerned for the contemporary ecclesiastical scene. Wales, it seems, has no archaeological parallel as yet to Tintagel, Glastonbury, Church Island, or Ardwall Isle, but just a few meagre early remains whose validity rests largely on tradition: for example, the foundations of the so-called cell and oratory of St Seiriol at Penmon, Anglesey, and some traces of an early hermitage on nearby St Seiriol's islet, or the fragmentary walls of a small oratory under the later church of the seventh-century Saint Beuno at Clynnog Fawr, Caerns.; and at Burry Holms, Glam., excavations still in progress suggest the presence of a small pre-Norman foundation on the site of the twelfth-century church.[2] For the traditional well-attested major monasteries of the early and later sixth century, among them those at Llancarfan, Llantwit Major, St David's, Bangor (Caerns.) and Bangor Is-Coed, no material evidence has so far come to light.[3] The well-known group of pre-Norman memorial crosses reflects the existence at Llantwit Major, from the ninth century at least, of an important religious centre, yet excavation locally has revealed merely the remains of a monastic grange of the twelfth and following centuries.[4] One must hope that Llancarfan nearby or some other site will some day prove more rewarding. The 'port' or anchorage of Illtud mentioned in his *Vita* (cc. 13, 15) is now more plausible, certainly for the twelfth century. A recent C^{14} dating from the remains of an old oak breakwater there well out on the beach has yielded a date of *c.* 1400 A.D., thus proving, by what seems a rapid rate of erosion, that the coastline at least was utterly different in the earlier centuries and could well have provided a haven for local seafarers.[5] It may have implications too for St David's and the neighbouring Porth Mawr and Porth Clais.[6] The western sea-ways were certainly much used at this time, for Irish and Gallic influences on certain cultural features are plain; and a glance at the imported material from a site like Dinas Powys – the sherds of fine red ware and amphorae, the glass and metal fragments – provides, somewhere apparently within the sixth and seventh centuries, a quite unexpected quasi-commercial setting for the travels of the Welsh Saints.[7] It is on a sherd of imported ware from Dinas Emrys in north Wales that a Chi-Rho monogram appears, but its relationship to structures on the site is at the moment uncertain.[8] Material from Dark Age sites, we are warned, must be used with caution, but it seems to illustrate clearly enough, with regional variations, an economic background both pastoral and agricultural in character, and the common use of domestic objects made from bone, iron, wood, leather and wool.[9] In most respects it would seem to represent a continuation of the local Romano–British way of life, except that occasional dry-stone buildings, as at Dinas Powys, probably replaced the well-built villas of the Roman period.[10] Settlement studies indicate too that the poorer classes, whether free or bond, may have lived largely in nucleated hamlets as well as in isolated wood-built homesteads.[11]

Such in outline are some aspects of the economic and social background of the early monastic centres of Wales, themselves, it seems, conforming to the general pattern of timber construction, though direct evidence is lacking.[12]

There is, however, one indisputable survival of contemporary documentation, that of the early commemorative and inscribed stone monuments.[13] These have proved a most fertile field for many theories concerning racial, linguistic, political and other problems of our period, in particular the thorny question of the scope and character of Irish settlement in Wales.[14] A fuller and perhaps more proper assessment of their ecclesiastical significance, however, depends, it seems, on more critical evaluations of these monuments, especially on a local and regional basis and utilizing the modern aids now available for comparative studies.[15] A fresh look might well be taken, for instance, at the so-called Cross of Illtud and the Pillar of Samson at Llantwit Major – both possibly misdated.[16] Meanwhile we see that the terms *sacerdos* and *presbiter* attest some organized form of fifth- to sixth-century Christianity in north Wales, where the Chi-Rho symbol is also found and the existence of a burial ground near Aberdaron is probably implied by the association of *presbyter* with the phrase *cum multitudinem fratrum*.[17] Nowhere on the earlier stones does the title *episcopus* occur. In the formula *hic iacet* (*iacit*) the influence of Gallic Christianity has been traced,[18] but this need not necessarily signify, as we shall see, any undue influx of missionary elements (or *peregrini*) from the continent. The association too with religious sites of many of the Ogam inscribed stones or those with an Irish name, several bearing Christian symbols as well, may indicate the faith of leading men among the goidelic element in west Wales, a suggestion of some significance, as we shall see later.[19] We may recall here that no site of a particularly Irish character has yet been identified in west Wales.[20] There are also a few stones which throw some light on social and political aspects of the time, but these are left to another context.

From this very brief survey, then, the archaeological contribution to our subject, especially when regarded in isolation, seems small and essentially indeterminate in character. Like *Britannia* to Gildas, it presents more tyrannical problems than facts.

II

But perhaps we can look for something better from the retrospective evidence?[21] For the direction of most early Welsh literary and historical traditions focuses unmistakably, if we exclude *Macsen Wledig*, on the fifth to seventh centuries.[22] The volume of material is large and varied, involving many cognate disciplines, and perhaps it may be said at once that, in spite of much recent valuable work in different directions, the specialists agree that no convincing synthesis is yet possible for many aspects of pre-Norman Wales.[23] One of the greatest needs, it seems, is for far more intensive work on the purely philological side of the later texts and documents in both Latin and Welsh, along the lines of Professor Jackson's masterly examination of the Life of St Kentigern.[24] Basic in particular to all research is the availability of technical aids and fully-collated texts, and here vernacular studies seem so far to have the advantage. It is gratifying to know that modern editions of the *Life of St David* and the *Latin Versions of the Welsh Laws* have just been published, but a complete text of the *Life of Cadog* is still only available in typescript form.[25] Valuable ancillary studies too, such as those on the settlements of the Welsh Saints and the Welsh tribal system, have thrown much new light on the historical and topographical background of the monastic milieu and the diffusion of cults in the early Welsh Church.[26] The possibility of later dedication or rededication of many churches, perhaps on the occasion of rebuilding or under external stimuli, need not invalidate well-attested tradition associated with the founders of the major settlements, *e.g.*, St David's; and it has rightly been emphasized, to take a special case, that the Norman preference for Llandaff over Cardiff as their cathedral centre may have its roots in a pre-existing ecclesiastical site governed originally by the line of a Roman road across the river Taff.[27] It is such possibilities that affect a number of related problems, such as the original home of the *Book of St Chad* or the theory of the transfer of a territorial episcopal title to a later cathedral centre. A word of caution, however, may be necessary concerning the apparent correlation between Welsh topography and some hagiographical statements, since the latter might well have their origin in the former and topographical accuracy by itself is no sure guarantee of general historical validity.[28]

Two points of view, broadly speaking, emerge from a fair amount of recent work on the ecclesiastical problems of our period.[29]

The first is more flexible and liberal in character. It would regard, for instance, the characters in the *Liber Landavensis* and the *Vita Cadoci* as substantially genuine, with due allowance made for certain twelfth-century editorial blunders; and then, on the basis of such documents together with the early genealogies, the *Vitae*, and other available literary and historical material, would reconstruct in some detail the sixth-century scene.[30] Monastic bishops and elastic lordship- or kingdom-bishoprics appear, with Dubricius and Teilo the first to bear the title in south Wales, while Illtud, Cadog, David and others are busy founding major monasteries, and the land is full of missionary spirit and activity. With the aid of later church dedications and genealogical and hagiographical traditions, their activities are then localized, *e.g.*, Dubricius in Erging,[31] and the monastic founders at their major settlements. Up to this point rational probabilities play their legitimate part. But then the old temptation to fill in the picture proves too strong. From the Welsh *Vitae* and the cognate Irish and Breton material, most of it apparently much contaminated, including even the prestigious *Vita Samsonis*, the saints are given the traditional imposing biographical treatment, so much so that even the enigmatic Docus has emerged once more hale and hearty from the shadows.[32] All this, we note too, in the almost complete absence of such material in the earliest Welsh vernacular literature, where religion or ecclesiastical saga, it seems, played little if any part.[33] This further step, which would seem to most a retrograde one, is largely subjective in approach, the result, apparently, of a special training necessary for dealing with 'the peculiar literature of Celtic Britain' and where 'experience in the handling of rational sources can be a misleading guide to the interpretation of material that is inherently irrational.'[34] But whatever the truth of the matter is, it seems far better to accept the luminous protreptic guidance of Delehaye and others and so avoid, as far as possible, the confused methodology, the arbitrary and eclectic use of sources, that still seem endemic to this field of study.[35] I have stressed this point, since we are apt to underrate not only the sensible contributions made by this approach, but the fact that it is chiefly in this area of comparative study that any slight hope of progress lies. It has recently been re-emphasized, for example, that the repeated stress in the *Liber Landavensis* on Llandaff's claim to jurisdiction over the territory between the rivers Wye and Towy has not yet been satisfactorily explained.[36] The implications may be far-reaching, and an open mind and controlled imaginative insight, both necessary, must somehow be balanced by the observance of accepted canons of criticism.

The second point of view is much more critical and conservative in character.[37]

It would see in the *Liber Landavensis* a highly edited and partially forged compilation of Bishop Urban's *familia* to serve contemporary ecclesiastical claims, but would admit that the Cartulary of Llancarfan may well have its chief source in genuine grants, derived perhaps from marginal entries in Gospel books.[38] There is obviously much room for argument, but in general the orthodox view is presented of the ambiguous character of nearly all our early references to the Welsh episcopate, including the Celtic bishops that attended the meetings with Augustine, the ninth-century Welsh Archbishops Elfoddw of Gwynedd and Nobis of St Degui (Dewi), their titles assumed to be honorary, while there is also a reference to a *parochia* of St Degui (Dewi) and a 'bishop of Teilo' of the same date.[39] These later bishops, it is suggested, were closely associated with the mother *clas* church rather than with any formal territorial diocese.[40] Bangor and St David's were thus obviously important centres at an early time, but 'the true physiognomy of the Welsh Church before the Danish raids is hidden from us in impenetrable obscurity.'[41] To fill the gap, the organization of that church on a monastic basis in the sixth and seventh centuries must then be inferred largely from Irish and Breton analogies.[42] Bishops there were, but monastic and not territorial in character, for the foundation of major monasteries during the sixth century on their traditional sites is granted.[43] There was, however, no monastic 'explosion,' for the monastic system in Wales never seems to have developed as extensively or vigorously as in Ireland. The bishops, whether under the abbot or as abbot–bishops, would be responsible for all details of ritual both in the monastery and in those associated churches founded either by the monks or privately. There is no sign of any important central organization or, in the absence of towns, of any equivalent to a metropolitan. As for ritual and customs the Welsh church, as befitted its older connections with Rome, might have its own minor peculiarities, but in all essentials, such as doctrinal orthodoxy, it probably conformed to the general Celtic pattern and reflected the influence of the Gallic church.

It will be clear at once that this second attitude is much more cautious and negative in character. It stresses the monastic colouring of much of the available material, the panegyrical character of the commemorative anniversary sermons with dire consequences for sixth-century history, and ruthlessly excludes Kentigern from St Asaph and perhaps the Welsh Mass from Ireland.[44] But in some ways it is itself uncritical, for the validity of the Irish and Breton analogies is largely a tacit assumption. The Breton evidence[45] of the *Vitae*, influenced so much by the Carolingian revival of letters, is more suspect than the Irish, and as yet it is not at all certain how far the description of Irish society as 'tribal, rural, hierarchical, and familiar' in character truly reflects in the fifth and sixth centuries the nature of Welsh society with its legacy of long and direct contact with Rome.[46] The ground common to this and the more liberal view seems small and virtually confined to the acceptance of monastic bishops in the sixth century, the reality of monastic founders like Illtud, Cadog, David and Deiniol, and the presence of thinly scattered major monasteries with growing administrative as well as religious ecclesiastical functions. It is all as dauntingly dark and vague as its counterpart is attractively colourful and familiar.

The retrospective evidence then, I feel, has contributed little as yet of positive major value to the picture of the early Welsh Church that one finds in the comprehensive, though somewhat coloured and partly dated account of Hugh Williams and in the fresher, sober work of J. E. Lloyd.[47] The impact has been most fruitful in the field of topographical, linguistic and onomastic studies; *e.g.*, the reasons governing the location of monasteries or the meaning of Welsh place-names.[48] Whether the notable advance made in the attribution of much of the earliest Welsh poetry to the later sixth century[49] will be paralleled for a core of information in our own field remains to be seen. But better to live with a dearth of facts than rely for solutions on what may involve 'an amazing concatenation of circumstances.' The ancient wisdom is not amiss here: *melius est aliqua nescire.*

III

It is time now to turn to a more logical consideration of the origin of the early Welsh Church as the possible product and inheritor of Romano-British traditions.[50]

That paganism was active to some extent in the latter half of the fourth century is seen from the building of the Temple of Nodens on an isolated hill at Lydney, Glos., but probably other than purely religious motives made it a centre of pilgrimage, mostly for the well-to-do, to judge from the spacious and lavish lay-out.[51] As for Christianity the material traces are very slight. A certain Christian significance has been detected in the orientation of some burials at the Llantwit Major Villa in Glamorgan, but this can probably be discounted until a much wider study has been made of villa graves.[52] It would seem that the only clear piece of Christian evidence is the small pewter bowl from Venta Silurum (Caerwent) with a Chi-Rho monogram on its base, which may bear witness to the presence of a house-church at least.[53] The identification of a so-called church there has been questioned by some competent to judge;[54] and the gnostic formula from Segontium (Caernarvon) is irrelevant.[55] In view of the tradition, stemming from the sixth century, of the martyrdom of Julius and Aaron, which probably took place *c.* 250–60 A.D. at Caerleon, this absence of virtually any Christian material remains in Wales is all the more surprising.[56]

With the one important exception of the early Christian inscribed stones and the doubtful interpretation of possible symbols on the Llangeinwen (Anglesey) lead coffin, the fifth century too presents much the same picture of the lack of direct evidence for Wales.[57] There are some literary references, but these are secondary and suspect. The traditional connection of Germanus, for example, with northeast and south central Wales, the region of later Powys, where from place names and dedications like Llanarmon the saint seems to have had a special cult, and where he is associated with Vortigern in Nennius, may be due to legendary accretions to his *Vita* or to Welsh oral saga connected with fifth-century British leaders.[58] The same influence may be seen too at work in the later hagiographical references to Illtud and Paulinus as the disciples of Germanus, for in this way the mantle of the illustrious saint would fall indirectly on the sixth-century Gildas, Samson, David and Paul Aurelian.[59] Nor can we draw any plausible inference at all for Wales *c.* 478 A.D. from Sidonius Apollinaris's oft-quoted visitor Riocatus, described as *antistes ac monachus*, for his home might well have been Brittany at this time.[60] It seems that the only literary source for any convincing evidence of the British Church in a large part of the fifth century lies in Patrick's *Confessio* and *Epistola ad Coroticum.*[61] Even here the much-debated problem of Patrick's personal contact, if any, with Gaul raises many difficulties. But among the few facts that may be inferred is the continued existence in Britain of a diocesan church with a hierarchical structure and occasional synods. It would seem too that Patrick regarded his compatriots in Britain as still *cives* and *Romani* and to that extent nominal Christians at least. This is significant for north Wales in the light of the evidence of two inscribed stones dated at present to the late fifth/early sixth century, one of which mentions a *Venedotis cives* with a *magistratus* for cousin, and the other commemorates a *medicus* or doctor.[62] We must, of course, make due allowance in all this for literacy only in Latin and semantic uncertainties, but the impression is certainly given of some organized system of society, probably in process of adaptation to 'tribal' conditions after long association with Rome, in an area of north Wales with contemporary epigraphic evidence of a definitely Christian character, such as the Chi-Rho monogram and the specific ecclesiastical titles mentioned earlier.[63] It all suggests that Christianity in some form or another was the accepted official religion of a stable kind of society in northwest Wales towards the end of the fifth century, and intrusive elements need play but little part in it.[64] This picture harmonizes very well with the implications of Patrick's words for a slightly earlier period; and there seems no reason, in the light too of some other epigraphic material in Welsh areas, why we should not extend the same general acceptance of ordered ecclesiastical life, even if mostly at an official or upper-class 'tribal' level, to the whole of fifth-century Wales.[65] We may infer too from Patrick's words the presence in Britain in the first half of the fifth century of schools under *grammatici* at least, and probably some under rhetors, where Latin was acquired and taught as a living language.[66] The study, however, of Patrick's latinity as possibly reflecting his British schooling and training is bound to be extremely complicated, for like Jerome, at least in title, Patrick was a *vir trilinguis*. It was during this century, according to the Celtic philologists, that various loan words passed into Irish from British Latin, words both secular and ecclesiastical in character;[67] and since some scholars would locate Patrick's birthplace, *Bannavem Taburniae*, somewhere in the Bristol Channel area, it may be that this transmission took place from south Wales.[68] But this is just so much guesswork; and I mention it simply to illustrate how, in this period and for Britain as a whole, we ourselves eagerly scan Patrick's works for some light on that shadowy British Church from which other scholars are themselves hoping for illumination on Patrick.[69] For the objective historian it is a somewhat sad predicament, and were it not for one final consideration from the Age of the Saints nothing further would now be left us, for we have already glanced at that excessive dosage of the drug of secondary sources supplemented by a full magnum of autosuggestion against which Dr Binchy's hisperic eloquence has already warned us.[70] It is in this setting of ecclesiastical shadow and uncertainty that we now turn briefly to evidence for the early Welsh Church from Gildas.

IV

In recent times the revival of doubts about the unity of the *De Excidio Britan-*

niae of Gildas has caused a marked reluctance on the part of some scholars to make full and adequate use of this work.[71] Yet the validity of Gildas's testimony, as that of the only contemporary literary source for the history of the British Church in the early sixth century, is crucial to any discussion. A detailed and definitive critical study of Gildas's works as a whole, dependent as it is on advances yet to be made in other cognate fields, is still not possible, but one vital aspect of the problem is more fully illustrated in M. Kerlouégan's contribution. Meanwhile, as a convenient method of approach, it may not be out of place to make just a few preliminary observations before looking briefly at the *De Excidio* as it relates to the problem of the early Church in Wales:

(1) The text, as established by Mommsen, is generally sound;[72] and to his MS. evidence can now be added that of two leaves, probably of the ninth century, containing some later chapters of the work.[73] All the better MSS., including the lost eighth-century one that formed the basis of the Leyden Glossary, favour unity. Josselin's edition too of 1568, the basis with Cotton Vit. A. VI of any text, wisely calls it just *Epistola Gildae*.[74]

(2) There is wide agreement that Gildas was writing in the first half of the sixth century, probably in its second quarter.[75] To Gildas the Saxons are *deo invisi* (*i.e.*, pagan: 23 (38. 13, 14); cf. 38 (49, 22)), and very many Christian shrines are now isolated and cut off from the *cives* (natives, *c.* 10).[76] But there has been a long period of comparative peace over the large part of Britain still British, an area which is conveniently called, as Gildas himself implies, *Britannia* or *patria* and covering the Roman province of *Britannia Prima* at least.[77]

(3) The primary source of any information about Gildas and his times must be his own works. Secondary sources, including the *Vitae*, are all in varying degrees suspect, and at best provide only traditional and not direct corroborative evidence.[78]

(4) Of the other works attributed to Gildas, viz. the *Penitential*, the *Epistolary Fragments*, the *Lorica*, and the *Oratio Rythmica*, only the first, as probably the earliest genuine Celtic Penitential, merits at present a real claim to consideration.[79] Since all, however, including some other Welsh canons, are in various ways controversial, and in any case are concerned chiefly with general monastic discipline or prophylactic charms, they are not taken here into account.[80]

(5) The *De Excidio* belongs to a well-known earlier literary genre, in which a theological and moral retributive view is taken of history.[81] Gildas himself, with his tendency to dramatic presentation, might have put his message simply thus: 'I know, Maelgwn, that you and the other princes think me of little account, but at least learn the lesson of your country's history and heed God speaking through the Scriptures, if not through my own flood of words. Otherwise, not only Hell awaits you, but God has plague and the cursed Saxons just around the corner. And this is the message for the

people too, you officials and Church dignitaries, that you should proclaim by your own words and actions.' Only in this didactic context should one think of Gildas as *historiographus*, however seriously and critically he himself takes the historical side of his task.[82] Thus the *historia* and *epistola* are mutually essential elements in the same message; and from 1 (27.2) where the phrase *ingenitum quid* looks forward to the unfolding tale of *insipientia* and *levitas*, and from the links between later and earlier chapters, the unity of the *De Excidio* is evident. This is quite clear too from its partly sophisticated and rhetorical style, as if Gildas is making it plain that he can meet on their own ground the contemporary counterparts of Patrick's *dominicati rethorici*, the *sapientes et legis periti et potentes in sermone* of a later day who may have imbued the clergy with that passion for the *ineptae saecularium hominum fabulae*[83] so detested by our author. Yet he is more often quite lucid and direct.

(6) Finally the geographical and personal setting of the *De Excidio*. Somewhere within the extensive area of *Britannia* already mentioned Gildas was writing at a centre which served as a clearing house for all kinds of political, social and ecclesiastical news and provided too some library facilities.[84] From indications, however, like the order in which the princes are enumerated, various personal touches in their description, especially the fuller and more intimate treatment of Maelgwn, and from linguistic and some other signs and the fact that the *Scotti* lie to the northwest, we can very plausibly infer a Welsh milieu and that by the sea for our author.[85] But at this point our only aid is tradition, as reflected especially in the first *Vita Samsonis*, which associates a flourishing monastery at this time with its earlier founder Illtud, a teacher of secular and sacred learning, and the site is identified with Llanilltud Fawr (Llantwit Major) in the Vale of Glamorgan or Ynys Bŷr (Caldy Island) off the coast of Pembrokeshire.[86] The important group of inscribed stones at the former place, the long tradition of a surrounding Romanized environment, and a haven affording easy contact by sea with Dumnonia and the urban area, however decayed, of the lower Severn, these considerations, it seems, would strongly favour Llantwit Major. It is tempting to see here in Illtud the 'accomplished teacher of almost the whole of Britannia' who instructed Maelgwn and to link the literary implications of the *elegantem magistrum* with the Gildas who, to Vinnian's query, *elegantissime rescripsit*.[87] But all that can now be said is that the internal evidence of the *De Excidio* as a whole points to cherished familiarity with monastic activities and a certain failure to appreciate the various practical demands of worldly affairs. Was Gildas perhaps a deacon, as has been suggested, when he wrote this work?[88] Or a lay monk and *doctor* (teacher) at Illtud's monastery?[89] The question is very much open.

Bearing these observations in mind we can now look briefly at the evidence of the *De Excidio* for the ecclesiastical scene in *Britannia* as a whole.

It is expressly stated in *c.* 26 that the initial Saxon expansion and raids on the west did not vitally undermine the earlier post-Roman organized pattern of society implied in the words: *reges*, *publici*, *privati*, *sacerdotes*, *ecclesiastici*, *suum quique ordinem servarunt*.[90] Due allowance, however, must be made for social and political variety in rural and still partly urbanized regions, a difference reflected perhaps in the native equivalents of terms like *reges*, *rectores*, *tyranni* and *speculatores*.[91] The church certainly lived on in an environment of *serenitas* (*c.* 26), which has infected all elements in society with the poison of *levitas* and *insipientia* (*c.* 1, a 'witless indifference' to the claims and responsibilities of true religion).[92] Gildas is careful, however, to emphasize the presence of some noble and good elements too in every sphere, a fact often forgotten in the injustice commonly done to his personal portrait.[93]

Against this background the details given of the church, though lacking precise and clear definition, are striking enough, and seem to be quite free from anachronisms.[94] The scene presupposes a long tradition of established Christianity in *Britannia*, organized on a secular and episcopal basis, but already embracing some monastic settlements.[95] Bishops, presbyters, deacons and *clerici* in unspecified minor orders abound, but there is no mention of archbishops, metropolitans, and synods.[96] The clergy have their *parochiae* (parishes) and *greges* (flocks),[97] probably on a restricted territorial or local church assembly basis as regional differences demanded, and although there is no direct mention of monastic bishops and only one indirect reference to an abbot who offered the right of sanctuary,[98] Gildas's concept of the *mater ecclesia*[99] could well include them. Bishops, it is noted, are skilfully versed in the complexities of worldly affairs and are obviously of social and political importance to their rulers.[100] Celibacy is not incumbent.[101] The priests minister to the people in churches (*domus ecclesiae*), where the celebration of the eucharist is the focal point of worship and oaths are confirmed at the altars.[102] In these churches too, to judge from expert opinion about the quotations used so effectively and relevantly by Gildas, the Vulgate is coming more into use, but the preference for the Old Latin versions of the Gospels and of some of the Old Testament books, especially for a very early Old Latin literal rendering of Job, presupposes in itself a continuous history of Christianity reaching well back into Roman Britain.[103] In matters of ritual and belief the church is oriented towards Rome and seems largely orthodox. Belief in the Trinity, for example, is emphasized,[104] and there is no sign of heresy, though perhaps some lingering Pelagian influence may be detected in Gildas himself.[105] There is no sign either of paganism, though the presence of *increduli* (unbelievers) as well as the faithful calls for missionary service within the existing church framework.[106] Moral failings and malpractices, especially simony, are found along with nobler elements among the clergy, some of whom, ambitious timeservers rejected by their own *parochiae* for preferment, first carefully prepare the way and then travel abroad to acquire episcopal rank, returning as proud prelates and obviously a fertile source of Gallic influences.[107] Others, significantly again for us, are depicted as given to what may include secular literature and entertainments.[108] While we may make every allowance for homiletic exaggeration, conditioned nevertheless by contemporary acquaintance with the facts, yet it is a scene evocative in some ways of the declining *romanitas* of fifth-century Gaul rather than the somewhat restricted and austere background usually associated with the tendentious accounts of early British monasticism and the Age of the Saints. In many respects it is an altogether unexpected picture and one never to be inferred without Gildas's contemporary testimony.[109]

In this formal setting of long-established Christianity, for Gildas himself distinguishes no regional differences and the epigraphic evidence would seem partially corroborative, the exhortations to repentance addressed to the ageing Vortipor (Voteporix), prince of Demetia, and to Maelgwn, the powerful king in north Wales, take on a new significance.[110] In spite of earlier harsh words about the *grassatores Hiberni* (*c.* 21), Gildas makes no reference to Vortipor's Irish antecedents, but by calling him 'wicked son of a good father' points to an older Christian tradition in the family. It makes one wonder too whether the phrase *patriaeque amator* in the hexameter line of the Paulinus inscription from Cynwyl Gaeo, Carms., is not more appropriate to a fifth- not sixth-century date, reflecting perhaps the flight of refugees from Saxon pressure described in the *De Excidio*.[111] As for Maelgwn, usually only Gildas's famous reference to the bardic panegyrists at his court is mentioned.[112] But for us his importance lies in the proof afforded of the existence of an already established monastic centre, where the king himself spent some time as a monk before returning to the old ways.[113] The words of Gildas, too, imply generous gifts of Maelgwn to the church, but nowhere is the founding of a monastery recorded.[114] We hear also, in connection with his *conversio*, of monastic rules, the use of psalmody, and the emphasis put on scriptural instruction for the young;[115] and we recall how Gildas himself in *c.* 70 gives a vivid practical demonstration of the allegorical method of teaching scripture. It is all a fitting setting for the rise of monastic penitential discipline, as seen in Gildas's example, though the question of public or private penitence in the established church and its particular form is not made clear in the *De Excidio*.[116]

The continuity of the Christian tradition in these far western areas, however formal in character, is probably even more true for south Wales, with which region it seems likely we should not identify the kingdom of Aurelius Caninus.[117] Here the more pronounced Roman tradition of earlier days[118] might well have seen the continuation or development of some quite unsuspected features. We recall, for instance, the use of the Roman measures *himina* and *sextarius* in Gildas's penitential, and the casual mention of *pecunia*, *obolus*, and *denarius* in the *De Excidio*.[119] The context seems to imply more than just a literary usage. But whatever their significance, Gildas's contemporaries must surely have been living out at this moment the very last declining days of *romanitas* in Glywysing (roughly Glamorgan), where the *Llys* at Dinas Powys reflects one aspect of the social and political background.[120] But only the *De Excidio* allows us with some confidence to make this the setting for a long-established church in south Wales and adjacent areas, organized in a pattern of *parochiae* (parishes) centred probably in decaying urban communities and in lordships or hamlets or private and monastic churches.[121] But we are already in the dark shadows, where, ironically enough, the only hope of possible illumination must seem to rest in – the *Vitae!* The wheel has turned full circle!

Such then is our reading of the significance of the *De Excidio* for the Welsh Church in the post-Roman period ending with the earlier part of the sixth century. At least three main points emerge:

(1) There was no break in the continuity of the Christian tradition in Wales since the Roman period.
(2) The monastic element seems small in *Britannia* at the time of the composition of the *Epistola*.
(3) The so-called missionary activities of the Welsh 'Saints' should be viewed as a natural *internal* ecclesiastical development that rules out the need for any vigorous intrusive evangelization via the western seaways; and this development took place increasingly later under the aegis of the larger focal points of religious life, the monasteries, to meet the social challenge of an evolving complex political system which we conveniently call 'tribal.'[122]

Notes

1. Basic are chs. VII and VIII in *PEW;* Alcock, L., *DP* (1963) and *WHR* (1964), 1–7 as a convenient summary. I am greatly indebted to them. Cf. Nash-Williams, V. E. (ed.), *A Hundred Years of Welsh Archaeology:* 1846–1946 (Gloucester, 1947). For Williams and Lloyd, see *CEB*, *HW*.
2. Radford, C. A. R., 'The Celtic Monastery in Britain', *Arch Camb*, CXI (1962), 1–24; O'Kelly, M. J., 'Church Island Near Valencia, Co. Kerry', *PRIA*, LIX (1958) 57–131; Thomas, C., 'Ardwall Isle: The Excavation of an Early Christian Site of Irish Type' (1964–5), *TGNHAS*., vol. XLIII, 1966; Hague, D. B., 'Burry Holms Excavation' 1965–6, *Journal of the Gower Society*, vol. 17, 1966 (Mr Hague has very kindly informed me that the 1967 excavations have now confirmed the presence of an earlier timber frame structure under the later church and brought to light elsewhere, along with some samian, a few sherds of possibly Romano-British or Dark Age pottery. I am also grateful to Mr C. H. Houlder for the following communication: During rescue operations of prehistoric structures in a field at Llandygai, nr. Bangor, Caerns., in 1966–7 a number of medieval graves were found. Amongst these was one at the centre of the foundation trench of a rectangular wooden structure, 12′ x 14′. Though it cannot be proved that this structure was roofed, the presence of a simple early church is a strong possibility at this site. For the present church nearby, cf. *RCAM*, *Caern. Inventory*, vol. I, p. 103–5); 'St Tudwal', *Trans. Caernarvonshire Hist. Society*, XXI (1960), 6–13

Notes

3. Alcock, L., *PEW*, 199; *HW*, 144, 155, 175; *Arch Camb*, LXXX (1925), 432–6 (St Deiniol's, Bangor, Caerns.); cf. Johns, C. N., 'The Celtic Monasteries of North Wales', *Trans. Caernarvonshire Hist. Society*, XXI (1960), 14–43
4. Nash-Williams, V. E., 'The Medieval Settlement at Llantwit Major, Glamorgan', *BBCS*, XIV (1952), 313–333; *id*, *ECMW*, no. 223 (a pre-Norman foundation). See also note 86
5. I am very much indebted to my colleague, Professor C. Kidson, for obtaining the radio-carbon dating of the sample. The date is 550 B.P. ± 95, hence theoretically it could be between 1305 and 1495 A.D., with *c.* 1400 a probable mean
6. Cf. Wade-Evans, A. W., *Life of St David* (London, 1923), 68–70
7. Alcock, L., *PEW*, 185–6; id. *DP*, 55–60 and *passim*. For a conservative view of the extent of trade, Grierson, P., 'Commerce in the Dark Ages: A Critique of the Evidence', *Trans. Royal Historical Society*, 5th ser., vol. IX (1959), 123–140. Cf. note 107
8. I am grateful to Dr H. N. Savory, the excavator, for this communication. On Dinas Emrys, id., *Arch Camb*, CIX (1960), 13–77 (Chi-Rho, 44, 51, 53). For archaeological comment on early Welsh literature, Bowen, E. G., in *Llên Cymru*, VIII (1965), 150–167
9. For caution, Alcock, L., 'Pottery and Settlements in Wales and the March, *A.D.* 400–700', *CE*, 301–2 (with his reservation, *Arch Camb*, CXV (1966), 185–6)
10. No evidence for a Dark Age *llys* has been found at Degannwy; Alcock, L., in *CBA Summary of Excavations in* 1966
11. Jones, G. R. J., 'The Tribal System in Wales: A re-assessment in the Light of Settlement Studies', *WHR*, 1 (1961), 111, 130–2; Alcock, L., *DP*, 195–199
12. So too for Ireland, Henry, F., *Irish Art* (1965), 49. Cf. metaphors from building, *DEB*, 26 (41.10), 67 (63.14); the simile of a bright lamp in a house, 93 (77.14–78.1; the purpose of Gildas largely precludes any undue emphasis on preciosity; his literary figures would be understood, whatever their contemporary relevance)
13. Cf. *ECMW; LHEB*, 149–193. To be supplemented now by several subsequent finds, e.g. *Arch Camb*, CVI (1957), 118; CVII (1958), 123–4; CX (1961), 144, 154; CXII (1963), 184
14. *LHEB*, ch. 5 *passim;* Richards, M., 'The Irish Settlements in South West Wales', *Journal of the Royal Soc. of Antiquaries of Ireland*, XC (1960), 133–162
15. E.g., for palaeographical comparison, various volumes in Lowe, A. E., *Codices Latini Antiquiores*, vols. I-XI (Oxford, 1934–1966); cf. Bu'Lock, J. D., 'Early Christian Memorial Formulae', *Arch Camb.*, CV (1956), 135, 137–8 (regional differences); Richards, M., *op. cit.*, 147f. (onomastic research); Löfstedt, B., *Der Hibernolateinische Grammatiker Malsachanus* (Uppsala, 1965) 81–149 (latinity in general). For particular studies cf. that of the Idnert stone at Llanddewibrefi, Cards., *BBCS*, XVII (1957), 185–93, *ibid.* XIX, 231–4 (with possible historical implications for David); cf. the new stones in *Arch Camb* in note 63
16. *ECMW*, 222, 223. Cf. Morris, J., 'Dates of the Celtic Saints', *JTS*, XVII (1966), 380, note 1. 'Different strands of epigraphic tradition' (*LHEB*, 168, note 1) probably still await identification, especially in the light of the implications of *DEB* 67 (63.9–64.9) and the contemporary script used by Gildas himself, and in the implied scriptorium necessary for disseminating copies of the *Epistola*. Cf. too the weakness of the typological system, Alcock, L., *PEW*, 202
17. *ECMW*, 77, 78, 83, 101. *sacerdos* possibly 'bishop,' *ibid.* 33; *episcopus* once, but late, *ibid.* 255; the Trinity twice, but late, *ibid.* 220, 240; D(is) M(anibus) once and probably early, *ibid.* 285. Cf. DEB, where *sacerdos* is equated with *episcopus* and *pontifex*, 74 (67.31ff.), 108 (83.26ff.); *antistes*, 95 (78.30); and the Trinity is stressed, e.g. 70 (65.13ff.), 73 (67.11ff.), 110 (85.12ff.). Cf. Foster, I., *PEW*, 214f.

Notes

18. *ECMW*, pp. 8, 55; *LHEB* 164; Bu'Lock, J., *op. cit.*, 138 (map)
19. Richards, M., *op. cit.*, 144
20. Cf. Simpson, G., *Britons and the Roman Army* (London, 1964), 162–3
21. The literature is extensive. For full bibliographies, *Bibliography of the History of Wales* (2nd ed. Cardiff, 1962), with Supplement 1 in *BBCS*, XX, 1963, Suppl. 2 *ibid.*, XXII, 1966; sections too in the bibliographies of Bonser, W., 1957 (Anglo-Saxon and Celtic), 1964 (Roman Britain)
22. Bromwich, R., *SEBH*, 83–136, and *Trioedd Ynys Prydein* (Cardiff, 1961), lxvii
23. Cf. Dodd, A. H., in *Celtic Studies in Wales*, Davies, E. (ed.) (Cardiff, 1963), 67
24. Jackson, K., *SEBC*, 273–357. For outstanding problems and needs, Foster, I., *PEW*, 235; Morris, J., in *Medium Aevum*, XXXIII (1964), 162–4
25. James, J. W., *Rhigyfarch's Life of St David* (Cardiff, 1967); Emanuel, H. D., *The Latin Texts of the Welsh Laws* (Cardiff, 1967) (his text and study of the *Vita Cadoci* is deposited, as a thesis, in the National Library of Wales, Aberystwyth). For a conspectus of the Welsh genealogies, Bartrum, P. C., *Early Welsh Genealogical Tracts*, (Cardiff, 1966) (contains too 'The Pillar of Eliseg' and 'The Expulsion of the Déisi'); and for British and Irish Latin works, Latham, R. E., *Revised Medieval Latin Word-List* (London, 1965)
26. Cf. *Bowen* (1954); *SEBH*, 173–188. See also note 11
27. *Lewis* (1960*b*), 59
28. Cf. Delehaye, H., *The Legends of the Saints* (London, 1962), 177
29. Most scholars in this field have been 'critical' in their approach in varying degrees, but subjective factors, especially the use of 'constructive imagination,' often lead to widely divergent interpretations
30. E.g., James, J. W., 'The Book of Llandav', *Journal of the Hist. Soc. of Church in Wales*, IX (1959), 5–22 (a reply to Brooke, C., (1958), 201f: see note 39); 'The Concenn Charters in the Book of Llan Dav', *THSC* (1963), 82–95; *Church History of Wales*, 1945
31. *Bowen* (1954), 33–9; cf. Brooke, C., in *Celt and Saxon* (ed. Chadwick, N. K., Cambridge, 1963), 319; Radford, C. R., in *The Land of Dyfed in Early Times*, ed. Moore, D. (Cardiff, 1964), 21–2; Morris, J., 'Dates of the Celtic Saints', 372
32. On Docus, Morris J., *op. cit.*, 372–73, 378; cf. Chadwick, N. K., *The Age of the Saints in the Early Celtic Church* (Oxford, 1961), 73–4. For the *Vitae*, Kenney, p. 173; Chadwick, N. K., 'The Colonization of Brittany from Roman Britain', *Proceedings of the British Academy*, li (Oxford, 1965), 284 & *SEBC*, 128f. (*Life of St David*: cf. James, J. W., *THSC*, 1961, 177, and his edition in note 25 for a full account of the MSS.). For the *Vita Samsonis*, Kenney, 173f.
33. For a few possible traces, Bromwich, R., *Trioedd Ynys Prydein*, 201–4. For our attitude to *Bonedd y Saint* (ed. Bartrum, P. C., *op. cit.*, 54f.), cf. Bromwich, R., *op. cit.*, 187 (a likely ecclesiastical fiction mentioned); *SEBH*, 177, n. 1 (Welsh Laws)
34. Morris, J., 'Dark Age Dates' in *Britain and Rome*, ed. Jarrett, M. G. and Dobson, B. (1965), 145. For appreciation of method, Morris J., *op. cit.* (1966), 347f.; *CEB*, 311; Gougaud, L., *Christianity in Celtic Lands* (London, 1932), 52f.; Chadwick, N. K., in *SEBC*, 18–21. The restrictive character of later monastic traditions has encouraged devolution
35. Among the best guides, Delehaye, H., *op. cit.*; *id*, *Sanctus* (Brussels, 1927). Cf. Chadwick, N. K., *op. cit.* (1961), 3–4. 'Saints' could be men of action and affairs, cf. Chadwick, N. K., *op. cit.* (1965), 276–7. Outstanding *sancti* were perhaps few in Gildas's day, *DEB*, 65 (61.21ff.), 69 (64.17ff.), 92 (76.37ff.), 106 (82.20ff.); cf. Williams, H., *Gildas* (London, 1899–1901), 64–5. See note 33
36. Lewis, C. (1960*a*), 57f. and (1963), 127f.; id. (1960*b*), 56f.; cf. Rees, W., *A Historical*

Notes

Atlas of Wales (London, 1959), 19
37. Cf. Brooke, C., in *SEBC* and *Celt and Saxon*
38. Brooke, C., in *SEBC*, 221. For text, with facsimiles, Evans, J. G. and Rhys, J., *The Text of the Book of Llan Dâv* (Oxford, 1893); best introduction by Jones, E. D., *National Library of Wales Journal*, IV (1945–46), 123–57
39. Brooke, C., in *Celt and Saxon*, 317, 319; *Lewis* (1963), 142 (with the suggestion of a movement towards territorial organisation later in the pre-Norman period, 142–4)
40. The problem is well stated in *EA*, 474f., 593; *HW*, 205f.
41. Brooke, C., in *Celt and Saxon*, 322
42. Cf. Chadwick, N. K., *The Age of the Saints*, 70f.; *EA*, 469–70
43. For this and what follows, cf. Brooke, C., in *Celt and Saxon*, 315f.; *EA*, 479–80; *CEB*, 475–6; Chadwick, N. K., *The Age of the Saints*, 77. No sure conclusions can be drawn for the sixth century from *BDA* (c. 40 sites) or Rees, W., *Atlas*, pl. 27 (for *clas* churches, *HW* 218); cf. the implications of *EA*, 588 for an 'explosion', Morris, J., 'Dates of the Celtic Saints', 351. On the possible existence of both territorial and monastic *parochiae*, Hughes, K., *The Church in Early Irish Society* (London, 1966), 73–4. For origin of usages, cf. Chadwick, N. K., *Poetry and Letters in Early Christian Gaul* (London, 1955), 205–6
44. Jackson, K., *SEBC*, 315; Hughes, K., *op. cit.*, 72
45. Cf. Durtelle de Saint-Sauveur, E., *Histoire de Bretagne*, (Rennes, 1935), 41 (*Vita Samsonis* accepted, 52–3); Chadwick, N. K., 'Colonization of Brittany', 275, 281, 284ff.
46. Foster, I., *PEW*, 226 (quoting Binchy, D. A., who makes a reservation concerning former Roman provinces in *Studia Hibernica*, 1, 1961, 13). Cf. Alcock, L., *DP*, 42
47. The best account of the 'Age of the Saints' is still that of *HW*, Ch. V, 124–159
48. Cf. *Bowen* (1954), 118f.; Williams, I., *Enwau Lleoedd* (place-names) (Liverpool, 1945); Richards, M., *op. cit.* Cf. Chadwick, N. K., *Age of the Saints*, 93–4, and James, J. W., *THSC* (1961), 178 for Merthyr
49. Cf. Foster, I., *PEW*, 233
50. The evidence for Christianity in Roman Britain is presented in *Toynbee* 1953; Frend, W. H. C., 'Religion in Roman Britain in the Fourth Century A.D.', *JBAA*, XVIII (1955), 1–18. Cf. Frere, S., *Britannia* (London, 1967), 331–4, 378
51. Richmond, I. A., *Roman Britain* (1963), 139f.
52. Nash-Williams, V. E., 'The Roman Villa at Llantwit Major in Glamorgan, *Arch Camb*, *CII* (1953), 103, 129. So too *BDA*. The site, however, seems to need expert re-evaluation, but its setting may be clearer once the current excavations at nearby Whitton are completed (cf. *Morgannwg*, X. 1966). Any association with Illtud is illusory. Cf. Alcock, L., *DP*, 199
53. Boon, G. C., *BBCS*, XIX (1962), 338–44; *id JRS*, LII (1962), 196. For a reported engraved spoon from Monmouthshire, *Toynbee* (1953), 22
54. For the 'quasi-basilican character' of the building, cf. Nash-Williams, V. E., *BBCS*, XV (1953), 165, where two Near Eastern parallels to the 'wide-winged' narthex are adduced from Kaufmann, C. M., *Handbuch der Christlichen Archäologie*, Paderborn (1922), p. 201, fig. 79, 1 and 12. Mr G. C. Boon, of the National Museum of Wales, to whom I am very grateful for advice, has serious reservations about any positive identification. Cf. Alcock, L., *DP*, 63, n. 1. For later Christian traditions at Caerwent, *HW*, 279
55. Wheeler, R. E. M., 'Segontium', *Y Cymmrodor*, XXXIII (1923), 129–30; Boon, G. C., *BBCS*, XXI (1964), 98–9; *RIB* No. 436
56. For the earliest reference to the martyrs, *DEB* 10 (31.14–22). They do not appear in the *Hieronymian Martyrology;* Delehaye, H., in *Proc. Brit. Academy*, XVII (1931), 300.

Notes

On the date, *CEB*, 102; Frend, W. H. C., *op. cit.*, 4. For 208–9 A.D., Frere, S., *op. cit.*, 332. Caerleon tradition would be known in south Wales (cf. note 85)

57. Cf. Hughes, K., *op. cit.*, 29–32. For the coffin, *ECMW*, 27
58. Cf. Chadwick, N. K., *Poetry & Letters*, 270–1; Hughes, K., *op. cit.*, 29; Rees, *Atlas*, pl. 26; Ralegh-Radford, C. A., *Antiquity*, XXXII (1958), 22–3. A forthcoming study of Vortigern by my colleague, Dr D. P. Kirby, will deal with the problem of Germanus
59. The tradition is accepted by Wilson, P. A., 'Romano-British and Welsh Christianity: Continuity or Discontinuity?' (*WHR* III, Oct. 1966, 5–21; Dec. 1966, 103–20), 117. Cf. *HW*, 144, n. 96. Germanus is not referred to in the *DEB*
60. Sid. Apollinaris, *Epist.* IX, 9, 6. Cf. *LHEB*, 13f. For recent views on the British emigration, Fahy, D., 'When did the Britons become Bretons?' *WHR*, 2 (1964), 111–124; Chadwick, N. K., 'Colonization of Brittany', 258ff.
61. A continuous Christian tradition of some one hundred years is implied. Cf. Hanson, R. P. C., *St Patrick, a British Missionary Bishop* (Nottingham, 1966), with convenient references; Morris, J., 'Dates of the Celtic Saints', 358f. *Synodus I S. Patricii*, 33 (Bieler, L. (1963), p. 59) is too controversial for use here
62. *ECMW*, 103, 92. *Medicus* occurs twice in the *DEB*, 21 (37.14), 108 (83.34) (in an elaborate medical metaphor); *medicina* once, 21 (37.14); *medicamen* twice, cc. 70 (65.14), 108 (83.33)
63. *ECMW*, 14; cf. Foster, I., *PEW*, 216f.; Alcock, L., *DP*, 70. The word 'tribal' offers difficulties for our period, probably with regional variations; cf. *ECMW*, 103 (*Venedotis cives*), 126 (*Ordous*) and *DEB*, 31 (43.20, *Demetae*); Jones, G. R. J., *op. cit.*, 131. Cf. *Arch Camb*, CX (1961), 147, 151. The word *contribulis* was known to Gildas. Roman influences on native ways of life may have been restricted, *LHEB*, 117. Cf. *CBA* (7), 98 (Dumnonia)
64. For Gallic influences in the inscriptions, *ECMW*, 8 and *passim; LHEB*, 163f. A British intruder (from Elmet, Yorkshire) appears in *ECMW*, 87
65. Cf. *ECMW*, 294 (Llanerfyl, Montgomeryshire, with the possible theological connotation of *in pace*); *Arch Camb*, CX (1961), 154–5 (Trawsfynydd)
66. *LHEB*, 118f. Cf. Bieler, L., *Works of St Patrick*, 81 (on *Confess.* 9, where there may be some literary pretension; *id Libri Epistolarum*, Part 2, 113)
67. *LHEB*, 122f.
68. Bury, J. B., *Life of St Patrick*, p. X; Grosjean, P., *Anal Boll*, LXIII (1945), 65–72; Tolstoy, N., *THSC* (1964), 305–7; James, J. W., *THSC* (1961), 177
69. Hanson, R. P. C., *op. cit.*, 20
70. Binchy, D. A., 'Patrick and His Biographers: Ancient and Modern', *Studia Hibernica*, 2 (1962), 173
71. Examples are the late Rev. A. W. Wade-Evans and Father Paul Grosjean. Cf. Emanuel, H. D., 'The Rev. A. W. Wade-Evans: an Appreciation of His Contribution to the Study of Early Welsh History', *THSC* (Part 2) (1965), espec. 265–9 (utilising Grosjean's letters). Grosjean 'Romana Stigmata chez Gildas' in *Hommages á Max Niedermann* (Brussels, 1956, 128–39), 128, like Wade-Evans (1959), 11–12, distinguished *DEB*, 2–26 from the *Epistola*, 1, 27–110; *id* 'Notes on the De Excidio Britanniae', *Anal Boll*, LXXIII (1957, 185–226), 205 *passim;* for Malmesbury, *id* 'Remarques sur le De Excidio attribué à Gildas' (*Archivum Latinitatis Medii Aevi*, XXV (1955), 155–87), 176 and 'Notes on the De Excidio', 212–22. Wade-Evans, *op. cit.*, 159, accepted Gildas's picture of the sixth-century church; Grosjean made but few comments on the content of the so-called *Epistola* section, e.g. in Gordon, D. (ed.), *Memorial Essays to F. Saxl* (London, 1957), 70–76

Notes

72. In *MGH*, *Auct. Ant.*, XIII, Pars 1, Berlin, 1894, 5–85 (with *Epist. Fragmenta*, *De Paenitentia*, and two *Vitae*). Text (Mommsen's mostly) of *Opera* with notes and translation in Williams, H. (1901 dated and translation faulty in places, but still valuable). There is much textual work yet to be done
73. The leaves, ff. 78^{r}–79^{v}, follow the *Prognosticum* of Julian of Toledo (cf. *Clavis Patrum Lat.*, 2nd ed. (1961), p. 283) and precede *Sermones* of Caesarius of Arles (*ibid.* p. 224) in MS. 414 of the Bibliothèque Municipale of Rheims. They may be provisionally ascribed to the ninth century and include the whole of *DEB*, cc. 27, 63, and parts of cc. 31, 42, 43, 46, 50, 59. The text is generally close to that of A (Avranches 162, s.XII *ex.*), with some links with D (Camb. Dd. I. 17), but a full account will appear elsewhere. I am most grateful to Mons. F. Kerlouégan for drawing my attention to the MS. and to Dr H. D. Emanuel for palaeographical guidance
74. As Gildas himself, *DEB*, 1 (25.1), 93 (77.30); elsewhere *historia*, 37 (48.15), *opusculum*, 62 (60.12), 94 (78.2). For unity, cf. reference in 65 (61.28) to 26 (41.5f.), and *sicut et nunc est*, 21 (36.13)
75. The problem is the attitude to be taken to two key dates in the *Annales Cambriae*, viz. 516 A.D. (Battle of Badon) and 547 A.D. (death of Maelgwn). Cf. Morris, J., *Britain & Rome*, 178, n. 30
76. For *cives*, *DEB*, 10 (31.19), 26 (40.16), 28 (42.1), 32 (44.6); *contribulibus* is found in an Old Testament context, 39 (50.3). Cf. *ECMW*, 33, 103. The term *civis* no longer evokes Claudian's vision of *Roma mater* (*De laudibus Stilichonis*, III, 150–53). It seems literary and neutral in character, with the general meaning of 'native' (Briton) predominating, but perhaps differentiated regionally in ways now beyond precision
77. *Patria* is Roman Britain in *DEB*, 1–26 (allowing for neutral colouring in 1, 2, 26), afterwards Celtic Britain, 27 (41.19), 30 (43.6), 62 (60.16), 64 (61.12), 67 (64.4). For an idea of the large area designated *patria* (note use of *omni insulae*, 93 (77.27)), cf. Blair, P. H., *Roman Britain and Early England* (Edinburgh, 1963), 166, 175; Evison, V. I., *The Fifth Century Invasions South of the Thames*, London (1965), 79f. (Cf. Alcock, L., 'Roman Britons and Pagan Saxons: An Archaeological Appraisal', *WHR*, III (1967) 235f.). For *Britannia Prima*, cf. Mann, J. C., in *Antiquity*, XXXV (1961), 319
78. On the *Vitae*, Mommsen, *op. cit.*, 3–4
79. For the *Penitential*, Bieler, L. (ed), *The Irish Penitentials* (Dublin, 1963), 60–5, McNeill, J. T., and Gamer, H. M., *Medieval Handbooks of Penance* (New York, 1938), 174–8: the *Oratio*, Strecker, K., in *MGH*, *Poetae Lat. Med. Aevi*, IV, Pars III, (Berlin, 1914); cf. Meyer, W., *Göttingen Nachrichten* (1912), 48–108: the *Lorica*, cf. Kenney, J. F., *Sources for the Early History of Ireland* (New York, 1929), 270f.; Esposito, M., *JTS*, XXX (1929), 289–91 for the Verona MS
80. The Welsh Canons are in Bieler, L., *Penitentials*, 66–73
81. See now Hanning, R. W., *The Vision of History in Early Britain* (London, 1966), 44–62
82. Cf. *DEB*, 4, 10; Stevens, C. E., 'Gildas Sapiens', *EHS* (1941), 357; Blair, P. H., *op. cit.*, 157. For extreme criticism, Lot. F., in *Medieval Studies in Memory of Gertrude Loomis* (Paris & N. York, 1927), 229–264
83. *DEB*, 66 (62.22); Patrick, *Conf.* 13
84. It seems very unwise to read into a number of brief and sometimes vague classical reminiscences in the *DEB* a complete training along the old lines in the *artes liberales*. Patristic works (including the *transmarina relatio* of 4 (29.22) e.g. *Orosius*), supplemented probably for the most part by manuals of extracts and *loci communes*, do not make a Vivarium: cf. Deanesly, M., in *Memorial Essays to F. Saxl*, 65, 68;

Notes

Riché, P., *Éducation et Culture dans L'Occident Barbare* (Paris, 1962), 356–7. For the quotations, Grosjean, P., 'Notes on the De Excidio', 189–94. There is no trace of the knowledge of Greek. Rome now lives for Gildas through the idea of the *Sedes* or *Cathedra Petri Apostoli* (e.g., 66, 67)

85. There may be some synoptic significance in *DEB*, 3 (28.12) (no trade as formerly in the Severn area), 10 (31.14–22, Gildas must be writing in the west), 14 (33.13, Irish *a circione*), 19 (35.8, 9, *tithicam vallem* and *curucis* in a Scottic as well as Pictish context), 23 (38.19, *nostra lingua* with *cyulis*), and perhaps some other features, e.g. possible triadic elements in style, Bromwich, R., *op. cit.*, lxiii
86. For Llantwit Major, *HW*, 144; cf. Doble, G. H., *Saint Iltut* (1944), 44 ('the chief centre of the cult of S. Iltut'). For Caldy, *CEB* 325f.; James, J. W., *Church History of Wales* (1945), 3; Loyer, O., *Les Chrétientés Celtiques* (Paris, 1965), 27
87. See *DEB*, 36; Walker, G. (ed.), *Sancti Columbani Opera* (Dublin, 1957), 8 (*Epist.* 1). Cf. the first *Vita Samsonis*, c. 7 (Illtud as *egregius magister Britannorum*)
88. Chadwick, O., *JTS*, V (1954) 78–81 (commenting on *DEB*, 65 (61.23) *episcoporum vel ceterorum sacerdotum aut clericorum in nostro quoque ordine*). Cf. Grosjean, P., in *Memorial Essays to F. Saxl*, 70f.; *id*, 'Notes on the De Excidio' (1957), 205. For probably contemporary evidence for the monks and clerics of Gildas, *Praefatio de Poenitentia*, can. 3 (Bieler *Penitentials*, 60)
89. Significant here may be *DEB*, 1 (27.4) *veluti conspicuo ac summo doctori;* 93 (77.21, 22) *scientiae lampade;* the illustration of allegorical methods of scriptural interpretation, e.g. 1 (25.20ff.), 70 (65.13ff.). 'For Gildas . . . the pre-eminent, almost the only function of the Christian priesthood is to be a ministry of teaching and guidance,' *CEB*, 461; cf. Williams, H., *Gildas*, 160. He wrote *fratrum religiosis precibus coactus* (c.1)
90. Officials 'have no time to breathe,' *DEB*, 1 (27.9; *spatium respirandi non habent*)
91. The words are given some precise significance by Morris, J., in *Britain & Rome*, 173. *Rectores*, *DEB*, 1 (27.7), 6 (30.6) (and 14 (33.10): 'rulers,' 'government'); cf. 11 (32.12), 15 (33.22); *speculatores*, 1 (27.7) only: *tyrannus* means 'prince', pejorative in a moral rather than constitutional sense: cf. 9 (31.5), 14 (33.11), 27 (41.15) and *passim; protector* does not occur. The social picture is indicated in 27, 66. Some towns at least still existed in the area, but in a rundown state, due largely to internal *native* dissension and stresses (cf. *squalent* 26 (40.21))
92. Strabo's very words with others for the Celtic temperament! Cf. *Geography*, IV, 4, 5 ἡ κουφότης, τὸ ἀνόητον
93. The good are few in number, *DEB*, 1 (25.20ff.), 50 (53.25ff.), 65 (61.27ff.), 69 (64.17ff.), 92 (77.1ff.), 110 (85.23). Gildas writes in a spirit of modest and passionate sincerity, not pious bigotry
94. Cf. Deanesly, M., in *Memorial Essays to F. Saxl*, 69. A good picture of the Gildasian Church is given in Davies, E., *The Character of the Early Christian Church in Wales*, B. Litt. Thesis (Oxford, 1934), 32–3
95. For the inference of monasteries, *DEB*, 28, 34. Gifts to the Church are indicated, 27 (41.20), 33 (44.26), 42 (51.26), 107 (83.24) (*ecclesiae donaria*), but there is no mention of the founding of a monastery or of a private church
96. *DEB*, 65 (61.23), 66 (62.3ff.), 69 (64.17), 76 (69.14), etc. Ordinarily a bishop seems to be elected by his *parochia*, 67 (63.9ff.). For the unique British ordination service, 106–9
97. The words used are *plebs*, *populi*, but cf. implications of *grex*, 21 (37.15), 32 (44.13ff.), 95 (78.18ff.) and *pastores*, 66 (62.4), 92 (77.4) *et passim*
98. 28 (41.28ff.)

Notes

99. 26 (1.7), 96 (79.15)
100. 50 (55.25ff.), 66–7. 'A socially acceptable class,' Hughes, K., *op. cit.*, 40
101. 108–9. Cf. Hughes, K., *op. cit.*, 42–3. For a vow of chastity by a widow, 32 (44.8) (may we infer the presence of nuns?). Family succession may be indicated in 67 (63.9ff.), and *subintroductae* in 66 (62.16–18)
102. 27 (41.18,26), 66 (62.3–15, cf. 69 (64.17ff.)). There is no sign of relics
103. Burkitt, F. C., 'The Bible of Gildas', *Revue Bénédictine*, XLVI (1934), 206–15. Cf. Williams, H., *Gildas*, 88–99, 129–39, 192ff.; *CEB*, 182ff., 449–52 (dated, it appears: cf. Grosjean, P., 'Notes on the De Excidio,' 203, n. 1). Further progress is now facilitated by works like the Beuron *Vetus Latina* (1949 onwards)
104. 73 (67.18), 74, 110
105. *Gratia* (grace) is found once only and in association with just retribution and judgement, 1; the periphrasis *gratuito munere* once, 10 (cf. same use and context, Alcuin, *Ep.* 122), *misericordia* or its cognates some six times. A quotation in 38 is from a Pelagian treatise, Morris, J., 'Pelagian Literature', JTS, XVI, Part 1 (1965), 36. Man's moral responsibility, expressed in terms of the need for repentance and the fear of judgement, meant much to Gildas. Cf. Bullock, J., *The Life of the Celtic Church* (Edinburgh, 1963), 111–13
106. 73 (67.15), 107 (83.17–18)
107. 67 (63.26–64.9). The words are striking: *praemissis ante sollicite nuntiis transnavigare maria terrasque spatiosas transmeare non tam piget quam delectat ut omnino talis species... vel venditis omnibus copiis comparetur.* Wide contacts between Gildas's milieu and elsewhere are implied in 26 (41.13) *quippe quid celabunt cives, quae non solum norunt, sed exprobrant iam in circuitu nationes?* (this is more than just homiletic scriptural overtones)
108. 66 (62.20ff., *ad ludicra et ineptas saecularium hominum fabulas . . . strenuos et intentos*). The contrast in the context with *ad praecepta sanctorum . . . oscitantes ac stupidos* perhaps implies some kind of secular reading, and may well include bardic recitals and various forms of social pastimes (*ludicra*, 'games' or 'shows') according to the domicile of the priest (bishop, etc.) in town, country or court: cf. Williams, I., *Lectures on Early Welsh Poetry* (Dublin, 1944), 51–2. Can some kind of heroic tradition lie behind *DEB*, 1 (25.5,6) *quia non tam fortissimorum militum enuntiare trucis belli pericula mihi statutum est quam desidiosorum?* It is noteworthy that the clergy are censured for moral failings, not for lack of education. Gildas is obviously writing for a circle capable of appreciating the content and significance of 3–26 (the *historia*). The scene in general faintly reflects that of Gaul in the later fifth century, simony and all; cf. *LRE*, 909, 978–9
109. Cf. *HW*, 128 (for Maelgwn); Morris, J., 'Celtic Saints', *Past and Present*, No. 11, 1957, 2–16
110. 31, 33–36. Cf. a dated contemporary inscription, *ECMW*, 104 (540 A.D.). Perhaps we should not be too much influenced in this field of study as well as others by 'the arbitrary nature of the binary classification of Britain into Highland and Lowland zones'; cf. Peate, I., in *CE*, 10 ibid., Daniel, G., 21
111. *ECMW*, 139 (*c.* 550 A.D.). A fifth century date is epigraphically possible: cf. Radford, C. A. R., *The Land of Dyfed in Early Times*, Moore, D. (ed.), Cardiff (1964), 20. For orthography, *LHEB*, 191–2. Gildas too is *patriae amator*. On fifth century refugees in the west, *Roman Archaeology in Wales*, Wheeler, R. E. M., Cardiff (1957), 26
112. 34 (46.11–15). We may see here among Maelgwn's *comitatus* (cf. the *parasiti* of 35 (46.25), 43 (52.6)) the setting for the early stages of the Macsen Wledig saga. Cf. Williams, I., *op. cit.*, 52

Notes

113. 34 (45.14ff.). Was the monastery that of Deiniol? Cf. *HW*, 130
114. 33 (44.26)
115. 33, 34, 36. For Illtud and Maelgwn, *HW*, 145
116. 70 (65.13ff.). See note 88 and McNeill, J., and Gamer, H., *op. cit.*, 20–22. This would seem the natural ecclesiastical setting too for *Canu Aneirin*, ll. 61 and 72 (*ket elwynt e lanneu e benydu* – 'though they went to churches to do penance') and other Christian references in the poem. I am grateful to my colleagues, Professors T. Jones and C. Williams, for help on this and other points
117. 30 (43.3ff.) shows some intimate knowledge of Aurelius's family; but if we identify Gildas with a south Wales milieu, was it politic to attack the prince of the region? The lower Severn area seems indicated for Aurelius, leaving the ruler (or petty kings) of Glywysing free from moral stricture. For some archaeological aspects, Savory, H. N., in *Dark Age Britain*, 57–58. The *DEB* does not mention *reguli* or *subreguli*
118. Cf. Alcock, L., *DP*, 42
119. The instances are: *pecunia* once, 66 (63.1, *paene omni pecunia redimentes*, sc. *sacerdotium*); *denarius* once, 66 (62.25, *uno sane perdito denario maestos*); *obolus* twice, 66 (62.15), 107 (both perhaps with a literary flavour); phrases like *terreno pretio mercari*, *venditis omnibus copiis*, *sacerdotia emunt*, *coemptionis condicio*, all in 67 (63.9ff.). For the Penitential, Bieler, *Penitentials* 3, 60–1 (*himina Romana lactis . . . tenuclae vero vel battuti lactis sextario Romano*: 'a Roman half-pint of milk . . . also a Roman pint of whey or buttermilk'). Continuity of coinage as a medium of exchange after 430 A.D. is rejected by Frere, S., *op. cit.*, 372 (following Kent, J. P.); but cf. Sutherland, C. V., in *Dark Age Britain*, 3–10
120. Alcock, L., *DP*, 71; Rees, W., *Atlas*, pl. 17; Bartrum, P. C., 'Some Studies in Early Welsh History', *THSC* (1948), 279–302. Note that *DEB*, 3 (28.12) implies a lack of trade at this time in the Severn (Bristol Channel?) area: cf. Stevens, C. E., *op. cit.*, 354. *Vinum* is mentioned twice in *DEB*, 21, 31
121. We recall the existence and state of rural parishes in Gaul, Sid. Apollinaris, *Epist.* VII, 8 (a fate undoubtedly suffered by many churches in Gildas's day). For rural bishops, rural and private churches in the Roman Empire, *LRE*, 879, 901
122. The so-called Heroic Age of the Saints thus represents a natural extension of forces and pressures operating in every sphere of contemporary Welsh life and leading to the more discernible features of succeeding centuries. The saints of history have largely been swamped by the saints of legend

Le Latin du De Excidio Britanniæ de Gildas

F. Kerlouégan

Mon propos, en abordant ici l'étude du latin du *De Excidio*, est d'en donner une image, non pas complète, mais dessinée dans ses grands traits.

Ce latin a, ou plutôt a eu, si mauvaise réputation qu'il importe d'y regarder de près. Quand je dis: ce latin, je devrais préciser: le style du *DEB*. On l'a trouvé entortillé, prolixe, ampoulé, déclamatoire; bref, Gildas aurait été un piètre styliste et le seul intérêt du *DEB*, quand encore on voulait bien l'y voir, était dans les allusions historiques de la partie que nous appelons *Historia* (chapitres 3 à 36). Ceux de nos contemporains qui ont lu Gildas se montrent en général plus nuancés. Gildas certes écrit un latin rhétorique et compliqué mais ils savent que ce latin a eu ses heures de gloire et ils s'efforcent de replacer le *DEB* dans son contexte. Quant à la syntaxe, nous disposons jusqu'ici de quelques appréciations qui s'appuient sur une lecture sérieuse du texte mais aucun travail ne lui a encore été spécialement consacré.[1]

Les savants qui s'intéressent à la Bretagne des 'Dark Ages' se sont assurément posé la question: ce clerc auquel on attribue le *DEB*, quel est le niveau linguistique de son ouvrage? quel latin était-il capable d'écrire? quels renseignements sur sa formation, sur son attitude à l'égard de la langue, sur ses rapports et ceux de son milieu avec les traditions antérieures peut-on découvrir en examinant son latin? C'est d'abord à ces interrogations que je voudrais répondre.

Mais je pense nécessaire de ne pas en rester là. Car, si le *DEB* apparaît vers 530 comme une lumière isolée entre deux zones d'ombre importantes – Qu'y a-t-il dans les Iles entre Patrice et Gildas, entre Gildas et Colomban? Quelques anonymes, des textes mal datés et en petit nombre – ces mêmes Iles, à partir de Colomban, produisent toute une littérature, encore mal connue dans ses détails, mais dont les caractères essentiels sont à peu près dégagés: correction relative de la grammaire, quand on compare avec la production contemporaine sur le Continent; recherche de l'expression savante ou pseudo-savante, goût pour l'élégance alambiquée qui s'accommode sans contradiction de vulgarismes que la seule fréquentation de la Bible peut expliquer; nombreuses traces enfin de l'influence des langues vernaculaires.[2] On sait assurément que le latin insulaire du VIIème siècle est un latin d'école; on en devine l'origine ou les origines. Mais ne serait-il pas intéressant de pouvoir jeter un pont entre les derniers écrivains du Bas–Empire, dont les écrits et le rayonnement ont pu atteindre la Bretagne, ou même les écoles romaines ouvertes dans l'île, d'une part, et, d'autre part, les moines du VIIème siècle? Mlle Mohrmann, dans l'article cité ci-dessus, a remarquablement mis en lumière que, vers 600, Colomban écrit un latin anachronique, héritage des auteurs de la latinité tardive. L'étude du latin du *DEB* nous permettrait-elle, chemin faisant, de découvrir une île nouvelle de cet archipel étiré entre deux continents?

On s'étonnera peut-être que j'aie considéré jusqu'ici le *DEB* comme une oeuvre composée en une seule fois par un seul et même homme. Des voix se sont élevées, nous le savons, pour mettre en doute l'unité de l'ouvrage; je ne citerai que les deux derniers champions de cette thèse: A. W. Wade-Evans et le P. Grosjean.[3] Leurs arguments – je pense surtout au P. Grosjean– ne sont pas dénués d'intérêt et leurs travaux ont ranimé la curiosité sur Gildas. Reste que le *consensus doctorum* se maintient en faveur de l'attribution du *DEB* à Gildas. Si aucune preuve péremptoire n'a encore été avancée contre l'interpolation (découverte d'un manuscrit complet du VIème siècle, par exemple!), aucune preuve du même ordre n'a été donnée jusqu'à présent pour défendre cette interpolation. L'étude du latin du *DEB* apportera peut-être quelques indications et nous pourrons revenir sur cette question en conclusion.

Auparavant, j'aurai, dans une première partie, situé *grosso modo* le niveau linguistique du *DEB* et, dans les deux parties suivantes, précisé les traits qui donnent à ce latin sa physionomie originale.

* * *

Au premier abord, et compte tenu du temps et du lieu auxquels la tradition rapporte le *DEB*, on s'attendrait, sinon à trouver un témoin de la langue parlée au début du VIème siècle, du moins à lire un texte farci de vulgarismes et rédigé dans un style voisin de celui de l'exposé oral destiné à des oreilles simples et peu formées.

Or même les critiques les plus violentes n'ont jamais taxé, sauf exception, le *DEB* d'incorrection grammaticale et l'examen des faits nous montre de façon positive que Gildas écrit un latin de bonne tenue qui soutient la comparaison avec celui des meilleurs auteurs de la période précédente.

Les vulgarismes sans doute et plus généralement les faits attestant une évolution de la langue ne manquent pas. Mais il s'agit le plus souvent de tours qui avaient acquis droit de cité dans la langue des écrivains de la fin du Vème siècle.

Il faut reconnaître que certains des vulgarismes du *DEB* ne se rencontrent habituellement que chez les traducteurs ou les auteurs d'ouvrages techniques, gens de plume sans prétentions littéraires.

Ainsi:

(1) *le datif complément du comparatif*

18 (34.23): *gentibus nequaquam sibi fortioribus.*

Ce datif est surtout utilisé après *inferior* et les comparatifs irréguliers.

Mais *fortior* + datif se rencontre chez Oribase.[4]

(2) *le réfléchi remplaçant l'intransitif*
108 (83.33): . . . *quod tumore iam uel fetore sibi horrescens cauterio et publico ignis medicamine eget.*
Sibi horrescens semble correspondre à *sibi fugire* (français s'enfuir), *sibi uadere* (fr.s'en aller) etc. . . . Quel que soit le sens ici (être dégoûtant ou donner la nausée), nous avons sans doute un exemple de cette construction avec le réfléchi au datif qui se rencontre en particulier chez Lucifer, Chiron et dans les *Vitae Patrum*.[5]

(3) *quam plurimi équivalent de multi ou de plurimi*
Gildas emploie 4 fois *plurimi* et toujours avec *quam*. Le sens de "le plus nombreux possible" n'est jamais très défendable. Ainsi:
21 (37.16): *ebrietate quam plurimi quasi uino madidi torpebant;* "dans leur majorité", "pour le plus grand nombre" paraît satisfaisant.
Svennung donne des listes d'exemples pour *quam plurime* et *quam plurimi;* ces exemples sont le plus souvent tirés d'auteurs techniques.[6]

(4) *prior pour primus*
En 11 (32.7): *ut* (*Albanus*) . . . *priorem carnificem tanta prodigia uidentem in agnum ex lupo mutaret*, si *priorem* signifie: en premier, le premier, d'abord, *primum* serait la forme attendue. Or comparatif et superlatif tendent à se confondre dans la langue parlée. Ainsi la Vetus Latina traduit πρῶτος par *prior*, mais la Vulgate donne *primus*.[7]

(5) *in + adjectif neutre substantivé, à l'ablatif singulier et pluriel*
Des expressions comme *in uno*, *in quantis* sont surtout en usage chez les auteurs techniques.[8]

(6) *l'emploi de l'impératif futur*
A la deuxième personne du singulier, Gildas se sert 9 fois de l'impératif présent et 3 fois de l'impératif futur. D'après Svennung, ce futur, évité par les personnes cultivées comme rustique, se serait conservé plus longtemps dans les classes inférieures de la société.[9]

(7) *le participe remplaçant un verbe personnel*
Dans la description de la Bretagne, au chapitre 3, les principales ne présentent que des participes (présent et passé). On peut encore citer: 28 (42.9): *et hoc ne post laudanda quidem merita egit*, *nam multis ante annis crebris alternatisque faetoribus adulteriorum uictus* . . . (participe passé coordonné au verbe personnel) et: 20 (36.1): *igitur rursum miserae mittentes epistolas reliquiae ad Agitium . . . et post pauca querentes . . . nec pro eis quicquam adiutorii habent* (participes présents antéposés et coordonnés à un verbe personnel).
Ces constructions ne paraissent pas représentées chez les meilleurs auteurs.[10]

Faut-il ajouter à cette énumération quelques fautes qui peuvent passer pour des ignorances du latin correct, comme:

72 (66.31): *ita ut intueri poterit* (à côté de 21 (37.10): *ita ut potuerit*, correct), 102 (81.15): *quis uestrum sponte expleuerit id quod sequitur* (à côté de 103 (81.30): *quis . . . uestrum . . . custodiuit id quod sequitur*)?

Ces fautes ne s'expliquent pas, à ma connaissance, par des faits de langue: futur (*poterit*) pour subjonctif parfait (*potuerit*)? Subjonctif parfait (*expleuerit*) pour parfait (*expleuit*)? Faut-il y voir de simples fautes de copiste?[11]

On pourrait allonger la liste donnée un peu plus haut, en dépit des difficultés à bien isoler les vulgarismes typiques des auteurs techniques. Mais, au total, nous n'aurions pas une masse de faits au vu desquels nous pourrions conclure au caractère populaire du latin de Gildas. Comme contre-épreuve, on remarquera du reste l'absence de nombreux vulgarismes courants au VIème siècle:

- *excepto* figé: Gildas emploie 4 fois ce participe mais il fait toujours l'accord. Ainsi 26 (41.5): *exceptis paucis*.[12]
- accusatif absolu: aucun exemple.[13]
- adverbes formés de préposition + adverbe: *in certe*, *in uane*, *in simul*, *in antea*, etc.: aucun exemple.[14]
- prépositions composées: *abante*, *deante*, *desub*, etc. . . .: aucun exemple.[15]

Revenons maintenant aux faits largement attestés dans la langue littéraire, qui, par suite de circonstances diverses, était devenue plus perméable à l'évolution linguistique. Je relève, par exemple:

(1) *confusion ablatif-accusatif* (*avec in*)
in + ablatif pour *in* + accusatif:
4 (29.9): *ante aduentum Christi in carne*
65 (61.22): *in optato euectus portu*
109 (85.11): *ut in caelis nequaquam ascendatis*
in + accusatif pour *in* + ablatif:
67 (63.27): *in parochiam resistentibus sibi . . . commessoribus*
95 (78.29): *quem . . . uestrum sequens testimonium non in profunda cordis arcana uulneret?*
Ces confusions sont fréquentes en latin tardif; on en a des exemples dès les premiers textes latins.[16]

(2) *préposition + adjectif neutre substantivé à l'accusatif singulier*
Cet usage est attesté dès Salluste et se répand à l'époque post-classique.[17]
On relève dans le *DEB : ad integrum*, *in unum*, *in altum*, *in medium*.

(3) *emploi de la négation*
(a) deux négations se renforcent au lieu de se détruire:[18]
69 (64.28): *quis eorum . . . nullum Deo aduersantem . . . non admisit?*
(b) *ne=ne . . . quidem* :[19]
22 (38.5): *tantam . . . multitudinem . . . sternit quantam ne possint uiui humare*.

(4) *quidam = aliquis*[20]
une douzaine d'exemples.

(5) *alii = ceteri*[21]

au moins 6 exemples.

(6) *proprius* pour *suus*
très utilisé par Gildas et très fréquent en latin tardif; mais il ne s'agit peut-être pas d'un vulgarisme.[22]

(7) *le subjonctif plus-que-parfait au lieu du subjonctif imparfait*
En 50 (55.29): *quis* (=*quibus*) *ex corde ad Deum repedantibus . . . uindictam non potuissent inducere*, le sens appelle *possent*. Cette tendance est largement représentée en latin tardif, le plus-que-parfait évinçant pour finir l'imparfait (cf. l'origine de l'imparfait du subjonctif en français).[23]

(8) *la conjugaison du perfectum passif*
Gildas présente constamment au parfait le type *amatus sum;* au subjonctif parfait, 1 ex. de *–fuerim* pour 4 de *–sim;* au plus-que-parfait indicatif et subjonctif, à l'infinitif passé et au futur II, constamment *–fueram*, *–fuissem*, *–fuisse* et *–fuero*.

C'est en gros la conjugaison que donnent Schrijnen-Mohrmann[24] et Leumann-Hofmann-Szantyr.[25]

(9) *l'infinitif après facio*
Le *DEB* n'a aucun exemple de *facio ut* + subjonctif. Le tour *facio* + infinitif, qu'il emploie, est usuel en latin tardif.[26]

(10) *l'emploi de l'adjectif verbal en –ndus*
(a) avec *sum*, comme équivalent du futur indicatif passif[27]
94 (78.4): (*haec scripturae sacrae testimonia*) *simpliciter congesta uel congerenda sunt*.
(b) attributif.[28]
93 (77.30): *haec . . . testimonia huic epistolae inserta uel inserenda*

(11) *le participe futur substantivé*
23 (39.6): *barbari, ueluti militibus et magna . . . discrimina pro bonis hospitibus subituris, impetrant sibi annonas dari.*
27 (41.21): *in sede arbitraturi sedentes*
Le tour est fréquent en latin d'argent et tardif.[29]

(12) *dum au sens de cum temporel;*[30] *dum causal*[31]
Dans le *DEB*, aucun emploi de *dum* (6 ex.) ne paraît recouvrir 'jusqu'à ce que' ou 'pendant tout le temps que'. C'est *donec* (2 ex. sur 2) qui rend 'jusqu'à ce que.'[32] *Quoad* n'est pas représenté, ce qui est le cas chez de nombreux auteurs.[33]

(13) *licet concessif + indicatif*
1 exemple en 9 (31.4). La construction est largement répandue en latin tardif.[34]

(14) *disparition de cur, remplacé par quid*[35]
Dans le *DEB*, 17 *quid* interrogatifs; 5 *quare;* 1 *ut quid;* 0 *cur*.

(15) *l'emploi de l'indicatif dans l'interrogation indirecte*[36]
9 exemples au total: après *quis*, 4; *quare*, 1; *quantus*, 2; *quantum*, 1; *quam*, 1.

(16) *l'emploi de dico quod, dico quia complétifs*[37]
dico quod : 6 ex., dont 5 avec le subjonctif
dico quia ; 2 ex., avec l'indicatif.

Ces faits, choisis parmi d'autres, montrent bien que le *DEB* reproduit l'état de langue couramment attesté chez les écrivains du Vème siècle. Il faut noter du reste que, comme les auteurs les plus soignés, Gildas utilise le plus souvent le tour classique dont l'école et les livres assuraient la survie. Ainsi:

- *licet* + subjonctif: 5 ex.
- interrogation indirecte au subjonctif: 36 ex.
- *dico* + proposition infinitive: plus de 30 ex.

Vue dans son ensemble, la syntaxe du *DEB* ne paraît donc pas plus marquée par la langue parlée que celle de la majorité des auteurs du Vème siècle.

Considérons maintenant le style de Gildas. Sur ce style si souvent décrié, on pourrait faire des remarques analogues. Il se rattache pour l'essentiel à la tradition des rhéteurs du Vème siècle et, mis à part quelques traits sur lesquels je reviendrai, la prose de Gildas n'est pas plus compliquée que celle de Sidoine ou d'Ennodius.

On retrouve dans le *DEB* les trois types de phrase que nos auteurs ont coutume d'employer, dans des proportions évidemment variables:

(1) la période, qui appartient en propre au style conservateur des Panégyristes gaulois et d'Hilaire.
(2) la cathode, petite phrase construite sur un parallélisme ou une antithèse; elle relève du style moderne.
(3) la phrase complexe où les parenthèses, les subordonnées, les participes s'accumulent et s'entremêlent; ce sont ces phrases qui donnent aux textes de Sidoine et d'Ennodius cette impression de complication.

Voici, du *DEB*, à titre d'exemple:

Période :

1 (26.7):
ista ego et multa alia ueluti speculum quoddam uitae nostrae in scripturis ueteribus intuens,
conuertebar etiam ad nouas,
et ibi legebam clarius quae mihi forsitan antea obscura fuerant,
cessante umbra ac ueritate firmius inlucescente.

Cathode :

1 (26.22):
sciebam misericordiam Domini
sed et iudicium timebam ;
laudabam gratiam
sed redditionem unicuique secundum opera sua uerebar ;
oues unius ouilis dissimiles cernens
merito beatissimum dicebam Petrum ob Christi

integram confessionem,
at Iudam infelicissimum propter cupiditatis amorem,
Stephanum gloriosum ob martyrii palmam,
sed Nicolaum miserum propter immundae haereseos notam.

Phrase complexe :

34 (45.14): *Nonne,*
subordonnée – *postquam tibi ex uoto uiolenti regni fantasia cessit,*
participes – *cupiditate inlectus ad uiam reuertendi rectam,*
– *diebus ac noctibus id temporis conscientia forte peccaminum remordente,*
– *de deifico tenore monachorumque decretis sub dente primum multa ruminans,*
– *dein popularis aurae cognitioni proferens,*
monachum sine ullo infidelitatis (ut aiebas) respectu
coram omnipotente Deo, angelicis uultibus humanisque,
participe (abl. abs.) et relative – *ruptis (ut putabatur) capacissimis illis, quibus praecipitanter inuolui solent pingues tauri moduli tui, retibus, omnis regni, auri, argenti et (quod his maius est) propriae uoluntatis distentionibus ruptis,*
perpetuo uouisti et tete,
comparaison developpée – *ac si stridulo cauum lapsu aerem ualide secantem saeuosque rapidi harpagones accipitris sinuosis flexibus uitantem*
ad sanctorum tibi magnopere fidas speluncas
refrigeriaque salubriter rapuisti
suite de la comparaison – *ex coruo columbam?*

65 (61.21): *Quam enim libenter hoc in loco*
participes – *ac si marinis fluctibus iactatus et in optato euectus portu remis,*
subordonnées – *si non tantos talesque malitiae episcoporum uel ceterorum sacerdotum aut clericorum in nostro quoque ordine erigi aduersus Deum uidissem montes,*
– *quos me, secundum legem, ceu testes, primum duris uerborum cautibus,*
dein populum,
si tamen sanctionibus inhaeret,
(subordonnées intercalées dans la précédente) – *non ut corporaliter interficiantur, sed mortui uitiis uiuant Deo,*
– *ne personarum arguar exceptionis,*
suite de *quos me . . .* *totis necesse est uiribus lapidare,*
uerecundia interueniente quiescerem!

Quant aux figures de style, antithèses, parallélismes, allitérations, rimes, anaphores, chiasmes, disjonctions, figures étymologiques et jeux de mots se présentent à chaque page, en particulier dans l'*Historia*.

Examinons pour finir l'ordre des mots. Le fait le plus frappant est, à propos du groupe adjectif-substantif, la fréquence de l'antéposition de l'adjectif déterminatif (*Romanus*, *ciuilis*, par exemple), alors que l'ordre normal est la postposition.[38]

Ainsi *Romanus* est 10 fois antéposé contre 2, *sacerdotalis*, 8 contre 0, *propheticus*, 7 contre 3, *humanus*, 8 contre 2, *ecclesiasticus*, 5 contre 0. On a 3 *ciuilia bella* contre 0 *bella ciuilia*, 2 *popularis aura* contre 0 *aura popularis*. Au total, la proportion est de 4 antépositions pour 1 postposition.

Il arrive que l'antéposition se justifie, par exemple dans une opposition: *externis bellis sed non ciuilibus*. Mais le plus souvent on n'en trouve pas de raison. Nous avons là, semble-t-il, un tic stylistique, un abus du procédé qui tend à lui faire perdre toute signification et n'est que le signe d'une recherche de l'élégance à tout prix.

Or ce trait, des sondages dans la prose de Sidoine et de Salvien nous le font apparaître comme l'une des marques de la prose soignée du Vème siècle; ses origines peuvent même être plus anciennes.

Autre notation: la fréquence des disjonctions dans le même groupe. M. Marouzeau a remarqué qu'à date tardive la disjonction, qui, chez un écrivain ménager de ses effets, a pour rôle d'attirer l'attention sur l'un des termes disjoints, tourne elle aussi à l'abus.[39]

Cet aperçu sur la manière d'écrire de Gildas me confirme dans mes vues. Le style du *DEB*, comme sa syntaxe, appartient à une langue littéraire de bonne tenue; l'un et l'autre nous rappellent la tradition des derniers rhéteurs du Vème siècle.

Le fait mérite d'être souligné et je proposerai les conclusions suivantes:

(1) Gildas n'a pas été formé 'sur le tas,' dans un milieu qui pratiquait le latin sans souci particulier de correction et d'élégance, ni même dans une école de piètre niveau, mais dans une école qui transmettait, en même temps sans doute que certaines règles de la rhétorique traditionnelle, l'usage des auteurs en vogue au cours des décennies précédentes. Gildas, comme le roi Maglocunus, a certainement profité des leçons d'un *magister elegans*.[40] En plus de la Bible, les élèves de cette école devaient lire, sinon des textes *in extenso*, du moins des extraits importants de ces textes. A première vue, à s'en tenir aux indications marginales de Mommsen dans son édition, les citations non bibliques de Gildas sont peu nombreuses. Mais cela ne signifie pas que Gildas avait peu lu. L'état de sa syntaxe et la qualité – tout jugement esthétique mis à part – de son style me feraient plutôt penser le contraire.

(2) Ainsi, bien avant la jeunesse de Colomban, en somme vers les années 500, existaient, au moins en Bretagne, une ou des écoles bien organisées. Nous relevons au passage que l'une des marques du latin insulaire, la correction

grammaticale, apparaît déjà dans le *DEB*. Il faut sans doute tenir compte du rôle des écoles de l'Ouest breton dans la transmission du latin antique aux fondations monastiques d'Irlande et la formation du latin des Iles.

(3) La survie des traditions de raffinement verbal est, pour la Gaule du début du VIème siècle, un fait reconnu. Si nous n'y trouvons pas pour cette époque d'auteurs comparables à un Sidoine, il est certain que chez les Hagiographes au moins se maintenait le goût du bien-dire.[41] Mais en Bretagne, un siècle après le départ des Romains, que restait-il du latin et de la culture latine? Nous sommes déjà mal renseignés sur les écoles qui pouvaient fonctionner sous l'occupation romaine; il ne fait pas de doute cependant qu'elles ont existé et qu'elles enseignaient – ce qui est normal – un latin souvent conservateur, comme le montre la phonétique de certains mots latins empruntés par le brittonique.[42] Sur la période post-romaine, nos informations sont aussi chétives. Vraisemblablement, le latin n'était plus utilisé que par le clergé, quelques princes, comme Maglocunus, par exemple, et quelques lettrés de cour. Le *DEB* en tout cas semble prouver que, malgré l'effacement du latin, certains milieux cultivaient une langue encore digne du nom de littéraire. On peut supposer que la tradition des écoles romaines de Bretagne s'était réfugiée dans l'Ouest et le Sud-Ouest de l'île,[43] sans méconnaître le rôle qu'ont pu jouer les Gallo-Romains.[44] Dirons-nous alors que le latin de Gildas est déjà anachronique? Valable pour Colomban, ce jugement serait ici outré; reconnaissons cependant que vers 530 un tel latin fait figure d'exception.

Voilà donc une première idée du latin du *DEB*. J'ai situé Gildas linguistiquement et à grands traits, ce qui me paraissait essentiel: plus proche de Sidoine que des traducteurs ou même de Césaire d'Arles. Mais c'est presque un portrait-robot du bon écrivain des années 470 que j'ai donné; il me faut maintenant procéder aux retouches. Car, de 470 à 530, la situation linguistique a changé: Gildas n'est pas qu'un Ruricius.

* * *

Gildas, nous venons de le voir, a reçu une bonne formation. Mais prenons le cas d'un auteur des époques antérieures. Il a fréquenté l'école du grammairien et du rhéteur, il a appris le bon usage, Cicéron et Quintilien, Virgile et Térence. Or il vit dans un milieu où le latin se parle et se transforme; lui-même parle un latin qui n'est pas exactement celui qu'il a appris et qu'il lit. S'il a du tempérament, ce n'est pas le latin de son école qu'il écrira, mais un latin qui, selon les genres, fera la part plus ou moins grande au latin vivant. Le bon auteur qui écrit dans un milieu linguistique normal ne dédaigne pas de s'inspirer aux sources de la langue parlée.

Ce n'est pas, semble-t-il, le cas de Gildas. Il emploie sans doute des vulgarismes, mais ce sont les vulgarismes qu'il a appris à l'école, les vulgarismes intégrés dans la langue littéraire. Mieux encore, on le surprend souvent à appliquer des règles enseignées par l'école mais qui n'étaient plus suivies par les auteurs qu'occasionnellement, ou encore à imiter des traditions brillantes mais mortes, attitude qui dénote l'élève formé exclusivement à l'école, sans contact avec une langue vivante, attentif à suivre les règles dictées par le maître et non les écarts des auteurs. Je disais à l'instant que Gildas avait appris le latin à l'école; je dirai maintenant qu'il ne l'a appris qu'à l'école.

Venons aux faits. D'abord ceux qui relèvent du respect des règles apprises:

(1) après *dare* ou *habere*, on ne rencontre pas, en fonction de complément d'objet direct, *de* ou *ex* + ablatif: type *ut ex suis equis daret his qui amisissent equos.*[45]

(2) alors que le datif prédicatif (*esse auxilio*) tend à céder la place au nominatif (*esse auxilium*), Gildas emploie encore 3 de ces datifs, dont deux fois dans le type *esse alicui auxilio.*[46]

(3) aucun exemple de *si* interrogatif, attesté chez les meilleurs auteurs du Vème siècle.[47]

(4) l'adjectif possessif est en latin normalement postposé; l'antéposition, qui peut être majoritaire chez tel auteur, est en principe expressive.[48] Or la langue parlée tend à dire *meus pater* (cf. français: mon père). Gildas présente 57 cas de postposition contre 41 d'antéposition. Si l'on se souvient combien il affectionne pour les déterminatifs – et les possessifs en sont – l'ordre exceptionnel, on peut supposer qu'il s'agit là d'un bel exemple d'attention à suivre la règle de l'école.

(5) de même, le pronom personnel sujet de 1ère et de 2ème personne tend à être employé dans la langue courante sans intention expressive – contrairement à l'usage ancien.[49] Sur ce point, Gildas se montre réservé et la présence du pronom sujet, assez rare, est le plus souvent motivée.

(6) dans l'emploi de *suus/eius*, *se/eum*, Gildas est plus proche de l'usage classique que certains auteurs tardifs.[50]

(7) dès l'Empire, le participe présent accompagné de *sum* tend à se substituer au verbe personnel.[51] Le *DEB* ne présente jamais *amans sum* pour *amo.*

(8) *quippe* en latin tardif disparaît; quand on le trouve, c'est plus comme forme savante que comme forme populaire.[52] Or Gildas l'utilise plusieurs fois, et correctement.

(9) *cum* historicum et *cum* adversatif sont toujours construits avec le subjonctif, comme en latin classique.[53]

(10) *quare* a toujours le sens de 'pourquoi' et non celui de 'parce que.'[54]

(11) *quominus*, qui tend à disparaître,[55] se rencontre 1 fois:
37 (48.16): *ne formidolosos nos aut lassos putent quominus illud Isaianum infatigabiliter caueamus.*

De même pour *quin.*[56] Or, fait curieux, Gildas, qui emploie plusieurs fois *quin etiam*, *quin potius*, écrit:
72 (66.32): *ita ut poterit* (sic) . . . *credere quin fortior fortior* (sic) *esset ad saluandum quam inimici ad pugnandum.*

109 (84.24): *unum ueredice possum dicere quin haec omnia in contrarios actus mutentur.*

Quin paraît être ici l'équivalent de *quod* complétif avec le subjonctif. Ce trait est, à ma connaissance, particulier à Gildas. Est-ce une extension de *quis ignorat quin?* ou une réaction contre la tendance à remplacer *quin* par *quod?* En tout cas la survie de *quin* est à noter.

(12) *dum*, qui dans le *DEB* est causal ou l'équivalent de *cum* temporel, s'emploie toujours avec l'indicatif.[57]

(13) l'ablatif absolu reste dans le *DEB* un syntagme très utilisé; la liste des occurrences est longue; de plus, je ne vois qu'un cas où le sujet du participe à l'ablatif reprend un mot déjà cité. Or un auteur comme Cyprien utilise surtout des formules du type *Deo iubente.*[58] Chez Patrice, l'ablatif absolu avec participe passé se limite à deux formules, les quelques exemples de reste étant au participe présent.[59] L'usage du *DEB* est au contraire très riche; j'y verrais l'influence de l'école.

(14) l'emploi de *et* et de *-que*
Je relève dans le *DEB* en gros 400 *et* et 200 *-que*. De Lucrèce à Velleius Paterculus, *-que* apparaît à égalité numérique avec *et* chez de nombreux auteurs. Chez Tacite, Suétone, Pline le Jeune, le rapport est encore de 1 à 2. *-Que* disparaît chez Ethérie et dans certains livres de la Vulgate mais il est encore assez bien représenté dans Grégoire de Tours et les *Vitae Patrum.*[60] La proportion du *DEB* est en tout cas beaucoup plus forte que chez ces derniers auteurs puisque elle atteint celle de Tacite, Suétone, etc.

En matière de style, je soulignerai deux faits:

(1) la place du verbe 'réel' (= non attributif, non copule) dans la proposition.[61]

A date ancienne, la place normale est la finale: César: 90%, Salluste: 80%, Cicéron, amateur de *uarietas:* 55%. Mais ce pourcentage tend à faiblir: Tite-Live: 70%, Apulée: 60%, Victor de Vita: 50%, Ethérie: 30%. Dans certains textes de basse époque, la position finale est exceptionnelle, le verbe se loge à l'intérieur de la proposition, ce qui préfigure l'état roman.[62]

Pour les 36 chapitres en question, j'ai relevé 60.7% des verbes à la finale. Connaissant le goût de Gildas pour l'expressivité et son abus, nous aurions attendu un pourcentage plus faible; notons, pour fixer les idées, que Gildas nous ramène au chiffre d'un auteur du IIème siècle.

(2) dans le syntagme participe passé + copule, l'ordre normal à date ancienne est *factum est.* Mais la langue parlée tend à préférer l'ordre inverse, qui sera celui des langues romanes. On voit par exemple un écrivain aussi peu soucieux d'élégance littéraire que Lucifer employer autant *est factum* que *factum est.* Chez Ethérie, on s'attendrait à la même situation. En fait, elle n'a, pour 315 *factum est*, que 13 *est factum*, et encore avec les formes non enclitiques *fuerat*, *fuisset* etc. ... Seul le souci de suivre une règle apprise peut expliquer ce fait.[63]

Gildas présente l'ordre normal 67 fois contre 7, soit 90.5%. Ce n'est pas tout à fait le pourcentage d'Ethérie, mais c'est beaucoup plus que Lucifer, et même que Ruricius, bon élève des rhéteurs: 79.4%.[64]

Par ailleurs, l'école pouvait transmettre ou Gildas avait pu acquérir par ses lectures des usages propres à certains auteurs, mais généralement hors de circulation:

(1) *gratia* postposé à un génitif est plus fréquent chez Gildas que *causa*. C'est un trait de Salluste et de Valère-Maxime.[65]

(2) Gildas emploie 2 fois *postquam* mais jamais *posteaquam*, alors que la tendance générale est inverse; on n'a même aucun *postquam* chez Cyprien et le traducteur d'Irénée. Mais Tite-Live et le *Bellum Africanum* ne connaissent que *postquam*.[66]

(3) la présence de *ni* dans le *DEB* (3 fois) est peut-être une trace de Tacite.[67]

(4) le participe futur attributif, qu'on rencontre au moins 8 fois dans le *DEB* (type *periturae Troiae*), est peu connu en latin tardif (sauf chez Prudence) mais il fleurit à l'âge d'argent.[68]

Il convient peut-être de faire la part du hasard. Des auteurs que je viens de citer, se détache cependant le lot des historiens, dont on sait qu'ils exercèrent, surtout par leurs préfaces, une grande influence sur les stylistes postérieurs. J'ai parlé plus haut du double datif. Or *DEB* 15 (33.21): *ut esset arcendis hostibus terrori, ciuibusque tutamini* ressemble assez à Tite-Live XXVI 2.10. . . . *praesidio sociis, hostibus terrori esse*. La convergence de ces remarques permet de voir là plus qu'un simple hasard: certains tours devaient être présentés par le maître comme plus distingués.

Au total, j'ai l'impression que Gildas, qui écrit habituellement le latin du Vème siècle, est plus marqué par l'école, plus conservateur que ses prédécesseurs. Ceux-ci, au contact de la langue parlée, oubliaient parfois ce qu'on leur avait enseigné, et c'est normal. Gildas, au contraire, écrit comme on le lui a appris; il a la plume scolaire et cette docilité n'est pas occasionnelle, comme ce peut être le cas pour Ethérie, par exemple, mais elle apparaît à chaque page. Timidité, manque de tempérament? Pourquoi ne pas supposer plutôt que Gildas, n'ayant pas subi l'influence d'un milieu linguistique naturel, ne connaît au fond que l'école et l'enseignement de ses maîtres? Il emploie le latin dont on lui a dit qu'il était le plus distingué et les libertés syntaxiques que ses devanciers se permettent sans scrupule sont accueillies chez lui avec la plus grande réserve.

Nous retrouverons le même caractère scolaire dans le latin des Insulaires du VIIème siècle. Mais il faut noter une différence importante. Les Irlandais, au contact cette fois de la langue parlée sur le Continent, réagissent contre ce qui leur paraît du laisser-aller. D'où l'apparition de fautes inverses, d'hypercorrections et d'hyperurbanismes dont il n'y a pas de traces notables dans le *DEB*:[69] Gildas, par exemple, use de *se/eum* plus correctement que sur le Continent, mais sans aller jusqu'à l'hypercorrection. Il est en fait plus coupé de la langue vivante que ses successeurs; une fois de plus, il apparaît que Gildas a été formé exclusivement par l'école.

Mais, s'il se montre peu empressé à utiliser le latin de ses prédécesseurs avec toutes ses innovations, il lui arrive en revanche de surenchérir en matière d'élégance et de rechercher des tours savants qu'on ne pouvait guère cultiver qu'en milieu fermé.

Depuis longtemps, mais surtout à partir du IVème siècle (Ausone par exemple), les écrivains précieux développent l'usage de procédés qui ne sont pas nouveaux mais qui, par leur conjonction, deviennent la marque d'un style: latinisation, voire introduction en alphabet latin de mots grecs, adjectifs en *-fer* et en *-ger*, en *-ōsus*, substantifs en *-men*, mots rares, combinaisons de mots inhabituelles. Soutenue par le goût des énigmes et des jeux littéraires, favorisée par la décadence des Lettres, cette tendance est certainement pour une bonne part à l'origine de la littérature dite hispérique, qui pousse au paroxysme la recherche du mot bizarre, comprise sans doute comme le comble de l'élégance verbale.

Malgré les efforts répétés de nombreux savants, l'Hispérisme n'a pas encore livré tous ses secrets. On n'est pas d'accord sur la date des *Epitomae* de Virgile de Toulouse; on ne sait pas quand et où ont été écrits les *Hisperica Famina*. Il paraît sûr toutefois que ces derniers textes, qui sont probablement des exercices d'école, étaient connus des latinistes celtiques, sans que leur origine soit pour autant à chercher dans les Iles; qu'il y a un rapport entre notre Virgile, les *HF* et l'école d'Aldhelm; que les *Scoticae latinitatis consuetudines*, ou faits de vocabulaire qui passent ordinairement pour caractériser le latin insulaire en dehors de toute influence de la langue vernaculaire, se rattachent à ce courant.

Peut-on proposer une vue d'ensemble de la question qui ne soit pas déraisonnable et laisse la porte ouverte à d'autres interprétations? A la fin du Vème siècle, dans le Sud-Ouest de la Gaule, sous domination wisigothique, à un moment où la culture reculait et où les demi-savants se prenaient d'autant plus pour des gens graves, se serait développée une école littéraire, héritière des traditions de l'Université de Bordeaux, et soucieuse, par pédantisme mi-plaisant peut-être, mi-sérieux, d'écrire un latin qui devait représenter la fine fleur de la latinité compromise. On peut supposer, après le P. Grosjean, qu'un de ces lettrés soit passé dans les Iles et qu'il ait ainsi répandu cette mode, que le goût des Celtes pour l'ornement contourné devait adopter avec ferveur.[70] Une telle formation aurait été largement diffusée dans les écoles des pays celtiques et, *mutatis mutandis*, elle serait devenue ce qu'était la rhétorique à Rome. On en trouve en tout cas des traces nombreuses dans tous les écrits insulaires, même après le Haut Moyen-Age. Les *HF* représentent sans doute une limite, mais, s'il s'agit bien d'exercices d'école, de rédactions, de textes d'application ou de modèles, bref, d'écrits à usage interne, on explique aisément leur caractère d'exception. Quelques autres pièces rivalisent avec eux en obscurité; elles peuvent être l'œuvre d'écrivains qui, à un moment donné de leur carrière et dans des conditions particulières, ont voulu s'essayer à un genre – il s'agit surtout de poèmes et de *Loricae* – et composer un chef d'œuvre que seuls les initiés pouvaient lire – n'oublions pas que la poésie celtique est elle aussi affaire d'initiés – alors que par ailleurs ils ont pu nous laisser des ouvrages plus accessibles, destinés à un public plus large. Par exemple, la fameuse lettre d'Aldhelm à Ehfrid nous montre le grand clerc rivalisant avec les Irlandais pour prouver que les Anglo-Saxons égalent leurs maîtres. Mais c'est une occasion exceptionnelle, ce qui n'empêche pas Aldhelm de pratiquer çà et là le même type de recherche dans l'expression.

Si cette mode est passée de bonne heure dans les Iles, on pourrait en trouver au moins l'écho dans le *DEB*. De fait, l'éditeur des *HF* a rapproché certains passages du *DEB* de ces écrits mystérieux: le mot *tithica*, rarissime, est commun aux deux textes. Mais, faute d'un index du *DEB*, il n'a pu pousser son enquête très loin.[71]

L'exploitation, même sommaire, des suggestions de Jenkinson trouvera donc ici sa place. Compte tenu du fait qu'un jargon du type hispérique n'est pas utilisable à jet continu dans une admonition destinée à un public aussi limité et aussi cultivé qu'on veuille le supposer, pouvons-nous dire que Gildas a connu et suivi, sinon les *HF*, dont la date est incertaine, du moins la rhétorique qu'ils véhiculent et dont ils ont pu être comme le point de cristallisation, utilise-t-il des procédés qui pouvaient exister avant d'être présentés en une sorte de concentré dans ce prolongement exubérant des tendances précieuses et pédantes du Vème siècle finissant que sont les *HF*?

J'utiliserai pour cela les traits dont la liste est donnée par Ehwald dans son édition d'Aldhelm:[72]

(1) *les mots grecs latinisés ou semi-latinisés*

Exemple, dans Aldhelm: *pantorum*, *climata*, *navarcus*, *ad doxam onomatis cyrii* etc. . . . cf. la fin de *Rubisca : Ymniste pantes trinon tonethnon.*

Gildas emploie des mots grecs, mais en dehors des christianismes courants (*angelus*, *anathema*, *episcopus*, *euangelium*, *etc*. . . .),[73] on ne trouve que quelques mots déjà acclimatés en latin: *amphibalum*, *celeuma*, *fantasia*, *flegma*, *mastigia*, *plasma*, *proto–*, *stigma.*

Je note l'absence dans le *DEB* de *pontus* et de *pelagus*, bien attestés dans les *HF*, dans Aldhelm et dans l'hagiographie celtique, alors que Gildas avait l'occasion de les employer, puisqu'il donne plusieurs fois *mare* et *Oceanus.*

(2) *les mots rares ou mots de glossaire*

Exemple, dans Aldhelm: *arcister*, *boatus*, *circulus*, *dodrans.*

La concordance est cette fois intéressante entre Gildas, les *HF* et Aldhelm:

(a) attestés dans le *DEB* et les *HF :*
coruscus, *tithica*

(b) attestés dans le *DEB* et dans Aldhelm:
circio, *catasta* = *caterua*, *epimenia*,[74] *refocillare*, *repedare*

(c) attestés dans les trois textes:
aluearium, *caespes* = *tellus*, *macerare*, *piaculum* = *peccatum*, *quis* = *quibus*, *ruminare*, *sablones*.

Ces listes seraient à discuter. Je note au passage que l'usage de *quis* n'est pas le même dans nos trois textes. *Quis* pour *quibus* est ancien et ce n'est qu'une nette prédominance de *quis* qui nous autoriserait à y voir un hispérisme. Or Gildas a 6 *quis* pour 20 *quibus*, soit 1 pour 3.33, ce qui est en gros la proportion de Virgile et de Tacite, alors que Pline le Jeune donne de nombreux *quibus* pour 0 *quis*, et Lucrèce, 28 *quibus* pour 5 *quis*.[75]

Dans les *HF* au contraire, 8 *quis* pour 5 *quibus;* chez Aldhelm, 11 *quis* pour 9 *quibus*.[76] Si l'emploi de *quis* est un poétisme (Tibulle 4 *quis*/3 *quibus*) repris par les *HF*, on ne peut guère admettre que Gildas se soit distingué de ce côté d'une honnête moyenne.

J'ajouterai que Gildas ne connaît pas *occiduus*, qui se trouve dans les *HF*, mais il emploie *occidentalis*, qu'ignorent les *HF*.[77]

(3) *les adjectifs en –ōsus et les substantifs en –āmen*
Je groupe ces deux séries, dont Niedermann a montré qu'elles étaient, par leur usage, caractéristiques des *HF*.[78]

–**amen**	*HF*	*Aldhelm* (*avec Carmina rythmica*)	*DEB*	*Ausone*[79]
Total des mots	23	24	8	15
Attestés ailleurs	6	21	7	14
–**osus**				
Total des mots	61	113	17	49
Attestés ailleurs	34	111	17	49

Le grand nombre des néologismes contenus dans les *HF* est l'argument principal de Niedermann. Leur rareté dans le *DEB* et chez Aldhelm attire de ce fait notre attention: ces deux auteurs sont plus proches d'Ausone. D'autre part, compte tenu du volume respectif des oeuvres et des différences de genre, les *HF* sont de très loin en tête pour l'emploi global de ces mots, suivis par Aldhelm, qui ne les méprise pas, puis par Gildas, nettement en retrait.

(4) *les adjectifs en –fer et en –ger*

	HF	*Aldhelm*	*DEB*	*Ausone*
Total	21	51	5	34
Attestés ailleurs	17	39	5	30

Là aussi, Gildas est en retrait.

(5) *les distributifs remplaçant les cardinaux*[80]
(a) l'emploi du type *bis bini* pour *quattuor :* c'est un procédé des poètes latins. Mais sa généralisation peut être hispérique.
Ainsi les *HF* emploient 2 fois *bis bini* pour *quattuor*
4 fois *bis seni* pour *duodecim*

sans aucun exemple du cardinal correspondant.

Chez Aldhelm, *bis bini* et le cardinal sont attestés; dans le *DEB*, on trouve 3 fois le type *bis bini* mais 10 fois le cardinal.

(b) en latin le singulier du distributif peut servir de cardinal (*centeno gutture* à côté de *centum uoces*), mais les *HF* utilisent couramment le pluriel: *quini* pour *quinque*.

Aldhelm écrit *deni leprosi*, *quinis uersibus*, non distributifs, à côté de *decem*, *quinque*, tandis que cet usage est inconnu de Gildas.

(6) *les combinaisons de mots*

Le P. Grosjean, après Ehwald et de façon systématique, a signalé que les phrases des *HF* présentent un ordre courant et presque constant:[81]

A épithète – verbe – substantif

supernam compaginat camaram

B deux épithètes – verbe – deux substantifs

aquosi luteas irrigant fluuii uenas

La répétition de ces types de phrase semble indiquer qu'il s'agit bien d'un exercice d'école. Qui ne se souvient d'avoir traduit des phrases comme: *bona puella ornat pulchram aram?*

Ce qui me retient ici, c'est l'ordre des mots.

La type A est fondé sur la disjonction adjectif-substantif avec antéposition de l'adjectif, quel qu'il soit: deux tics dont nous avons déjà parlé et que nous ne sommes pas surpris de retrouver ici.

Le type B m'intéresse davantage. Quelle est l'origine de cet ordre bizarre, que je schématise ainsi: *E*1 *E*2 *V S*1 *S*2?

A première vue, ce n'est pas un ordre simple, un ordre de prose, mais une manière recherchée de s'exprimer. Or tournons-nous vers la poésie; nous remarquons que les Latins affectionnent, parmi d'autres possibilités, le type: *E*1 *E*2 *V S*2 *S*1 (appelons-le I):

Pharsale VII, 64: *Pacificas saeuus tremuit Catilina securis.*

Il s'agit d'une disposition savante, à double embrassement, qui convient à l'expression d'une grande idée, d'un sentiment puissant, d'un tableau majestueux.[82]

A cette disposition embrassée, peut se substituer une variante croisée: *E*1 *E*2 *V S*1 *S*2 (II)

Sidoine *Carmen II*, 411: *Picta peregrinos ignorant arua rigores.*

De II, par permutation d'un des groupes, on peut obtenir deux combinaisons, dans lesquelles *E*1 voisine avec *S*2 et *E*2 avec *S*1:

*S*1 *E*2 *V E*1 *S*2 (permutation de *E*1 *S*1) (III)

Culex 147: *Carmina per uarios edunt resonantia cantus.*

*E*1 *S*2 *V S*1 *E*2 (permutation de *E*2 *S*2) (IV)

Juvénal *Satires* VIII, 253: *Nobilis ornatur lauro collega secunda* (j'admets à titre de variante du type le déplacement du verbe).

Ces ordres savants et poétiques ont pu s'introduire dans la prose pour des raisons de recherche bien évidentes. Il ne semble pas cependant que Sidoine dans sa prose en use beaucoup. Mais les *HF* en seraient un bon exemple, avec l'emploi si fréquent de II.

On pourrait alors rapprocher Aldhelm, Lettre à Ehfrid:
p. 489.12: *priscam paterni uisitantem clientelam ruris*
p. 491.21: *fuscata tetrae occulitur latebra urnae*
p. 488.7: (sans verbe cette fois): *almae editum puerperae sobolem.*

Or ces types, et pas seulement II, sont bien connus de Gildas, qui emploie la variante sans verbe:
II 32 (44.22): *perpeti immortales igni animae*
34 (45.21): *stridulo cauum lapsu aerem*
73 (67.19): *primus in nouo . . . episcopus testamento*
III 28 (42.3): *latera regiorum tenerrima puerorum*
IV 32 (44.21): *taetro ignium globo aeternorum*
3 (29.1): *frigidum aquae torrentem uiuae.*[83]

Autant que je sache, le P. Grosjean ne précisait pas l'origine des deux combinaisons qu'il relevait dans les *HF*, son affaire étant alors d'établir l'origine de la rime. Je ne voudrais pas me risquer trop en avant sur un terrain mal connu mais je supposerais volontiers que les combinaisons si curieuses de Gildas, peu attestées avant lui chez les prosateurs, sont en rapport avec une mode qui empruntait ses procédés à la poésie et qui ferait partie du courant dont il est ici question, Gildas se trouvant du reste en pointe par rapport aux *HF* puisqu'il présente les types III et IV dont le P. Grosjean ne parle pas.

Il serait vain, nous l'avons vu, de comparer des fréquences relatives. Mais, même ainsi, Gildas paraît en retrait sur la rhétorique hispérique. Car, si par nécessité il devait mesurer l'utilisation de chaque procédé, il pouvait du moins les employer tous. Or seuls les mots de glossaire et les combinaisons adjectif-substantif se présentent de telle façon qu'on peut proposer un rapprochement avec l'hispérisme proprement dit. Je dirai même que Gildas ne craint pas de proposer à ses lecteurs une brochette de mots rares; l'aurait-il fait, si Maglocunus et les autres avaient ignoré ces subtilités? Si donc son public comprenait ces mots, pourquoi Gildas n'a-t-il pas eu recours aux autres recettes de l'hispérisme, s'il les connaissait? Or, quant au reste, il est en fait plus proche des poètes et des prosateurs d'art du IVème siècle et fait preuve d'une modération qui serait surprenante s'il avait été touché par les milieux où circulaient les tendances hispériques. Au contraire, Aldhelm, toute question de fréquence relative mise à part, paraît plus familier avec l'arsenal des *HF*. Il est donc permis de penser qu'Aldhelm ou ses maîtres ont connu l'acmè de l'hispérisme. De Gildas, on peut se demander s'il a fait un choix parmi les tics hispériques ou s'il est antérieur à leur vogue, l'hispérisme n'étant au début du VIème siècle qu'un mouvement en gestation et certaines tendances se trouvant ici et là plus cultivées que d'autres. La seconde hypothèse me paraît plus vraisemblable, je viens de le suggérer. Ajoutons que la plus haute date proposée pour Virgile de Toulouse est la fin du Vème siècle, début du VIème siècle. A cette époque, Gildas devait être en possession de ses moyens linguistiques; ce n'est pas l'enseignement de Virgile qui pouvait l'atteindre – s'il a eu lieu – mais plutôt une certaine atmosphère, disons prévirgilienne.

Quoi qu'il en soit de ces suggestions, je voudrais, revenant à mon sujet, souligner la présence, dans la prose de Gildas, de ce goût pour des vocables et des tours savants qui rendent incontestablement un son hispérique. Ce n'est certes pas du VIème siècle que date cet engouement pour le mot rare et la construction artificielle; ce n'est pas du VIème siècle que date l'introduction en prose des procédés de la poésie. Mais il est ici question d'expressions et de tournures dont l'apparition dans un texte de prose frappe l'attention. Ne serait-ce pas un indice que Gildas fait de la surenchère par rapport aux prosateurs du Vème siècle? Timide quant aux franchises syntaxiques, ne serait-il pas plus hardi quant aux recherches de style, introduisant en prose ce qui jusqu'alors était surtout l'apanage des poètes? L'élève qui apprend la syntaxe la plus distinguée – ce qui l'amène au conservatisme – est aussi soucieux de tourner sa phrase de la façon la plus recherchée – et cette fois il va plus loin que ses devanciers. Il n'y a pas contradiction et, dans les deux cas, c'est un latin scolaire, artificiel, étranger à la langue vivante qui se dévoile.

C'est à une conclusion semblable que nous mènerons les remarques suivantes sur les clausules du *DEB*.[84]

De la part d'un écrivain qui suit d'aussi près les derniers rhéteurs du Vème siècle et se montre parfois si attaché au bon usage, on s'attend, sur un chapitre de rhétorique aussi important, à un égal respect du système généralement utilisé.

On sait qu'à partir du IIème siècle la prose métrique se règle sur une formule unique et que, plus on avance dans le temps, plus les bonnes clausules tendent à s'imposer, au détriment de la variété. D'autre part, l'accent du mot, devenu accent d'intensité, prend de l'importance dans le rythme de la langue: dès Arnobe, l'étude de la typologie des clausules les plus employées met en valeur les sous-types où l'accent du mot coïncide avec l'*ictus* du pied, ces sous-types devant donner par la suite les trois clausules du *cursus* médiéval.

Au début du VIème siècle, il y a de grandes chances que la situation soit encore la même qu'au cours des décennies antérieures et que les clausules de Gildas appartiennent au type métrique.[85]

Or, si je prends les trois clausules les plus recherchées du IIIème au Vème siècle, j'obtiens, pour le *DEB*, le pourcentage de 32%, la prose amétrique arrivant à 27–29%.[86]

La prose de Gildas n'est donc pas amétrique, mais de peu et l'écart avec les auteurs précédents est important:

Arnobe: 80.8%, Quodvultdeus: 41.03%, Ruricius: 69.3%.

Considérons la typologie des clausules et relevons les cas où l'accent coïncide avec l'*ictus*:

Clausule 18: crétique + trochée[87]
Arnobe: 94.8%, Qvdeus: 81.6%, Ruricius: 94.8%, Gildas: 61.53%.
Clausule 9: dicrétique[88]
Arnobe: 94.5%, Qvdeus: 79.8%, Ruricius: 97.4%, Gildas: 80%.
Clausule 15: ditrochée (précédé d'un proparoxyton)[89]
Arnobe: 85.1%, Qvdeus: 68.1%, Ruricius: 83.7%, Gildas: 28.5%.

Le *DEB* n'a donc qu'une prose médiocrement métrique, par rapport aux canons du Vème siècle, et peu sensible à la coïncidence de l'*ictus* et de l'accent.

Ce dernier point nous laisse deviner que Gildas ne pressent rien des formules du *cursus* médiéval. Nous constatons en effet qu'étudiées de ce point de vue ses clausules arrivent loin derrière celles des bons représentants du *cursus :*

	Gildas	Desiderius (VIIème s.)	Pierre Damien (c. 1050)
Planus	22.5%	35%	31.4%
Tardus	20.5%	10.8%	16.9%
Velox	23%	35.8%	49.4%
	66%	81.6%	97.7%

Quelle conclusion proposer?

(1) Gildas néglige-t-il les clausules de propos délibéré?
On constate en effet que les *Sermons* d'Augustin, écrits pour le peuple, sans souci des fleurs de la rhétorique, donnent pour les trois clausules principales un total de 33% (Gildas: 32%). Mais une telle attitude serait surprenante de la part de Gildas. Contrairement aux *Sermons*, où le relâchement est volontaire, le *DEB* a quelque prétention au beau langage; il n'est pas destiné au vulgaire.

(2) Si nous écartons cette hypothèse, il faut peut-être supposer que Gildas suit d'autres modèles que les auteurs du Vème siècle. Mais, nous l'avons vu, depuis le IIème siècle, c'est une formule unique qui s'impose et qui est généralement pratiquée. Cependant, n'avons-nous pas laissé entendre que les historiens avaient pu influencer Gildas? Or M. Perret a montré qu'avant le IIème siècle plusieurs systèmes étaient entrés en concurrence, que Salluste s'était constitué une prose métrique à base de pieds du genre égal: dactyles, anapestes, spondées, et que Tite-Live avait repris et même valorisé cet héritage.[90]

Si je relève dans le *DEB* les quatre clausules chères à Salluste, je constate que Gildas les présente plus souvent qu'Arnobe ou Cicéron

	Gildas	Arnobe	Cicéron
Cl. 14	6%	0.4%	1.9%
4	3%	0.3%	1.8%
17	3.5%	2.7%	1.4%
19	20.5%	3.6%	6.4%

Gildas évite le ditrochée (14%; prose amétrique: 18.9%), comme

Salluste (9.1%) et Tite-Live (12%), alors que Cicéron le recherche (entre 25 et 26%); on sait que Denys d'Halicarnasse reprochait aux Asianistes l'abus de ce mètre.

Mais j'objecterai que:

(a) le système qui apparaît bien en place dans Salluste ne fonctionne pas comme tel chez Gildas. Les pourcentages de ce dernier, supérieurs assurément à ceux de Cicéron et d'Arnobe, sont inférieurs le plus souvent à ceux de Salluste et même de la prose amétrique:

	Gildas	Prose amétrique	Salluste
Cl. 14	6%	8.5%	11.1%
4	3%	4.9%	10.1%
17	3.5%	1.4%	4.3%
19	20.5%	23.7%	26%

(b) habituellement Gildas a plutôt un faible pour la préciosité, l'Asianisme. Peut-on concilier la tonalité générale du *DEB* et le refus des clausules asianistes?

(3) Il est cependant possible que Gildas respecte une tradition, variante du système courant. En effet, les clausules qui s'achèvent par un crétique sont particulièrement recherchées dans le *DEB* : ainsi, les clausules 5, 6, 7, 8, 9, 10 et 11, terminées par un crétique, représentent 30% du total (prose amétrique: 21.1%). Les clausules 3 et 18, avec crétique pénultième, représentent 16%, contre 10.3% pour la prose amétrique. Il y aurait donc là un système, qui se rattache au système cicéronien, mais très simplifié. Ce système, qui semble jusqu'à présent peu attesté, a cependant des garants. La valorisation du crétique remonte à Quintilien et s'affirme dans Terentianus Maurus.[91] Les hymnes de Marius Victorinus, écrites, en lignes de prose à peu près isosyllabiques mais terminées très régulièrement par un unique crétique, en seraient une illustration.[92] On peut donc supposer une tradition du crétique qui serait parvenue jusqu'à Gildas, sans doute par l'intermédiaire de l'école.

Ce point acquis, reste à expliquer l'insensibilité relative de Gildas à l'accent. Comment se fait-il qu'il respecte les quantités et non l'accent, dont nous avons dit qu'il était alors intégré au rythme de la langue? Sans doute parce que Gildas n'a pas l'oreille latine et que le latin n'est pas sa langue maternelle. La majorité des Bretons qui avaient parlé le latin l'avaient appris comme seconde langue; au temps de Gildas, ce devait être le cas pour ceux qui le parlaient encore. Ils peuvent le bien écrire; mais comment le prononcent-ils? K. Jackson a admirablement mis en lumière que les phénomènes phonétiques qui travaillent le brittonique dès le Ier siècle se transposent dans le latin des bilingues.[93] Les missionnaires qui transmirent aux Irlandais des mots latins prononçaient à la bretonne et disaient 'pader' pour *pater*. On peut supposer qu'ils accentuaient aussi les mots latins sur la pénultième, comme dans leur langue maternelle, ou du moins qu'ils tendaient à le faire, et que Gildas, formé dans un milieu linguistique assez semblable, pratiquait la même prononciation.

Ainsi je comparerais volontiers Gildas et nos étudiants en thème latin. Les meilleurs écrivent un bon latin cicéronien mais leur prose est amétrique, comme celle des dissertations du XIXème siècle, parce que nous prononçons le latin à la française ou à l'anglaise. Gildas faisait sans doute plus attention car il avait appris l'usage, mais son oreille le trahissait, dernier trait, je crois, qui fait du latin de Gildas un latin scolaire, coupé de la langue vivante, un peu, toutes proportions gardées, comme celui de nos thèmes latins.

Les clausules du latin insulaire n'ont pas encore, à ma connaissance, attiré l'attention des chercheurs. Lindholm, pour le Haut Moyen-Age, ne donne de chiffres que pour Bède. J'ai, pour ma part, dépouillé le *De Virginitate* d'Aldhelm et effectué des sondages dans Colomban et dans Adomnan. Du point de vue métrique, les clausules d'Aldhelm sont encore plus médiocres que celles de Gildas – je compare avec le système courant – mais Aldhelm paraît touché par la même tradition que Gildas. Quant à l'accent, il ne joue qu'un rôle modeste chez Bède et chez Aldhelm: Bède suit les formules du *cursus* dans 63.2% des cas, Aldhelm, dans 54.66%. Sous réserve d'un inventaire plus complet, je concluerai que les clercs du VIIème siècle prononçaient eux aussi le latin à l'insulaire et qu'ils étaient, comme Gildas, assez insensibles à l'accent du latin.

Je pense avoir suffisamment illustré la différence essentielle qui sépare le latin de Gildas de celui du Vème siècle. Alors que Sidoine est soutenu par un milieu linguistique vivant, Gildas est enfermé dans les traditions et les déformations d'une institution scolaire, seul support de la langue latine en Bretagne. Soumis à de telles conditions, le latin se fait artificiel; ce n'est plus qu'une langue d'école. Plus ou moins accentuées, nous retrouverons les mêmes caractéristiques un siècle plus tard dans le latin des grands monastères insulaires.

* * *

Si le latin de Gildas nous apparaît par certains côtés comme artificiel et déjà médiéval, il reste que le milieu de Gildas et Gildas lui-même sont encore attachés à une tradition profondément latine. On pourrait le montrer à propos des images, qui, lorsqu'elles ne viennent pas de la Bible, appartiennent au répertoire latin et non à la poésie celtique. De même, au point de vue linguistique, on note que l'impact des langues vernaculaires, sensible dans les Iles à partir du VIIème siècle, est presque nul dans le *DEB*.

La liste des celticismes a peut-être été grossie par les celtisants eux-mêmes. Aujourd'hui, des savants comme MM. Bieler et B. Löfstedt inclinent à la prudence.[94] Reste que certains faits sont incontestables, dans le vocabulaire surtout: *dexter* et *sinister* pour 'du sud' et 'du nord', *materia abbatis* pour 'futur abbé' (irl. moyen: *damna abbad*, cf. breton moderne: *danvez beleg*, 'séminariste') par exemple. Ajoutons en syntaxe l'emploi d'*alius* au sens de *quidam*, acception que peut avoir l'irl. *araile*.

Dans le *DEB*, je relève un mot d'emprunt, *curucus*, le *cwrwg* gallois, le *curach* irlandais; mais aucun décalque comme *dexter* ou *materia abbatis*. En syntaxe, on rencontre des nominatifs absolus, des ellipses de *esse*, des confusions *cum-ab-apud;* mais s'agit-il de celtisismes?

Le bilan est donc voisin de zéro. Cette imperméabilité à la langue vernaculaire, alors que Gildas savait sans doute assez de breton pour prêcher ou communiquer avec ceux de ses compatriotes qui ne parlaient pas latin, ne surprendra pas si l'on considère que cette langue était encore uniquement orale. Les bardes refusaient de la confier à l'écriture, comme ce fut le cas en Gaule, et les clercs devaient se méfier de cette littérature d'inspiration païenne, où la guerre et le carnage étaient exaltés. Dès lors, quel prestige pouvait avoir, aux yeux d'un écrivain formé dans une tradition où l'écrit avait tant d'importance, la langue qui véhiculait une culture exclusivement orale? Les celticismes apparaîtront quand la langue vernaculaire aura acquis un statut de langue écrite, c'est-à-dire quand les moines se seront ouverts à la poésie et aux légendes celtiques. Gildas et son milieu, quelques réserves que l'on puisse formuler, sont encore tournés vers Rome: *ita ut non Britannia sed Romania censeretur*.[95]

* * *

En conclusion de cette étude, le latin du *DEB* peut être ainsi décrit: c'est en gros le latin d'un bon auteur du Vème siècle finissant, avec cette différence importante que Gildas n'est pas à l'écoute d'une langue parlée: il applique des règles, il raffine en élégance et donne assez loin dans une certaine préciosité, il écrit sans avoir l'oreille latine. Je crois que l'étiquette 'latin d'école' convient parfaitement au *DEB*. Mais, quel que soit le degré d'artificialité de ce latin, c'est encore vers Rome que regarde Gildas.

En d'autres termes, je qualifierai ce latin de colonial. Gildas s'exprime comme les élèves d'une école coloniale: tourné vers la métropole, Rome en l'occurence, la grande Rome d'un passé assez récent; peu libre à l'égard des règles, parce que la langue du colonisateur s'apprend d'abord et surtout à l'école et qu'elle ne se parle généralement que dans les milieux issus de cette école; amateur en revanche de phrases curieusement tournées, car il ne faut pas paraître moins distingué que les gens de la capitale; capable donc de reproduire les tours de la langue, mais insensible à ce qu'elle a peut-être de plus difficile à imiter: l'accent. Pensons que dans l'*Historia* les Romains sont donnés aux Bretons comme exemple d'organisation et d'efficacité. Gildas ne serait-il pas au fond un nostalgique de la *Romania*, n'aurait-il pas le complexe de l'Empire? Il faut remarquer ici que l'Eglise de Bretagne est encore à cette époque une Eglise épiscopale: c'est en effet aux évêques que s'adresse Gildas, et les particularismes qui seront au VIIème siècle la source des conflits que l'on sait, s'ils existent, n'attirent pas encore l'attention.

Beaucoup de ces traits passeront dans le latin insulaire de la grande époque: correction grammaticale, recherche de l'élégance savante, d'autant plus que l'Hispérisme est au plein de sa vogue, peut-être aussi incapacité à bien rendre l'accent de la langue; c'est là, comme dans le *DEB*, un latin scolaire.

Mais le contexte aura changé. Déjà Colomban, qui voyage en Gaule, entend un latin différent de celui qu'il a appris: la correction tourne en hypercorrection; un peu plus tard, Cenn Faelad illustre la fusion des deux écoles, monastique et bardique; les deux civilisations s'entrepénètrent, les moines n'ont plus peur de Cú Chulaind et recopient les épopées celtiques: les celticismes font leur apparition; le prestige de Rome enfin est peut-être ramené à des dimensions plus modestes, le centre des missions est en Irlande, Colomban parle au Pape haut et fort; pour un peu, Rome ne serait plus dans Rome. Cependant, malgré ces restrictions de poids, le *DEB* m'apparaît bien comme un premier état du latin insulaire: Gildas, tourné vers le passé, préfigure largement l'avenir.

J'ai promis de parler de l'unité du *DEB*. Ces réflexions permettent-elles d'avancer la solution du problème? Il n'existe aucune différence notable entre la partie attribuée par certains à l'école d'Aldhelm – c'est-à-dire l'*Historia* – et le reste. La syntaxe est en gros la même et les mêmes types de phrase, les mêmes figures se retrouvent dans les deux parties, avec des proportions variables que la différence des genres pourrait expliquer. Le plus habile des plagiaires ne se serait-il pas livré quelque part? N'est-ce pas par la comparaison de la langue et du style que l'on démasque souvent les faussaires? Ici, le problème se complique, car le style de l'école d'Aldhelm possède assez de traits communs avec celui de Gildas pour qu'un de ses représentants ait pu sans grand mal faire passer sa prose pour celle du moine breton. Cependant le suspect pouvait lâcher dans sa rédaction quelques-uns de ces mots grecs chers à Aldhelm, dont nous ne trouvons pas de trace dans le *DEB*. Je ne pense pas par ailleurs que l'*Historia* soit un hors-d'oeuvre: avant d'admonester ses contemporains, Gildas rappelle le passé et montre que les Bretons ont été punis chaque fois qu'ils se sont écartés de Dieu. Peut-on encore supposer qu'un moine de Malmesbury, monastère saxon, ait osé écrire des lignes si dures pour les ancêtres de son peuple? La question appellerait d'autres développements, mais, pour l'instant, je penche en faveur de l'unité du *DEB*.

Notes

1. Sur le style et sur la syntaxe du *DEB*, voir: *LHEB*, 119, Mohrmann, C., *The Latin of Saint Patrick*, 53, 'The Earliest Continental Irish Latin', *Vigiliae Christianae* XVI (1962), 229
2. Sur la question du latin irlandais et plus généralement insulaire, se référer à l'important chapitre VII (81–156) de Löfstedt, B., *Der hibernolateinische Grammatiker Malsachanus* (Uppsala, 1965), et au compte-rendu que je donne de cet ouvrage dans la *Revue des Etudes Latines* XLIV (1966), 585–8

Notes

3. On trouvera l'essentiel dans Grosjean, P., 'Remarques sur le *De Excidio* attribué à Gildas', *Archivum Latinitatis Medii Aevi* (Bulletin Du Cange) XXV (1955), 155–87
4. *L. H. Sz. Lat. Gr. II*, 113–4
5. *Ibid.*, 293–4; Löfstedt, E., *Syntactica II* (Lund 1933), 390 *et seq.*
6. Svennung, J., *Untersuchungen zur Palladius und zur lateinischen Fach-und Volkssprache* (Uppsala, 1935), 281 *et seq.*
7. *L. H. Sz. Lat. Gr. II*, 162
8. *Ibid.*, 276; Svennung, *Untersuch.*, 276
9. Svennung, *Untersuch.*, 469 *et seq.*
10. *L. H. Sz. Lat. Gr. II*, 389; Bieler, L., 'Libri Epistolarum Sancti Patricii episcopi, Introduction Text and Commentary', Part II, *Classica et Mediaevalia* XII (1951), 143–4
11. Comparer avec Ernout, A., 'Les "Gynaecia" de Caelius Aurelianus', *Revue de Philologie, de Littérature et d'Histoire anciennes* XXX (1956), 189
12. *L. H. Sz. Lat. Gr. II*, 445
13. *Ibid.*, 143
14. *Ibid.*, 276 et 283
15. *Ibid.*, 224, 280 et 282
16. *Ibid.*, 276–7
17. *Ibid.*, 276
18. *Ibid.*, 804
19. *Ibid.*, 447
20. *Ibid.*, 197
21. *Ibid.*, 208
22. *Ibid.*, 179
23. *Ibid.*, 321
24. Schrijnen, J., et Mohrmann, C., *Studien zur Syntax der Briefe des hl. Cyprian II* (Nimègue, 1937), 29
25. *L. H. Sz. Lat. Gr. II*, 320 *et seq.*
26. Perrochat, P., *Recherches sur la valeur et l'emploi de l'infinitif subordonné en latin* (Paris, 1932), 210
27. *L. H. Sz. Lat. Gr. II*, 312
28. *Ibid.*, 374
29. *Ibid.*, 157
30. *Ibid.*, 629
31. *Ibid.*, 614
32. *Ibid.*, 629
33. *Ibid.*, 654
34. *Ibid.*, 605
35. *Ibid.*, 458
36. *Ibid.*, 538
37. *Ibid.*, 576–7
38. Voir sur ce point Marouzeau, J., *L'ordre des mots dans la phrase latine ; I Les groupes nominaux* (Paris, 1922), chapitre I
39. Marouzeau, *op. cit.*, 106 *et seq. ;* 231 *et seq. ; Traité de stylistique latine* (Paris, 1946), 334
40. *DEB*, 36 (47.14) *sed monita tibi profecto non desunt, tum habueris praeceptorem paene totius Britanniae magistrum elegantem*
41. Voir, par exemple, Hoogterp, P. –W., 'Les Vies des Pères du Jura, Etude sur la langue', *Archivum Latinitatis Medii Aevi* IX (1934), 233–4
42. Jackson, K., *LHEB*, 108–10

Notes

43. C'est le point de vue, me semble-t-il, de nombreux savants britanniques; voir par exemple Jackson, *op. cit.*, 119
44. Je me réfère ici aux travaux de Chadwick, N. K., en particulier à *The Age of the Saints in the Early Celtic Church* (Londres, 1961), 49 *et seq.;* Mohrmann, C., *op. cit.*, 229, exploite cette hypothèse
45. *L. H. Sz. Lat. Gr. II*, 58
46. *Ibid.*, 99–100
47. *Ibid.*, 543–4
48. Marouzeau, *L'ordre des mots . . . I*, 133 *et seq.*
49. *L. H. Sz. Lat. Gr. II*, 173–4
50. Cette question demanderait un long développement. J'ai utilisé surtout Löfstedt, B., *op. cit.*, 122 *et seq.*
51. *L. H. Sz. Lat. Gr. II*, 388
52. *Ibid.*, 510
53. *Ibid.*, 621–2 et 624–5. Voir aussi Ernout, A., -Thomas, F., *Syntaxe latine* (Paris 1951, 2ème éd. 1953), 367
54. *L. H. Sz. Lat. Gr. II*, 541
55. *Ibid.*, 680–1
56. *Ibid.*, 679
57. *Ibid.*, 614
58. Schrijnen-Mohrmann, *op. cit.*, I, 35 *et seq.*
59. Bieler, *op. cit.*, 102
60. *L. H. Sz. Lat. Gr. II*, 474
61. Mon relevé n'a porté que sur les 36 premiers chapitres du *DEB*
62. Marouzeau, J., *L'ordre des mots dans la phrase latine*; *II Le verbe* (Paris, 1938), 47 *et seq.*, en particulier 106
63. *Ibid.*, 104 *et seq.*
64. Il s'agit, pour Ruricius, d'un relevé personnel
65. *L. H. Sz. Lat. Gr. II*, 133
66. *Ibid.*, 598–9
67. *Ibid.*, 667–8
68. *Ibid.*, 390
69 .Löfstedt, B., *op. cit.*, 154–5
70. Grosjean, P., '*Confusa Caligo*, Remarques sur les *Hisperica Famina*', *Celtica* III (1956), 85
71. Jenkinson, F. J. H., *The Hisperica Famina* (Cambridge, 1908), XIX–XXII
72. *MGH*, XV, 487–8
73. Une quarantaine au total
74. *HF* n'a que *circius*, que présentent aussi Gildas et Aldhelm et qui est la forme ordinaire; *HF* ignore *catasta* mais donne *caterua ; epimenia* est peut-être simplement un mot technique, voir Stevens, C. E., 'Gildas sapiens', *EHR*, vol. LVI (juillet, 1941), 369
75. Sauf pour Gildas, les chiffres utilises sont tirés des *indices* existants
76. Ni *quis*, ni *quibus* dans la lettre à Ehfrid
77. On voit tout l'intérêt qu'il aura à comparer systématiquement le vocabulaire des *HF* et celui de Gildas
78. Niedermann, M., 'Les dérivés latins en –ōsus dans les *Hisperica Famina*', *Archivum Latinitatis Medii Aevi* XXIII (1953), 75 *et seq.*
79. Pour Ausone, j'utilise les listes que donne Delachaux, A., *La Latinité d'Ausone* (Neuchâtel, 1909)
80. *L. H. Sz. Lat. Gr. II*, 212

Notes

81. Grosjean, '*Confusa Caligo*', 79 *et seq.*
82. Marouzeau, J., *Traité de stylistique latine* (Paris, 1946), 320–1
83. Il ne s'agit là que de quelques exemples
84. J'utilise pour cette étude: Hagendahl, H., *La prose métrique d'Arnobe* (Göteborg, 1937); *La correspondance de Ruricius* (Göteborg, 1952), chapitre III; Braun, R., édition de Quodvultdeus, *Le Livre des Promesses et des Prédictions de Dieu* (Paris, 1964), 675 *et seq.;* Lindholm, G., *Studien zum mittellateinischen Prosarhythmus* (Stockholm, 1963)
85. Voir Cavallin, S., 'Les clausules des hagiographes arlésiens', *Eranos* XLVI (1948), 133 *et seq.*
86. Le pourcentage varie selon les spécialistes
87. Les sous-types en question donneront le *cursus planus*
88. Les sous-types en question donneront le *cursus tardus*
89. Les sous-types en question donneront le *cursus velox*
90. Perret, J., 'Salluste et la prose métrique', *Revue des Etudes Anciennes* LXV (1963) 3–4, 330 *et seq.*
91. Quintilien, *De Institutione oratoria*, IX, 4, 107; Terentianus Maurus, *De Metris*, vers 1436 *et seq.* (*Grammatici Latini*, ed. Keil, H. (Leipzig, 1923), VI, 368)
92. Hadot, P., édition de Marius Victorinus, *Traités théologiques sur la Trinité* (Paris 1960), Commentaire, 1058 et 1071
93. Dans la Ière partie, chapitre IV, de *LHEB*
94. Bieler, L., *The Irish Penitentials*, 37 *et seq.;* Löfstedt, B., *op. cit.*, chapitre VII (voir, par exemple, 117 *et seq.*, et 149)
95. *DEB :* 7 (30.19)

Pagan Motifs and Practices in Christian Art and Ritual in Roman Britain

Jocelyn M. C. Toynbee

The title of this paper, 'Pagan Motifs and Practices in Christian Art and Ritual in Roman Britain,' obviously involves a far larger and more fundamental question, which can only be touched upon here. Is not *all* art unchristian and therefore pagan (and by 'art' I mean, of course, all renderings whether abstract or representational, in such media as sculpture, painting, mosaic-work, metalwork, and so forth, not only those renderings that might be regarded as being of the first flight aesthetically – an impossibly subjective principle of definition)? Can there really be a Christian art, when the Decalogue, which the Christian Church inherited along with the rest of the Jewish Scriptures, appears, on the face of it, to ban art of all kinds absolutely?

As is very well known, some early Christian writers and Church authorities answered this question firmly in the negative: art is forbidden to the Christian. The texts setting forth this view have recently been conveniently collected by Theodor Klauser in an article entitled 'Thoughts on the Origin of Early Christian Art' in the *Zeitschrift für Kirchengeschichte* 1 and 2 (1965). Most uncompromising are the fulminations of the African Tertullian who, invoking the Decalogue, attributed all art to the Devil and roundly declared that an artist's career must be abandoned at the font. Tertullian's notorious rigorism naturally inclines us to take his diatribes with a large grain of salt. In the more mildly worded statements of Clement and Origen of Alexandria, to the effect that art is deceptive, that is, removed from reality and truth, and hence forbidden to a Christian, the influence of Platonic teaching, as well as of the Decalogue, can be detected. Passing from the third into the early years of the fourth century we find the thirty-sixth canon of the Spanish Council of Elvira forbidding paintings of sacred persons on the walls of churches. Whether this decision was caused by local abuses or by a specially rigorous attitude on the Spanish hierarchy's part we cannot tell. It would, however, appear to indicate that in Spain the walls of some pre-Constantinian house-churches had been painted, probably with biblical scenes, just as the baptistery in the house-church at Dura-Europos on the Euphrates, dating from the first half of the third century, had its scriptural murals. And this prompts us to wonder whether pre-fourth-century house-churches in other provinces, such as Britain, and, indeed, in Rome itself, had similar murals of which all traces have disappeared.

But to return to the ban on art – particularly interesting from the point of view of the most important item in this paper is the famous letter of Eusebius, bishop of Caesarea, to Constantine's sister Constantia, assuming this letter to be genuine, which many, including Klauser, hold, while others doubt.[1] Constantia has asked Eusebius to send her a 'portrait' (εἰκών) of Christ as he appeared in the flesh on earth (σαρκίου αὐτοῦ δὴ τοῦ θνητοῦ τὴν εἰκόνα φῂς παρ' ἡμῶν αἰτεῖν) and brings upon herself a sharp episcopal rebuke. Once again the Decalogue is cited as the bishop's basic reason for refusing a request which the royal lady ought to have known to be quite outrageous and wholly unchristian (ἢ ἔστιν ὅτε ἐν 'Εκκλησίᾳ τὸ τοιοῦτον ἢ αὐτὴ ἢ καὶ παρ' ἄλλου τοῦτο ἤκουσας;). Finally, towards the end of the fourth century bishop Epiphanius of Salamis in Cyprus, while travelling in Palestine, was scandalized to see hanging on a church door a curtain embroidered with a representation of a holy personage, either Christ or a saint. Epiphanius promptly ripped up the offending curtain and, on returning home, took upon himself to write to the bishop of Jerusalem urging him to suppress all such idolatrous practices in his diocese.

We have, then, unequivocal evidence that from the early third century until the end of the fourth century at least there were certain Christian leaders who continued to take the Decalogue's ban on art literally and wrote off all artistic manifestations as incompatible with Christianity. We can understand their attitude, living as they did in a still largely pagan, image-worshipping world. All the same, there was, of course, developing throughout this period another, very different school of Christian disciplinary thought, which promoted a flourishing and widespread art that was current in Christian circles and to a large extent specifically Christian in its content, an art known to us at first hand at points as far apart geographically as Rome in the West and Mesopotamia in the East. I am not convinced by Klauser's implication that all this art of wall-painting, mosaic-work, and sarcophagus-carving was of unofficial, lay inspiration as opposed to an official, clerical condemnation of it. Certainly the Church authorities in Rome did not share the latter attitude. As we learn from the *Elenchos*, a work written in Greek early in the third century, probably by Hippolytus, Pope St Zephyrinus charged St Callixtus, round about the year 200, to found and organize the first underground Christian cemetery, τὸ κοιμητήριον (*the* cemetery), which is represented by the oldest part of the catacomb beside the Via Appia that bears St Callixtus' name today; and the principal catacombs dug from that time onwards were official, public burial-places, sponsored, and presumably frequented, by the pope and other ecclesiastics of the Roman Church, who must have seen the paintings in them. And what of the fourth-century apse-mosaic in the Constantinian basilica of Old St Peter's? What of the early-fourth-century floor-mosaics in bishop Theodor's cathedral at Aquileia? What, again, of the third-century wall-paintings in the baptistery of the Dura-Europos house-church, to which I have already alluded? We have no reason to believe that the Dura Christian community was either heretical or run entirely by layfolk, unsupervised by a bishop or by priests.

It would, indeed, seem that by the first half of the third century the main stream of Christian opinion, the general instinct of the Church, interpreted the ban on graven images in the Decalogue as many of the Jews had interpreted it, namely as applying, not to art *per se*, but to the worship of works of art as objects of cult in their own right. The Ark of the original Covenant was adorned with Cherubim of beaten gold: on the veil of the Tabernacle were embroidered Cherubim. In Solomon's Temple there were sculptural representations of Cherubim, lions, oxen, bulls, palms, gourds and pomegranates. On Solomon's throne there were a bull or a lamb and fourteen lions carved. And among the Jews of the Diaspora, both before and after the destruction of Jerusalem by Titus, representational art was widely practised. The paintings and reliefs in the Jewish catacombs of Rome and, above all, the great biblical cycles painted on the walls of the Dura synagogue will suffice as examples. Moreover, to the Christian the Incarnation, Resurrection, and Ascension have made all the difference. God by becoming Man in Christ and remaining Man in Christ for all eternity has endowed human nature with a share in his Divinity; and in this way he has bestowed a new significance and dignity upon the works of man, including his works of art, when they are viewed in their right perspective and given their appropriate place in the hierarchy of values. There was no doctrinal disagreement between the two schools of thought in the early Church: both were equally convinced of the sinfulness of image-worship. But while the one school was obsessed by the dangers of art as possibly opening a door to idolatry, the other school was convinced of its value for expressing the creed of the faithful in a visual language and for instructing them through the eye in its tenets. To this second school of thought the *raison d'être* of religious art was to be the medium of a sacred message. The figure or scene is never an end in itself: it always points to something beyond itself.

If we may, then, legitimately speak of an early Christian art in the Roman Empire as a whole and in Roman Britain in particular, there is one more well-known fact to recall about it. It was essentially a decorative art, born of the natural human urge to fill empty surfaces, in other words, an art that was applied to, and subordinated to, places, structures such as vaults, walls and floors, and objects such as sarcophagi, textiles, and metal items used by Christians. Independent works of Christian art of the period running from *c.* 200 to *c.* 500, such as sculptures in the round and self-contained 'easel' paintings, were extremely rare and perhaps deliberately shunned as resembling too closely pagan cult statues and votive pictures. Practically all that we have from this period of possibly Christian statuary in the round are the small figures of sheep-bearing shepherds – figures which could, as Klauser has argued elsewhere,[2] have been regarded as symbols of the virtue of *philanthropia*, pagan as well as Christian,[3] but to which the Christians would surely have given a more particular interpretation as the Pastor Bonus in the light of Matthew xviii. 12–14, Luke xv. 5, and John x. 11–16, as also of Psalm 23, Ezekiel xxxiv, and Isaiah xi. 11. This distinction between applied and 'pure' art, so to speak, does not, of course, meet the case of the paintings in the Spanish churches or of Epiphanius' curtain. But it might, perhaps, partly, although by no means entirely, help to explain Eusebius' letter to Constantia. From the context it appears that the 'portrait' of Christ that she wanted was a relatively small, self-contained, portable picture, probably painted on a wooden tablet, since the bishop maintains that such things must at all costs be avoided lest Christians should be thought to carry about their God in image like the idolaters (ἵνα μὴ δοκῶμεν δικὴν εἰδωλολατρούντων τὸν Θεὸν ἡμῶν ἐν εἰκόνι περιφέρειν). And in fact most of the representations of Christ that we have in the art of the third and fourth centuries show him either symbolically, as the Pastor Bonus, for example, or with other figures in a scene, not isolated in a way that might be suggestive of a cult-image.

The examples of Romano-Christian art in Britain which provide our special interest here are all of the applied, decorative kind – designs on mosaic pavements, wall-paintings, and representations on minor objects. And our concern is with those works in Roman Britain in which pagan motifs, either by their association, close or remote, with specifically Christian subjects, motifs, and inscriptions, or for some other concrete reason, appear to have been regarded as capable of a Christian interpretation and to have been utilized to express Christian ideas and teaching. This utilization would certainly have outraged Tertullian, Clement, Origen, the Spanish bishops at Elvira, Eusebius, and Epiphanius. Yet it was no insular idiosyncracy, but a widespread phenomenon throughout the early Christian world; and elsewhere in the Roman Empire, although not in Britain, this 'baptism,' so to speak, of pagan motifs can also be deduced from their presence in definitely Christian places of cult and burial.

The large mosaic pavement discovered in 1963 in a field in the village of Hinton St Mary in northern Dorset and acquired by, and relaid in, the British Museum in 1965, is now well known and has been published and fully illustrated by me in the *J.R.S.* 54 (1964), 7–14, frontispiece and plates I–VII. I do not propose to recapitulate my detailed description of the pavement here: I shall merely recall its essential features and make a few additional points connected with it (see pl. 1). It carpeted a room measuring 28 by 19 feet – a room which was either an integral part of, or closely associated with (this point has yet to be established by excavation), a country villa of the fourth century. The room, which has an east–west long axis, is divided into two unequal portions by two short cross-walls (already, at the time of the discovery, largely robbed out) that project at right-angles from the long walls and are linked in the central area of the chamber by a mosaic panel of *peltae* pattern. The eastern (in the British Museum, western) and larger portion of the pavement is a square, in the centre of which is a roundel containing the famous male bust, originally facing east, with the Chi-Rho monogram behind the head and flanked by pomegranates.

Four half-circles or lunettes surround the central roundel, one containing a tree, each of the other three a lively scene in which a hound chases or confronts a stag or hind. In each corner of the square is a quarter-circle or quadrant containing a male bust: two of the busts are flanked by pomegranates, two by rosettes. The western (in the British Museum, eastern) and smaller portion of the pavement is of oblong shape and comprises a central square, in which is inscribed a circle, flanked by two rectangular panels. In the circle is the scene, originally facing west, of Bellerophon on Pegasus slaying the Chimaera; and in each of the lateral panels is an animal-hunt scene of the same type as those in three of the lunettes, but on a larger scale and more elaborate as regards the wooded setting. It is to be noted that no human hunters are depicted in any of the hunting-scenes and that in none of them do the hounds wound or kill the stags and hinds, who seem to be rather enjoying the chase.

In their general scheme of composition, as well as in a number of stylistic details, into which I need not enter here, the Hinton St Mary mosaic and the most familiar of the three figured Roman pavements found in the late eighteenth century at Frampton in western Dorset resemble one another so closely that there can be no doubt that they are products of the same firm or workshop. (The Frampton mosaics (see pls. 2, 3) are lost, but are known from the fine coloured drawings of them published by Samuel Lysons in his *Reliquiae Romano-Britannicae I* (London 1813)). On this piece, as on that from Hinton St Mary, the smaller portion of the pavement consists of a central square containing a circle and flanked by oblong panels and is linked to the larger portion by a mosaic panel of *peltae* pattern connecting the inner ends of two short projecting cross-walls; while the larger portion of the pavement is a square with a central roundel surrounded by four lunettes.[4] The main deviations from the scheme of the Hinton St Mary pavement are that here the corners of this large square are filled by small squares, instead of by quadrants, and that one side of the large square throws off an apse, with the famous Chi-Rho monogram placed in the centre of the running floral scroll in the narrow panel on the chord.

As is well known, the Chi-Rho monogram was employed by pagans as a numerical symbol and as a ligature certainly before, and possibly during and after, the time of Constantine. But I know of no example in pagan art of the appearance of the monogram on so large a scale and in such positions of prominence as on the Hinton St Mary and Frampton pavements. No unequivocally pagan personage was, to my knowledge, ever shown with the Chi-Rho behind his head. On both of these floors the monogram occupies a central place of honour that would seem to preclude it from being regarded as the random choice of a Christian symbol by a pagan proprietor. On these mosaics it must be deliberately Christian, the monogram of Christ.

We may take it, then, that this Frampton pavement and that from Hinton St Mary are works of Christian art or at any rate Christian-sponsored works. How do the other motifs on the Frampton floor, all of pagan origin, fit into a Christian context? Before attempting to answer this question in regard to each motif, I should like to recall the important fact that by the fourth century the representation in *pagan* art of the traditional Graeco-Roman myths, gods, and personifications and of many motifs from daily life (such as hunting-scenes) had increasingly tended to shed their literal meaning and assume an allegorical, symbolic, and quasi-spiritual significance. This is particularly evident in the sphere of funerary iconography. But there can be little doubt that the selection of themes for domestic wall-paintings, mosaics, and other forms of decoration was not infrequently determined by ideas concerning death and the life beyond the grave to which a spiritual rebirth in this world forms the prelude. If in pagan circles such motifs were regarded, not as depicting actual events and persons, but as allegories and symbols that conveyed moral truths and other-world concepts, their adoption by Christians is easier to understand.

Next to the monogram at Frampton is a mask of Neptune, with a couplet in heptameters describing his functions and a procession of dolphins converging upon him from all four sides of the larger square. In pagan art Neptune or Oceanus and sea-beasts are common symbols of the voyage of the dead to the Blessed Isles; and on occasion Christian art adopted them to symbolize the journey of the soul to paradise. Painted Oceanus masks occur in the Roman catacombs;[5] and a procession of dolphins, complete with Neptune's trident, appears on the lid of an unequivocally Christian sarcophagus discovered beneath the pavement of Old St Peter's.[6] Into one of the four files of dolphins at Frampton is intruded a Cupid, also named in an inscription. Cupids are very familiar symbols of souls in bliss in paradise both in pagan and in early Christian art. In Christian contexts they are found, for instance, among catacomb paintings,[7] on the mosaic pavement of the fourth-century cathedral at Aquileia,[8] and on the fourth-century Christian sarcophagus of Junius Bassus.[9] In the central roundel on the smaller portion of the Frampton pavement is Bacchus mounted on a panther. Bacchus was, of course, a 'saviour-god,' a token of triumph over death and of after-life beatitude; and painted Bacchic masks, figures of Maenads, and so forth are known in the catacombs.[10] In the two panels flanking Bacchus are hunting-scenes, this time with human hunters engaged, such hunts being allegories of the pleasant pastimes of paradise to the pagan, of struggle with the forces of evil to the Christian. In the small squares in the corners of the larger square are scenes, one of which was already lost, apparently from the story of Venus and Adonis – perhaps an allegory of the power of love to bring back life from the grave. The contents of the four lunettes were also already lost. Since the Hinton St Mary discovery the scene in the central roundel of the larger square has taken on a new interest. Only part of this scene was intact when the mosaic came to light. Lysons restored it as a mounted hunter spearing a feline of some sort. Yet the feature in front of the rider's leg is not easy to explain except as the spring of the wing of Pegasus; and Mr David Neal of the Ministry of Public Building and Works has done for me what I personally consider to be a very convincing restoration of the scene as that of Bellerophon slaying the Chimaera (below). If this restoration is right, we have a second instance from Dorset of the story of Bellerophon rendered on a work of Christian art in Roman Britain.

Reconstruction as Bellerophon and the Chimaera of the Frampton mosaic 'Hunter' Roundel

On the Frampton pavement Christ is represented by his monogram. At Hinton St Mary we have his bust with the monogram behind his head. In the *J.R.S.* I have argued at length that this person is undoubtedly no pagan, nor an ordinary Christian, clerical or lay, nor a Christian emperor (he has no imperial dress and no imperial insignia), nor a Christian saint (there is no name inscribed beside him and he has no distinguishing attributes), but that this must be the εἰκών of Christ himself. The long locks of hair falling beside the neck, the dress, *tunica* and *pallium*, and the pomegranates, familiar symbols of immortality, in the field – all support this interpretation. In the art of the fourth and fifth centuries there are many more examples of Christ with the monogram behind the head, with or without a nimbus, than there are of any other persons so equipped, whether emperors or saints. For myself, I find this εἰκών, with its composed expression and large, dark, rather penetrating eyes, most impressive. Eusebius of Caesarea, had he visited Hinton St Mary, would have been, most probably, deeply shocked, in spite of this being a decorative, non-portable picture. It does, moreover, show Christ in relative isolation and neither symbolically nor as a figure in a scene. Epiphanius of Salamis in Cyprus would certainly have smashed up both the Frampton and the Hinton St Mary mosaics and have lodged a stinging protest with the local ordinary. And one wonders what both of them would have thought of the juxtaposition on these two pavements of Christ and Bellerophon.

The explanation of Bellerophon slaying the Chimaera in a Christian *milieu* is not far to seek. The scene is an allegory of the victory of life and virtue over death and evil, of truth over error – a Christianized pagan allegory, drawn from that traditional storehouse of Graeco-Roman mythology that was the fourth-century Christian's cultural heritage. Notions of this kind would in no way – and certainly not at this time – have involved that worship of false gods or idols which St Paul so roundly condemned, or placed pagan deities on a par with Christ. Personally I can see no difficulty in a Christian allegorical Bellerophon – or in a Christian allegorical Hercules, if we had one in Roman Britain; and Professor Marcel Simon of Strasbourg University shares my view, as is revealed by his book *Hercule et le Christianisme* (Paris 1955) and by a recent article, 'Bellérophon chrétien,' which was inspired by the publication of the Hinton St Mary mosaic.[11] Just as the Old Testament stories of David and Goliath, Samson and the Lion, and so forth were used by the early Christians as types of Christ's victory over evil and death, so (allowing for the difference between historical and mythological personages) we can imagine the pagan converts to Christianity saying: 'We, too, have had our ideals of heroic courage, our Hercules and our Bellerophon, typifying the fulfilment to come.' And if the question is asked – 'Why should the Christian owner of the Hinton St Mary room have chosen a pagan episode to illustrate allusively Christ's victory over death and evil instead of a straightforward Christian one?' – the answer lies, I think, in the strongly marked preference shown by all Christian art of the third and fourth centuries for scenes that refer indirectly, rather than directly, to New Testament events and teaching. Old Testament episodes far outnumber New Testament ones in catacomb-painting in Rome and on early Christian carved sarcophagi – partly, no doubt, to emphasize the fact that Israel's history was fulfilled in Christ and because to the Christians of the time the Old Testament was still, as it was to Our Lord, *the* Scriptures. Similarly, the choice of a pagan myth may have been partly determined by the wish to emphasise that the pagan world had also had its *praeparatio Evangelii* and that some light had relieved its darkness.

Marcel Simon's application in his new paper to pagan legend of the phrase 'le vestibule de la vérité' becomes especially pointed when we consider the use

1

1 Mosaic Pavement from Hinton St Mary, Dorset

2

3

2 and 3 Mosaic Pavements found at Frampton, Dorset

4

5

4 Mosaic Pavement (Bellerophon and the Chimaera) from Lullingstone, Kent

5 Mosaic Pavement (Europa and the Bull) from Lullingstone, Kent

6

6 Mosaic Pavement (Orpheus and the Beasts) from Barton Farm, near Cirencester

to which the mosaic room at Hinton St Mary could have been put. The fact that the two main pictures face in opposite directions seems to me to indicate that they were on occasion screened off from one another by a strongly marked partition, such as a wooden folding door or a heavy curtain, between the ends of the cross-walls. Could it be that this room was sometimes used for formal Christian worship, say on Sundays, and that the western portion was a kind of narthex, while the eastern portion formed a chapel proper? When Mass was celebrated in the early Church the catechumens were, as everyone knows, admitted to the first part only, to the part known as the 'Liturgy of the Word,' preceding the 'Liturgy of the Eucharist,' that is, the actual sacrifice, which begins with the Offertory. Up to that point we can think of the priest standing sideways on the *peltae* panel, praying with and reading to all the people in the whole room, whereas at that point we can imagine a door between the two portions of the room being closed or a curtain being drawn across and the catechumens being left in the western portion, with Bellerophon, while the baptised Christians occupied the eastern section. In that section, in the space between the *peltae* panel and the central roundel, where the mosaic shows distinct discolouration, there is room for a small portable altar and for a priest standing behind it and facing east as he celebrated in full view of the people, who could have filled all the remaining spaces round the Chi-Rho bust medallion. The people would then have looked across the εἰκών of Christ on the floor to the altar on which he was present sacramentally. At the Communion the members of the congregation could have stood in their places, while the priest passed round to distribute the sacred species to them. There would, of course, have been no communion rail. Obviously, no church of standard type would have had its altar just inside the entrance from the narthex. But a house-church would have had to adapt itself to the space and arrangements available.

There remain some subsidiary motifs on the Hinton St Mary pavement to be considered. The Tree of Life was a conception shared by pagans and early Christians: ξυλὸν γὰρ ζωῆς ἐστιν ὁ Χριστός, wrote Asterius the Sophist in his First Homily on the Psalms.[12] Harder to interpret are the four corner busts in the large square, with their upstanding, wind-blown locks of red hair above the brow. It is, in fact, these locks of hair that give us the clue to the busts' identity, combined with the evidence of the other two figured mosaics found at Frampton.[13] One of these shows the bust of Oceanus in the central roundel surrounded by four octagons each containing the bust of a Wind-personification with a conch and upstanding locks of red hair. I would not like to claim that the crosses on this mosaic are true Christian crosses and not just abstract motifs from the mosaicist's pattern-book: but the way in which they stand out is, perhaps, noteworthy. The possibly Christian symbolic use of Oceanus and of dolphins, the latter here depicted in the half-octagons and elongated hexagons, we have already considered in connection with the Chi-Rho Frampton pavement. The third of the figured Frampton mosaics was incomplete when found, but enough remained to show yet another set of four Wind-personifications, this time in roundels and with head-wings as well as conches. As I have already pointed out in my paper in the *J.R.S.*, St Irenaeus, writing *c.* 185, relates the number of the Gospels to that of the four main winds and of the earth's four quarters, to which is wafted the life-giving message of the Word of God;[14] and it could be that the Hinton St Mary busts are partly Winds, with rosettes and pomegranates, symbols of life and immortality, substituted for the head-wings and conches, and partly the Four Evangelists.

In the left-hand half of the third Frampton pavement there are some sea-beasts, but the central scene is lost. So is that in the right-hand half. There the small square panels that alternate with the Winds roundels seem to contain figures of gods – Jupiter (only the bearded head is left), Mars, Neptune, and possibly Apollo slaying the Python. Mars and Apollo could be taken as symbols of victory, Jupiter and Neptune as representing the created cosmic powers of sky and ocean. In a narrow panel, also in the right-hand half, is an animal-hunt scene, with two hounds chasing a stag and a hind in a setting of trees, precisely similar to the animal-hunts from Hinton St Mary. On both of these pavements the animal-hunt scenes could allude to the natural world as created by God or to the teeming life of paradise: the hounds, as I have said, do not wound or kill the stags and hinds. Or the stags and hinds could represent Christians pursued by sin and pleasure in the form of hounds.

Both at Hinton St Mary and at Frampton the Chi-Rho monogram and the rendering of Bellerophon were strictly contemporary, parts in each case of the same mosaic pavement. The only other quite certain mosaic representation of Bellerophon in Roman Britain so far discovered, that at Lullingstone in Kent, is more loosely in a Christian context. As is now very well known, this villa in its fourth-century phase comprised an apsed *triclinium* with figured mosaics and, immediately to the north of the *triclinium*, a series of three, possibly four, small, interconnecting rooms, which seem, to judge by the paintings on their walls, to have been set apart for Christian use (plan, p. 187).[15] I would not like to claim quite categorically that this complex was a house-church and that the largest chamber in it, that on the eastern side, was a chapel, since no liturgical fittings of any kind, comparable to the baptistery fittings in the Dura-Europos house-church, have come to light. But I would say that there is a strong probability in favour of this interpretation being right – for three main reasons. First there is the fact of this complex being made self-contained by blocking up access to the westernmost room from the western out-buildings of the villa and from the corridor leading to the apsed *triclinium;* and of the opening up in that westernmost room of a door leading into the room immediately east of it and of another door leading outside the house on the north. Secondly there is the discovery of Christian paintings that had fallen from the walls of two of these chambers – a row of six Christian figures, three at least in the *Orans* attitude, from the western wall of the so-called chapel, and three large Chi-Rhos, each in a wreath, one from the south wall of the so-called antechamber and two from the south wall and east wall respectively of the so-called chapel. Thirdly there is the fact that the coin evidence suggests that the Christian rooms continued in use after the domestic portions of the villa had ceased to function as such.

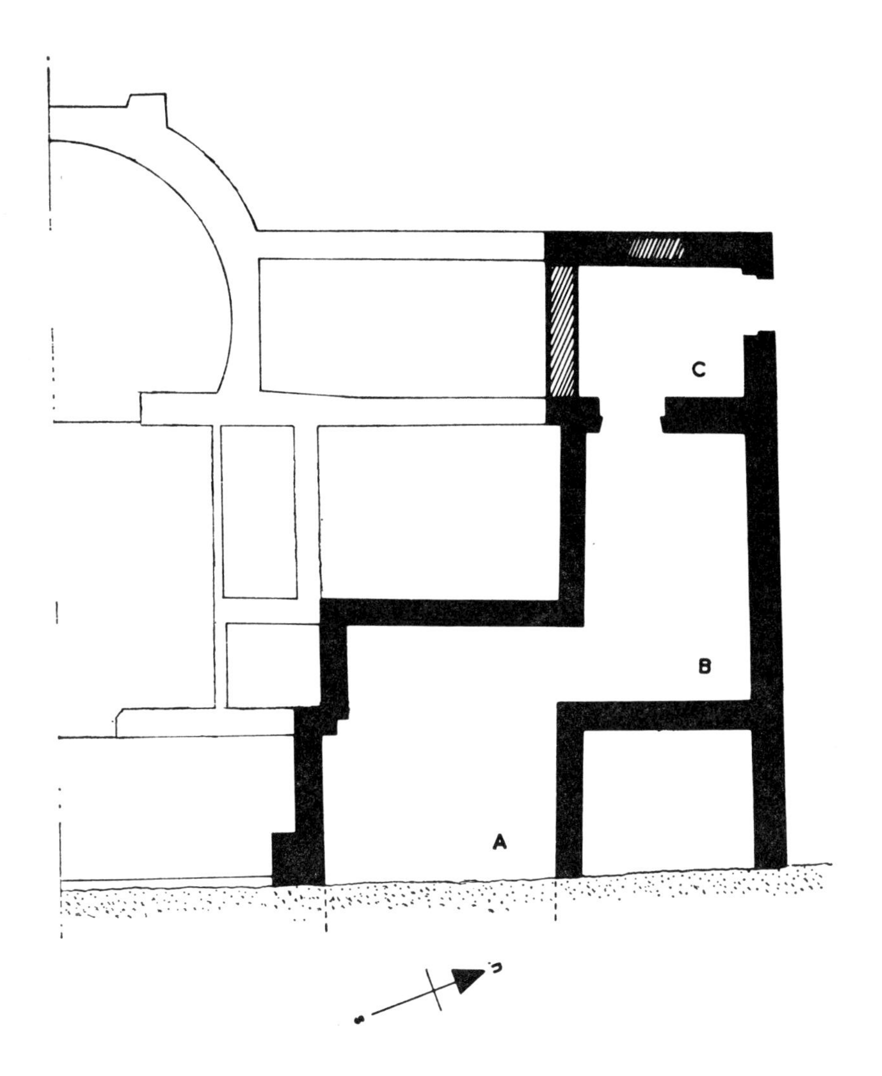

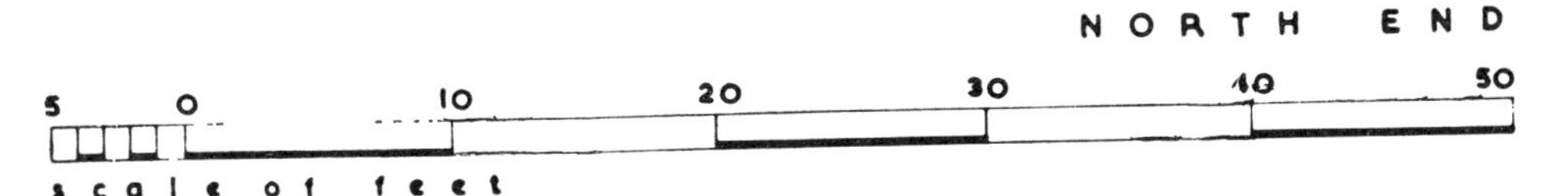

Plan of the Christian rooms in the Lullingstone Villa

The mosaics in the *triclinium* of the villa occupy both the square portion of the room and the apse, the Bellerophon scene covering the floor of the former, an Europa scene that of the latter (see pls. 4, 5).[16] Since these mosaics and the Christian paintings are not in the same room, but only in adjacent rooms, and the Christian rooms were definitely segregated from the *triclinium* by the blocking-wall already mentioned, I am inclined to believe that the mosaics were laid perhaps a decade or so before the owner of the villa embraced the Christian Faith and systematized the Christian complex. But at any rate he seems to have seen no reason, after he had been baptised, for covering over or smashing up his *triclinium* figured pavements. Both the paintings and the mosaics would appear to have led a peaceful, ecumenical coexistence.

Bellerophon would have been as acceptable to this Christian householder as he was to those at Frampton and Hinton St Mary. Nor would the busts of the Four Seasons that surround Bellerophon in this picture have caused him the slightest difficulty. Early-Christian art borrowed these personifications not infrequently from pagan funerary art, where they symbolize the blessings of the after-life or the endless cycle of eternity. We find them, for instance, on the mosaic floor of the fourth-century cathedral at Aquileia,[17] where, incidentally, Pegasus likewise appears, this time in his own right, as a symbol of resurrection from the dead.[18] But how would Europa have fitted into our Kentish Christian villa-owner's picture? Well, the elegiac couplet that accompanies the scene, with its playful allusion to the storm at sea in *Aeneid* I, gives this rather naughty episode a moral twist:—

invida si tauri vidisset Iuno natatus
iustius Aeolias isset adusque domos.

Jupiter was a married man and had no business to go a-wenching in this carefree style: he and his prize most certainly deserved a thorough sousing. Furthermore, even so lighthearted an episode as this could be seen to have its serious implications. In pagan funerary art such scenes of rape or carrying off very often appear as allegories of the violent sundering at death of soul and body and of the former's journey to the other world. We get, for example, the Rape of the Leucippidae by the Dioscuri, the Rape of Ganymede by the Eagle, the Rape of Persephone by Pluto and, on an elaborate grave-monument at Celeia in Jugoslavia, the Rape of Europa by Jupiter.[19]

Of all the stories from Greek mythology rendered in mosaic on Romano-British floors none was more favoured than that of Orpheus and the Beasts. At least nine examples are known to exist or have existed. All are of the fourth century; and there would seem to be a concrete reason for suggesting the possibility that all or some were crypto-Christian when we recall the well-known Christus/Orpheus paintings in the Roman catacombs[20] and Eusebius' statement, in his *De laudibus Constantini* 14, that the Logos tames mankind as Orpheus tamed wild beasts, where we have an explicit analogy drawn between Christ and Orpheus. The best surviving British Orpheus pavements are those from

Barton Farm, just outside Cirencester (see pl. 6), and at Woodchester, near Stroud.[21] Both are from the same workshop. And this particular scheme of the Orpheus scene, with the birds and beasts in procession in unbroken concentric circles, is only known, so far, on mosaics in Britain. Such mosaics would undoubtedly have met with Eusebius' disapproval had the persons who commissioned them been Christians. Yet they do, after all, but externalize the mental picture that his own words evoke.

The Vyne Ring (*from a drawing*)

A good instance of a British Christian object with a pagan motif, or rather of an object that was probably pagan originally before it passed into Christian hands, is thc famous gold signet-ring, long in the possession of the late Sir Charles Chute of The Vyne, near Basingstoke (above).[22] Whether the ring is still at The Vyne, I do not know. On the bezel is a female bust labelled *VENVS*. Engraved on the hoop, clearly at a later stage, is a secondary, Christian inscription reading *SENICIANE VIVAS IIN DE*(o). The engraver, through some blunder, doubled the *I* of *IN* and so left himself no room for the *O* of *DEO*. For myself, I am strongly inclined to agree with those who see no reason for not equating this ring with that mentioned in the well-known lead curse found on the site of the temple of Nodens at Lydney in Gloucestershire. On this tablet a certain Silvianus curses a certain Senicianus for being in possession of a ring which he (Silvianus) had lost after promising half of its value to the god Nodens. Did some Christian more zealous than strictly conscientious steal the ring to save it from being devoted to a pagan purpose? Did he have a Christian inscription engraved on it and did he present it to a Christian friend, Senicianus? And did Silvianus know that Senicianus had got it? The temple of Nodens dates from the time of the pagan revival under the influence of Julian the Apostate, when feeling between pagans and Christians might have been running high. The Vyne ring is said to have been found at or near Silchester. But since the Lydney temple had a guest-house attached to it, it is clear that devotees travelled there from distant parts of the province. Silvianus could have lost the ring before setting out from Silchester on a pilgrimage to the shrine of Nodens. At any rate, the Christian Senicianus seems to have had no scruples about possessing a ring adorned with a bust of Venus: he might possibly have looked upon it as a symbol of Christian love. This is not, perhaps, wholly fanciful when we recall that the late-fourth-century toilet-casket from the silver treasure found on the Esquiline and now in the British Museum, which was made as a wedding-present for a Christian couple, shows the scene of Venus at her toilet juxtaposed to the Chi-Rho monogram and the inscription *SECVNDE ET PROIECTA VIVATIS IN DEO* (below).[23]

The Lid of the Proiecta Casket in the British Museum

The title of this paper includes pagan practices in Romano-British Christian ritual. But of such things I know of only one possible instance. This is a burial found in 1901 in Sycamore Terrace, York, consisting of a coffin in which was a female skeleton together with glass vessels and jewelry and an open-work inscription in bone reading *S[OR]OR AVE VIVAS IN DEO* (below).[24] The grave-goods might well suggest that this burial was pagan, with a Christian object intruded. But that need not have been the case. The grave could have been

Bone Mount in the form of an inscription, from York

Christian, the goods being placed there to honour the dead, not for her use in the after-life. Of such a Christian attitude we have again from Rome a striking example. On the south side of Old St Peter's there once stood a circular Roman mausoleum which was converted into the Church of Santa Petronilla. When this building was demolished in 1544 it was found to contain, among other important burials, that of Maria, wife of the emperor Honorius. Lanciani, in his *Pagan and Christian Rome*, published in 1895, gives a vivid account (203–5) of this discovery. There lay the body of the Christian empress, accompanied by two silver caskets that contained cups, lamps, jewelled vases, jewelry, and toilet articles, a number of these items having been her wedding-presents. The objects themselves have, needless to say, long since vanished. But Lanciani quotes from a contemporary, sixteenth-century record. What was done in Rome could surely have been done in provincial Eburacum.

Notes

1. *PG* 20. 1845–50: *Epistola ad Constantiam Augustam*
2. Klauser, T., 'Studien zur Entstehungsgeschichte der christlichen Kunst I', *Jahrbuch für Antike und Christentum* I (1958), 20–51; *ibid.*, VIII, 8–9 (1965–6), 126–70
3. The only other early-Christian sculptures in the round known to me are the marble group in the Cleveland Museum, U.S.A., said to come from Antioch, attributed to the fourth century, and showing four episodes from the story of Jonah – Jonah being swallowed by the whale, Jonah being vomited by the whale, Jonah reclining beneath the gourd-tree, and Jonah praying (*Archaeology* xix (1966), 280–1). These, however, are narrative sculptures, 'reliefs in the round' meant to be viewed principally from one side: they could not have been regarded as objects of cult, any more than paintings, mosaics, and reliefs on sarcophagi depicting these events were so regarded. (My attention was kindly drawn to these pieces by Mr R. M. Harrison.) The marble Jonah group from Asia Minor now in the Metropolitan Museum of Art, New York, shows the ship worked in the round, while the figures in the episodes of the whale's swallowing and vomiting Jonah are in high relief
4. Lysons, S. *Reliquiae Romano-Brittanicae I* (London, 1813), pl. V

Notes

5. Wilpert, J., *Die Malereien der Katakomben Roms* (Feiburg-im-Breisgau 1901), pl. CXXXIV, a
6. Toynbee, J. M. C., and Ward Perkins, J. B., *The Shrine of St Peter and the Vatican Excavations* (London, 1956), 90–1, pl. XXIX
7. Wilpert, *op. cit.*, pls. V, LIII
8. Brusin, G., and Zovatto, P. L., *Monumenti paleocristiani di Aquileia e Grado* (Udine, 1957), 108, fig. 48
9. Gerke, F., *Der Sarkophag des Iunius Bassus* (Berlin, 1936), pls. XXXII, XXXIII
10. Wilpert, *op. cit.*, pl. VIII; De Rossi, G. B., *Roma sotterranea II* (Rome 1867), pl. XVIII, 1
11. *Mélanges J. Carcopino* (Paris, 1966), 889–903
12. *Asterii Sophistae Commentariorum in Psalmos quae supersunt:* homilia I, 5: ed. Richard, M., (Oslo, 1956)
13. Lysons, *op. cit.*, pl. IV
14. *Adversus haereses* III, xi, 8
15. Meates, G. W., *Lullingstone Roman Villa* (London, 1953), figs. 10–13, b; pls. XLII–XLVI
16. *Ibid.*, pls. III–IX
17. Brusin and Zovatto, *op. cit.*, 88, fig. 36
18. *Ibid.*, 26, fig. 3
19. Klemenc, J., *Rimske Izkopanine u Šempetru* (Ljubljana, 1961), pls. XXXIV, XXXVI
20. Wilpert, *op. cit.*, pl. XXXVII
21. Toynbee, J. M. C., *Art in Roman Britain* (London, 1962, 2nd ed. 1963), 198–9, nos. 185–6, pls. CCXXI, CCXXII
22. *Toynbee* 1953, 20, fig. 6; Goodchild, R. G., 'The Curse and the Ring,' *Antiquity* 27 (1953), 100–2
23. Dalton, O. M., *Catalogue of Early Christian Antiquities in the British Museum* (London, 1901), no. 304, fig. on p. 61
24. Toynbee, *op. cit.*, pl. IV, fig. 4; *Royal Commission on Historical Monuments (England); Eburacum* (H.M.S.O., 1962), 135, no. 150, pl. LXV

Sub-Roman Cemeteries in Somerset

Philip A. Rahtz

Sub-Roman cemeteries were first so-named by C. W. Phillips in his Dark Age map.[1] They can be defined as those cemeteries of the immediate post-Roman period in areas which were fully Romanized in the fourth century, but where there is a long gap between the breakdown of central Roman authority and the establishment of Saxon settlement. The gap is likely to extend into the fifth and sixth centuries over the greater part of western England, and well into the seventh century in Somerset and South Wales. Little is known about sub-Roman settlement in these areas, but it is generally agreed that land which was economically productive in the fourth century is likely to have continued in use, even if the population was somewhat reduced by economic disintegration, plague and violence. It is not easy to be sure which *are* sub-Roman cemeteries; they are likely to be at least nominally Christian in the mode of burial (extended inhumations with heads to west) and to be deficient in grave-goods. This serves to distinguish them from contemporary pagan Saxon cemeteries, but not from Christian cemeteries of Roman, Saxon, or later date. These, however, are more likely to be associated with churches, and with nuclei of Saxon settlement. Sub-Roman cemeteries on the other hand are usually associated with known late Roman sites. I have described them as if they were cemeteries of the lay population. But it is clearly impossible to separate them from monastic cemeteries, unless we can demonstrate that the settlement with which they are associated cannot be monastic. At least half of the cemeteries on the Dark Age map may indeed belong to Celtic monasteries, which are themselves associated with late Roman sites. Six are in Somerset and one in South Wales.

Of the seven cemeteries so-named, two are dug through the ruins of Roman villas; in two the graves are in and around the ruins of a Roman temple; one is near a building in use in the fifth century, one is outside a Roman town, and the last is on an open hill-top near a hill-fort. At Llantwit Major in Glamorgan, many graves were cut through tessellated floors in one wing of a Roman villa, the rest of which may have remained in use. At Winthill, Banwell, near Weston-super-Mare, many skeletons were found among the ruins of a large and prosperous villa. At Henley Wood, near Yatton, burials were cut through the destruction levels of a late Roman temple and also laid out in rows outside; close by is the hillfort of North Cadbury which has yielded sherds of imported sixth-century pottery. At Blaise Castle, Bristol, east–west graves cut across what is almost certainly another temple inside a hill-fort; at Brean Down, on the coast, there is an extensive cemetery, graves of which appear from time to time in the eroding sand-cliff. This cemetery is remote from any area of settlement, but close to a fourth-century temple, which was partly demolished to build an east–west structure, in use in the fifth century, as shown by the coin evidence.

These five cemeteries have so far only been examined superficially, but the other two have been excavated more thoroughly. At Camerton there is a cemetery outside the small Roman town on the Fosseway; it contained over one hundred graves, of which some contained Roman finds, and a few grave-goods of seventh-century Anglo-Saxon character. Miss Hyslop has recently described this as a Christian Saxon cemetery of late date,[2] but it may well have been a sub-Roman one in which the seventh-century finds belong to the latest phase.

The last cemetery, Cannington, has been largely destroyed by quarrying during the last century. The remaining part, of some 350 graves, was excavated in 1962–3.[3] If the area known to have contained graves had a similar density, the total number of interments must have exceeded five thousand. Only two graves, both babies, had associated finds; they include an amber bead and a glass polychrome bead of pagan Anglo-Saxon type, and a perforated Roman coin, a silver bracelet, and triple-foliated brooch of sub-Roman character – the brooch may be as late as the eighth century. The graves seem to have been clustered originally around the grave of a young girl under a mound. This was marked by a structure of slabs, and was approached through an area virtually free of graves, by a path. This was worn into the limestone rock and contained several finds of late Roman date. The only other structure was a circular trench on the hill summit, with traces of rough polygonal walls, with a single grave in the middle. This would be a late or sub-Roman shrine or mausoleum, or conceivably an early Christian church. It seems likely that the Cannington cemetery covered several centuries, with outside limits of the fourth and eighth centuries.

Its excavation prompted inquiries about the Christian settlement to which it belonged. Not far away at Combwich, at the mouth of the Parrett, parts of a considerable settlement have been found in clay pits at a depth of some eight feet – buildings, skeletons and finds – which were inundated by the marine transgression of the later Roman period. Flooding, and the vulnerable position of the mouth of the Parrett to piratical raiders, may have persuaded the inhabitants to move inland to a drier and more secure place. Close to our cemetery is a hill-fort: Cannington Camp. The main ramparts are Iron Age B, but there is a subsidiary rampart on the south side; an excavation behind this located a late Roman occupation layer and wattle and daub, but no I.A. material. Here then may be the settlement for our cemetery beginning in late Roman times and going on in the vicinity of the hill-fort for possibly three centuries or more.

Large-scale excavation of these cemeteries can thus provide much information not only on our sub-Roman Christians themselves from a study of their skeletons, and their religious practices, but also about their settlements and population. Of those I have described, only Cannington and Camerton can really be shown to be of sub-Roman date and culture, and not that of a monastic community. There must be many more, not only in Somerset and South Wales, but also in Devon and the West Midlands. Their discovery and excavation would clearly be very informative about sub-Roman Christian settlement.

Notes

1. Phillips, C. W., 'Map of Britain in the Dark Ages' (Ordnance Survey, 1966)
2. Hyslop, M., 'Two Anglo-Saxon Cemeteries at Chamberlain's Barn, Leighton Buzzard, Bedfordshire', *Arch. J.* CXX (1963), espec. 190
3. M.O.P.B.W. excavation by the writer, 1963; see note in *Med. Arch.* VIII (1964), 237

An Early Christian Cemetery at Ancaster

D. R. Wilson

Ancaster lies on Ermine Street about twenty miles south of Lincoln, where the limestone ridge of Lincoln Edge is interrupted by a gap allowing easy passage from west to east. An early Roman fort was placed on the low ground within the Gap itself at the natural crossroads, where an Iron-Age settlement already existed. A civilian settlement succeeded the fort and received a conventional defensive system of rampart, wall and ditches about the beginning of the third century A.D. Inhumation burials indicate the presence of cemeteries outside the walls of the Roman town on most sides. In the post-Roman period settlement is indicated at Ancaster by the early Anglian cremation cemetery beside Ermine Street south of the Roman town. There is then a gap in our knowledge of some 500 years, but the earliest fabric in the parish church can be assigned to the eleventh century. Mention should also be made of the local quarries on the ridge south of Ancaster. Ancaster stone was well known in medieval times, and it is credibly supposed that the quarries were first opened by the Romans.

Discovery of the ancient west cemetery was the direct result of digging graves in its modern successor, which was opened about the beginning of this century. Two stone coffins were lifted and now stand at the ends of the cemetery path. They look Roman rather than medieval. They are roughly dressed but not finished, in the state in which coffins would leave the quarry, as 'blanks' or 'rough-outs' to be carved and enriched by the monumental mason. We may suppose that such 'rough-outs' were available locally at advantageous prices in view of the modest transport costs involved.

In recent years other burials have attracted attention because of special features. In 1961 was found an inscribed stone recording the dedication of an arch to the god Viridios,[1] and in 1963 part of a life-size draped statue of a deity, whom we might suppose to be the same god.[2] Both stones had been trimmed for secondary use as lids or cover-slabs for stone-lined graves; they are now in the museum at Lincoln. The 1963 burial contained a grave-group comprising a grey-ware cup with three external cordons, still rather in the Belgic tradition, a bronze brooch of the Knee Brooch series, a bronze stud, and a piece of leather. The evidence, so far as it goes, would suggest a second- to third-century date.

Systematic excavation of the cemetery began in 1964 at the invitation of the Ancaster Burial Board. In addition to the burials themselves a hearth and two fragments of wall were found in 1966, indicating pre-cemetery occupation up to the later third century. Comparable results were obtained in 1964 when one of the graves was found to be cut through the construction-pit of a disused well, which contained third- to fourth-century pottery. The evidence from this portion of the cemetery, near its western limit, is thus for a *terminus post quem* in the early fourth century.

Stratigraphic evidence for a *terminus ante quem* is unfortunately lacking. Although one hearth and an area of paving could be shown to be later than the burials, they were not associated with any datable material.

In 1964–6, 91 burials were examined. If the twelve infants are excluded, 94% of the remainder lay with their heads to the west. In the virtual absence of any grave goods, this orientation strongly suggests that this part of the cemetery served a community in which Christian burial rites predominated. The lay-out of the cemetery is fairly orderly, with a tendency to place the graves in rows, but with slight overlapping of some adjacent burials. Such order suggests a master plan for the graveyard, but no surface markers for the actual graves and grave-plots.

In general, the skeletons lie on their backs, more rarely on their sides, in extended position; the hands may be placed on the chest, in the lap, or at the sides of the body. Two burials were exceptional. One lay on its side, with head to south and legs flexed. The other lay prone, with arms outflung, and was accompanied by a small baby in a similar position. This burial shows a complete lack of ceremony; and neither can have been contained in any sort of coffin. Elsewhere there is some evidence for wooden coffins in the form of iron coffin-nails, but these often seem too few to be derived from a complete coffin. On the other hand, stones along the edge of a grave quite often have the air of wedging something in position, and it is possible that certain burials were lined with loose planks.[3] Such burials would be the equivalent in timber of the stone-lined graves, in which re-used slabs were arranged to make a cist.

The most expensive burials were placed in limestone coffins, and four have recently been lifted. The one now removed to the Nottingham University Museum is a reasonably unblemished piece, though one corner has been damaged. The same defect can be seen in the second of the group, where it is evident that the damage took place at the quarry, before the interior was hollowed out. The finished product is serviceable, but misshapen – a manufacturer's 'second,' such as might have been available at a reduced price to local purchasers. The third coffin raises a number of questions. The body itself could be seen to have slid within the coffin towards the foot. Since it is unlikely that it would have been left so, if visible, we may infer that the sarcophagus was manoeuvred into the grave with the corpse inside and the heavy lid in position. The lid is notably heavy and seems rather ill suited to its purpose. It looks like the 'blank' for a *stela* bearing sculpture in high relief, prepared for supply to the mason, but then adapted to a funerary use. The actual shape of the coffin is unexpected, not only tapering towards the foot, but also narrowing sharply at the head, in a manner that looks disconcertingly medieval. Here also the foot of the coffin has lost a corner, but we can hardly account for the overall shape in terms of accidental damage. A satisfactory parallel for such a coffin from a Roman context would be very welcome.

The only grave-goods to come from the excavations of 1964–6 were a group of six bronze bangles, of which the most distinctive, a torque-like bracelet three inches in diameter, was found beneath the skull. In the absence of any *terminus ante quem* the date of the cemetery rests partly upon these, together with the grave-group previously described, partly on the character of the coffins, and partly on general probabilities. The only plausible alternative to a late Roman date would have been late Saxon; but this is excluded by the Roman cup and brooch and by the torque-like bracelet.[4]

In this late-Roman context we may wonder at the motives for re-using debris from a pagan sanctuary as cover-slabs for burials. Is this the act of a Christian triumphantly despoiling the heathen? Or of a pagan desiring the protection of sacred relics? Or is it simply the indifference of the ignorant and illiterate?

Notes

1. *JRS* LII (1962), 192, no. 7, LV (1965), 228, item (*a*)
2. *LAASR & P* XI (1964), 62ff
3. Mr Norman Cook has, however, drawn the writer's attention to the use of wooden pegs in Roman coffins found in waterlogged deposits in London
4. This evidence has been strengthened by the subsequent discovery of a simple penannular brooch and a typical Roman nail-cleaner in graves excavated in 1967

Britonia

E. A. Thompson

The purpose of this communication is simply to draw the reader's attention to a book which is not, I think, required reading for students of Roman and sub-Roman Britain. The book is by Pierre David and is called *Etudes historiques sur la Galice et le Portugal.* It was published at Lisbon in 1947. Its interest from the point of view of early Christian Britain is that it includes a discussion of a sixth-century settlement of Britons on the north coast of Spain.

The reader may know that Galicia – Gallaecia to the Romans – was occupied for much of the fifth century and the whole of the sixth by a Germanic people called the Suevi. They differed from some of the other great Germanic peoples who entered the Roman Empire in that they were not settled on the land as Federates (*foederati*) by the Roman government. There is no evidence that the Suevi were ever Federates. They seized Galicia in spite of the Romans and established an independent kingdom there before the middle of the fifth century. But like the Federate peoples, they appear to have kept the Roman administrative machine in existence so as to administer Roman law to the Roman inhabitants of the area under their control and also so as to collect the Roman taxes. That would account for the fact that we hear of a Roman provincial governor (*rector=rector provinciae*) as late as 460, several decades after the Suevi had seized Galicia.[1]

We do not know when exactly they became Arian Christians: but the conversion certainly took place sometime after the middle of the fifth century. And it was not until another hundred years had passed that they were converted to Catholicism. The conversion to Catholicism was brought about in the 550s and was largely due to the work of St Martin of Braga. Now, the Arian kings had no doubt been as liberal and tolerant to their Catholic Roman subjects as all the other Arian barbarian kings had been (apart from the Vandal kings of Africa). But at some date they banned the holding of Catholic synods and Church Councils.[2] We hear of no Catholic synod in Galicia until after the conversion of the Suevi to Catholicism; and then two were held – one in 561 and the other in 572. They both met at the royal capital, Braga; and the minutes of both have survived. What is important for our purpose is that the names of the bishops who signed the *acta* of these Councils of Braga have also survived. And at the Second Council, though not at the First, each bishop added the name of his see after his signature. One of these sees is called the *Britonensis ecclesia.*[3]

Now, David in the book which I mentioned at the beginning studies a sixth-century *parochiale* which has survived from Galicia in more than one version. It begins with a short preface which is later than the rest of the document and is not above suspicion in some ways. It gives its date as 569 (which may or may not be correct), tells of the establishment of Lugo as something like a second metropolitan see of the kingdom, and mentions that the bishops at a Council created new bishoprics and distributed the parishes between them.[4] The list which follows this preface gives the names of the thirteen sees of the kingdom and adds after each of them the names of the parishes which it comprised. The authenticity of the document (apart from the preface) can scarcely be questioned; and Claude W. Barlow, the learned editor of the works of St Martin of Braga, agrees with David that this *parochiale* without any doubt is a genuine document of the decade 572–82.[5] It is hardly necessary to emphasize the value of the list of parishes to the geographer, the student of place-names, and others. But two entries have a somewhat wider interest. The famous see of Dumium had been founded by St Martin of Braga himself and was later occupied by St Fructuosus, the greatest monastic founder of seventh-century Spain. Now, Dumium was in fact a monastery; and Isidore of Seville describes Martin as *monasterii Dumiensis episcopus*.[6] In David's *parochiale* Dumium has no regular parishes at all. The name of Dumium is followed simply by the words *familia servorum*. Does this mean, as David understands it, that the abbot of Dumium had the status and title of a bishop and had jurisdiction not only over his monks but also over the slaves of the monastic domains? If we look at David's critical note, we find that some of his texts read, not *familia servorum*, but *familia regia*, the royal slaves, a reading which rests apparently on a later misunderstanding. The point is one which deserves further study.[7]

But what concerns us is the last of the thirteen sees, the *sedes Britonorum*, as the writer of the document calls it. We can hardly disagree with David's remark that the *parochiale* is an historical witness of the first order on the emigration of the Britons in the fifth or sixth century. It shows us that the emigration carried some Britons not to Armorica but further afield – to the western part of the north coast of Spain. I say 'the western part' because the diocese of Britonia was later replaced by that of Mondoñedo, some 70 kilometres north of Lugo, west of the River Eo. I do not remember (though my memory may be at fault here) that any recent English historian of post-Roman Britain has mentioned this flight of Britons to Spain.

What can we learn about this British settlement? The document under discussion mentions a certain Maximus in a context which we shall look at in a moment. And if we turn to the list of signatories of the minutes of the Second Council of Braga – that is, the Council of 572 where the signatories give us the names of their sees – we find that the bishop of the *Britonensis ecclesia* is called MAILOC.

According to Professor Kenneth Jackson[8] this is a good Celtic name, indeed a name which is perhaps the earliest example of a sound-change of some interest to philologists. Our British community, then, included men with Roman names, like Maximus, and at least one man with a British Celtic name. When we look at the representatives of the *Britonensis ecclesia* who attended the seventh-century Councils in Spain we find that one of them has the Roman name Metopius but that the others – Sonna, Macteric, Sosa, Bela – have names which deserve the attention of someone who knows more about philology than I do. If they are Germanic, their bearers were either Suevi or Visigoths.[9] However that may be, Mailoc is certainly Celtic, but it is noteworthy that there is no Celtic name among the signatories at the First Council of Braga, that of 561.

Not the least interesting point in the text of the *parochiale* is the description which it gives of the *sedes Britonorum.* Instead of a list of parish names, such as it gives for all the other sees except Dumium, the writer speaks of 'the churches which are among the Britons (*ecclesias que sunt intro Britones*) along with the monastery of Maximus (*una cum monasterio Maximi*) and those (sc. churches) which are among the Asturians (*et que in Asturiis sunt*).' David (58) assumes, perhaps a little rashly, that the religious groups which existed among the Britons had as their centre the monastery of Maximus; and he says that this is a precise description of the organization of Celtic Christianity such as we know it in these islands from the fifth century, an organization based on the monasteries, in which the abbot of the chief monastery, the *monasterium Maximi*, was probably the bishop of the *sedes Britonorum.*

I am not convinced that the text can carry the hypothesis which David has erected upon it. Even if Maximus' monastery was the centre of the see, it would not follow that this was a specifically Celtic feature, for we have already seen that the abbot of Dumium was also bishop of the see of Dumium, and even the most fervent Celt would hesitate to claim Dumium and its illustrious St Martin as Celtic. But even so, the total absence of parish names and (apart from the monastery of Maximus) the uncharacteristically vague phrases of the entry, are mysterious: they almost suggest that the writer did not know, and could not find out, the names of the parishes. And the reference to a monastery is quite without parallel in the rest of the document. David may have overstated his case, but perhaps it would be unwise to reject that case out of hand.

Again, before the 570s the Britons had occupied an extensive area of land stretching presumably from the neighbourhood of Mondoñedo northwards to the sea and also extending across the River Eo to Asturia, where they had at least a few churches. Now, this is a very extensive tract of land, and its size suggests that it was no mere handful of Britons who landed in Spain. They can, of course, have been nothing like as numerous as those who went to Brittany, but they were not negligible. And what is most remarkable is that we hear of no other inhabitants of this see. The churches are described as being *intro Britones.* What, then, of the parishes of the native Hispano-Roman inhabitants of the region? What has become of the Hispano-Roman occupants of the area? So far as these documents go, they have disappeared. Had they been forcibly expelled by the invading Britons? If not, can we suppose that they were still pagan to a man and so had no parochial organization? Hardly.

Further, these Britons must be regarded as Catholics. Their diocese is listed among the Catholic dioceses, and their bishops attended the Councils of the Church on a par with the Hispano-Roman bishops. In a word, they were not Pelagians. It would be of the utmost interest to know whether they were already Christian when they took flight from Britain, or whether they, or some of them, were only converted after they had reached Spain. In the latter case they would presumably have had the parochial organization which was normal in Spain outside Dumium; but since they were not normally organized, we may suppose that they were Catholics when still in Britain and that they brought their British form of organization with them. That Catholic Christians should have fled to an Arian kingdom is not at all surprising. I have already mentioned the tolerant policies of the Arian monarchs of Spain; and examples could easily be cited of Catholic clerics migrating to Arian Spain both from France and from Byzantine Africa. Unhappily, the question which we cannot even begin to answer is *when* they landed in Spain. It is notorious that the history of the Suevic kingdom for almost a century before 560 is completely unknown, so much so that even the names of the kings have been lost.

But the essential point is that this was a settlement of Britons. That is put beyond doubt by the name of the see – *sedes Britonorum* or *Britonensis ecclesia* or in the seventh century *Britaniensis ecclesia* – and by the name of its first known bishop, Mailoc.[10]

Notes

1. Hydatius, 199 (*Chronica Minora* ii, 31)
2. Barlow, C. W., *Martini Episcopi Bracarensis Opera Omnia* (Yale 1950), 80, 103
3. *Ibid.*, 123
4. David, 30f.
5. Barlow, *op. cit.*, 100, n. 9
6. Isidore of Seville, *Hist Goth* 90 (*Chronica Minora* ii, 302)
7. David, *op. cit.*, 46
8. *LHEB*, 464
9. At IV Toledo in 633 the representative was called Metopius; at VII Toledo in 646 the representative was Sonna; at VIII Toledo in 655 the priest Mactericus represented the bishop Sosa; and at the Third Council of Braga in 675 the bishop Bela attended. Thereafter the see is not heard of in Visigothic times
10. See the signatures in Barlow, *op. cit.*, 115. There seems to be no good reason for identifying Mailoc with the Maliosus who appears there. I note that Jackson, *loc. cit.*, and Wallace-Hadrill, J. M., *The Barbarian West* (London, 1967), 118, refer to the settlers in Britonia as 'Bretons'. This may be; but to suppose that the fugitives from Britain had landed in Armorica before going on to Spain is perhaps to multiply

Notes

hypotheses, and in any case hardly alters the views put forward above. On the British Church in Galicia see now Mrs Nora K. Chadwick, 'The Colonization of Brittany from Celtic Britain', *Proceedings of the British Academy*, li (1965), 235–299, at 284, which appeared after the above Communication was written

Summary and Prospect

R. P. C. Hanson

I

Christianity in Roman and sub-Roman Britain is a subject with peculiar attraction for the scholar, for it contains quite enough darkness for him to imagine that there is much for him to discover, but enough evidence for him to decide that the task of discovery is not a hopeless one. Yet this subject is one which has been given surprisingly little attention by British scholars. The last full-scale, serious treatment of the subject by a single author was that of Hugh Williams, published as long ago as 1912. Since then there has been the composite volume edited by Mrs N. K. Chadwick, *Studies in the Early British Church*, and since that time quite a large spate of articles and minor or peripheral studies. It is however still a subject which receives little attention from people doing research in British Universities, partly because of the strange disinclination of British students, outside Scotland, Ireland and Wales, to take Celtic studies seriously. From the point of view of theological study, it has also been starved. There are two unmistakably British contributions to patristic literature, the works of Patrick and the works of Gildas. Neither appears in any recent series of Patristic texts such as *Sources Chrétiennes*, *Corpus Christianorum*, *CSEL* or Loeb. The best edition of Gildas is still that of Mommsen; the only recent edition of Patrick's text, and the only one based on a full survey of the available manuscripts, is that by Professor L. Bieler, a citizen of the Irish Republic; and the text with *apparatus criticus* of this edition is now almost unobtainable.

And yet this is a subject which unites the concerns of the students of a number of different disciplines to an unusual extent. The classical scholar who is interested in the late Roman Empire, the mediaeval historian whose particular expertise lies in the early part of this period, the student of patristic literature, the ecclesiastical historian, the expert in languages (Old Irish, British, Old Welsh, Breton, or Vulgar Latin), and, above all, the archaeologist can meet here. In fact students of all these disciplines did meet at the conference on this subject which was held in the University of Nottingham in April 1967. The interest aroused by this conference and the approval which it evoked from the large number of people who attended it were among the main inducements which moved the editors of this volume, representing by and large the proceedings of that conference, to take up their task.

The reader will quickly perceive that this book represents a cross-section of work in progress rather than a complete survey. It is intended to give readers, whether they are experts in the subject or not, a picture of what work is being done and can be done in studying Christianity in Roman and sub-Roman Britain, rather than a connected history or an exhaustive survey of the subject. That is why the industrious reader will find a number of conflicting opinions in the book. There are plenty of points within this subject which are still the centre of lively debate. One may instance the exact scope of St Ninian's work;[1] the connection of St Patrick with Britain;[2] the question of whether part of the not inconsiderable mass of fifth-century Pelagian literature which is in our hands is really British.[3] This is the reason also why smaller studies of much more limited scope appear in this book beside the longer essays which attempt a wide survey. It should be obvious that papers of this less ambitious kind can play an important part in suggesting new ideas and lines of research as well as in correcting old misapprehensions.

II

The picture of the early British church which emerges from this volume is certainly neither clear in its outlines nor rich in detail. But it can be said that a picture of that Church does emerge. The British church was evidently neither affluent nor a nursery of eminent writers nor ornamented with splendid and extensive buildings. Perhaps it is because we unconsciously expect the British church to display the outburst of ecclesiastical building that is visible in the church of the Mediterranean lands in the fifth century and to a lesser extent in the fourth that we experience a sense of disappointment at the meagre remains of the church buildings of the fourth and fifth centuries in Britain. But, as Dr Ralegh Radford reminds us,[4] the earliest Christian buildings were not usually luxurious, extensive or impressive structures. Roman Britain had a comparatively small population, few large towns, and not many members of the senatorial class. Perhaps it is significant that Britain produced two usurping emperors who were from the middle or lower ranks of society, Gratian II (who was a *municeps*)[5] and Constantine III (whom Orosius describes as coming *ex infima militia*).[6] There were few or none among British Christians who were the sort who could build large churches. It is unlikely that Christianity reached Britain through the upper classes of the society of the late Roman Empire. It almost certainly did not reach Britain through the Roman army. Mr Watson's paper should effectively exclude this possibility.[7] In fact the Roman Army, though it did have its proportion of Christians as time went on, must have offered during the first few centuries of Christianity stony ground for the seed of the Gospel. It seems very likely that the real motive-power behind Diocletian's persecution, as late as the beginning of the fourth century, was the Roman army. Even though St Alban was a Roman soldier, he did not, if there is any truth in the legend, pick up Christianity in the barrack-room. Traders, artisans and camp-followers are more likely to have been the people through whom Christianity reached this island. It is not insignificant that all the British bishops whose sees we know at the beginning of the fourth century are bishops of Roman towns.[8]

But clearly some of the native British upper classes had turned to the new religion well before the abandonment of Britain by the Roman government. The evidence of Christianity from the villas, such as Frampton, Hinton St Mary and Lullingstone, assures us of that. And if we accept the persuasive arguments of Professor Jocelyn Toynbee we will detect considerable depth and culture in these upper-class British Christians' choice of iconography.[9] By the end of the fourth and beginning of the fifth century the British church was producing very well educated men capable of making their mark in the wider world of the Western Church, such as Pelagius and Faustus of Riez. The learned clergy, experts not only in Scripture but also in law, who could discourse in an educated and elegant way, with whom Patrick contrasts himself, and who appear to have entertained considerable scorn for him, were almost certainly British. Towards the end of the fourth century the temporarily successful usurping Emperor Magnus Maximus, beginning his perilous imperial career in Britain, thought it profitable to declare himself, rather noisily, a Christian. Gildas, as M. Kerlouégan shows, has behind him a long tradition of intensive higher education in Latin literature and language, even though with him the tradition is beginning to enter the ivory tower.[10]

All the evidence shows that the first half of the fifth century was a period of rapid growth and steady prosperity for the British church. This period sees the missions of Ninian and of Patrick, in each case no doubt to places where a considerable Christian population already existed. Professor Thomas has argued persuasively that the kingdom of Rheged, lying probably along both the shores of the Solway, was largely Christianized during this period.[11] It seems most reasonable to assume that the soldiers of Coroticus, to whom Patrick writes his threatening letter about the middle of the century, are, with their commander, nominal Christians, and that this Coroticus had his headquarters at Dumbarton in the Firth of Clyde.[12] The Christian Gospel had spread very swiftly in this direction, even though it had to exist among bloodthirsty *tyranni*. But even bloodthirsty *tyranni* may be moderated by it. Patrick excommunicates unhesitatingly in circumstances in which Gildas, later, can only revile. During this period too the British church can afford the luxury of a heresy, Pelagianism, supported, as has been pointed out, by rich men.[13] It can encourage pilgrimages to the shrine of St Alban, such as Germanus of Auxerre and his companions made in 429, and it is deemed worthy of papal action in this very visit of Germanus.

When not long after the middle of the fifth century a large number of British families, under some sort of pressure (probably Saxon) emigrate to Armorica (later Brittany) they bring their bishops (and presumably also inferior clergy) with them. We know the names of two of them, Mansuetus, who attended a small council at Tours in 461, and Riocatus, who passes fleetingly through the correspondence of Sidonius Apollinaris about the year 476. The latter is a monk as well as a bishop. Even if we set aside the earlier evidence of monasticism in Britain, and ignore Constans and Patrick and Ninian (and I agree with Dr Frend that they should not be ignored)[14] here is incontrovertible evidence that there were monks in Britain by about 450. Finally there is the fascinating sketch at the end of Professor Thomas' essay of what could have been the distribution of the territory of North Britain into tribal dioceses.[15] We may safely assume that the same hypothetical diocesan divisions could be made for the rest of Britain not in possession of the Saxons at about the year 500. Here, as Dr Morris reminds us, was a Romanized country after the collapse of the Roman Empire which had managed to halt the barbarian invaders for some considerable time.[16] And in this country we can discern the lineaments of a Christian church, adapting itself, of course, to the altered conditions, but still not completely isolated and not violently unconventional.

The rest of the story is, of course, largely darkness. We are afforded short glimpses of what is happening, such as that given us by Professor Thompson.[17] We have the witness of Gildas to give us some light. But for the most part we are thrown back on archaeology on the one hand and such literature on the other as the saints' lives which have been evaluated for us in Dr Morris' essay. The two sources can hardly yet be said to have been successfully integrated. The British church which Augustine of Canterbury meets when he surveys it coldly and uncomprehendingly at the turn of the sixth and seventh centuries is a different church from that which we can see making a brave show in the middle of the fifth. It has probably undergone a monastic revolution. It has been profoundly influenced by Irish Christianity, after itself, as Professor Greene's essay suggests,[18] first influencing the church of that country. It has suffered from isolation from the continent, considerable, but not complete. It has been compelled to yield a very great deal more territory to the heathen Saxons. But even here we can perceive that it has not ceased to deserve the name of a Christian church. The monastic movement associated with such names as St David and St Illtud was, as Dr Morris reminds us, a reassertion by the Church of its influence upon a society which badly needed such an influence.[19] The mission of St Kentigern, surrounded though it is with mists of legend, was a genuine achievement of the British Church in the sixth century. And British Christians played their part too in the extraordinary outburst of missionary expansion which broke out from Ireland between about 550 and about 650. In short, the early British church is a subject that in every sense deserves study by British scholars. It was not a wraith or a mere skeleton. It had its own life, its own achievements, its own personality.

III

When we turn briefly to the prospects for the study of Christianity in Roman Britain we are met by one solid fact. The future lies with archaeology. This is a comparatively recent discipline and it is only comparatively recently that archaeology has been applied in a systematic way to our subject. But clearly, any remarkable developments or extraordinary discoveries in this field are likely in the future to come from archaeology. The discovery of the Lullingstone wall-paintings is a very recent example of such a discovery. It is possible (but not yet by any means certain) that a British Christian church has been discovered at York. Whithorn has been excavated, but there are plenty of other places like Whithorn which have yet to be scientifically explored. Cemeteries in other places besides Ancaster[20] and Somerset[21] may be investigated. Presumably a bulldozer may some day turn up another villa like Hinton St Mary. St Alban's may yield some significant finds. The possibilities of archaeology for producing facts to illuminate (or confound) the labours of historians are well enough illustrated in this book, in the essays of the majority of the contributors. Archaeology is the growing-point in the study of the early British Church.

But it would be wrong to assume that archaeology will in future take over from the study of historical documents which is now played out; the essays in this book demonstrate this as well as anything else. What is needed to advance the study of this subject is a co-ordination of several disciplines, archaeology, the study of literature, and the study of language. It was to further this co-ordination that the original Conference was held in April 1967, and it was to illustrate the possibilities of this co-ordination that this volume has been produced. The study of the relevant ancient literature, scanty though it is, has by no means exhausted all its possibilities. M. Kerlouégan and Professor Davies have demonstrated what can be done by a rigorously minute investigation of Gildas. It can hardly be claimed that all that can be learnt of Gildas has already been learnt. A new edition of Gildas' text with a new English translation is much to be desired. A thorough and methodical examination of Gildas' biblical quotations and a comparison of these with the biblical quotations of Patrick should yield important information, especially now that Professor Bieler has given us a scientific account of Patrick's quotations.[22] Generally, we need to encourage far more research students to turn their attention to Gildas. Several dozen could well (dare I say it?) be profitably drafted from pursuing fairly useless researches on the New Testament. I am not convinced that Patrick's slender but significant output of literature has yielded all its information yet. I differ, with great respect, from Professor Bieler, in finding it impossible to believe that Patrick's relations with the British Church were mainly hostile, and that little therefore can be learnt about it from his writings.[23] I believe that there is more to discover from Patrick's very curious and unusual Latin, more even than the labours of Professor Jackson, Professor Christine Mohrmann and Professor Bieler himself have uncovered, valuable though they are.[24] Intensively though Bede has been studied, in comparison with the attention paid to Patrick and Gildas, we need not assume that he yet represents a worked-out source; indeed the use made of him by Professor Thomas in his essay suggests that there is more light still to be found in his pages.[25]

Again, the experts in ancient Celtic languages have not exhausted their contribution to this subject. Professor Greene's essay whets the reader's appetite for more. Professor Cameron's short paper opens all sorts of interesting possibilities.[26] One could institute a comparison of the places with *Eccles*-names, where we can be fairly sure that there existed a church in Roman or Sub-Roman times (including perhaps Paisley, if this word can really be derived from *Basilica*), with the list of cantonal capitals in Britain. Or it might be worth while simply to mark all these places on the map of Roman Britain and ask why should they have been placed where they were and why the fact that there was a church there should have been preserved in the place-name, while the record of the existence of other churches was presumably lost. Finally, Dr Morris' essay sketches the subject of almost a lifetime's activity in determining the bearing which the hagiography of the dark centuries has upon the history of the period, and also offers a number of immediate practical lexicographical and philological tasks which await the research student.[27]

What is needed above all is a type of scholarship which shall co-ordinate and keep in view all these disciplines simultaneously. For too long study of Early British Christianity has been departmentalized, the marginal concern of a number of people working in isolation from each other. The subject is admittedly full of darkness and difficulty. But it has many possibilities of development. It would be a dismal thing if British scholars failed to take advantage of these possibilities, leaving them (as they perhaps have tended to do in the past) to exploration mainly by scholars from the continent. The subject deserves treatment as a study on its own, and properly co-ordinated and integrated treatment. It is the hope of its editors that this volume will help towards this end.

Notes

1. See above, pp. 43–44, 94–105, 110–11
2. See above, pp. 77–78, 125–8
3. See above, pp. 59, 61, 62. I may say that, in spite of the above arguments of Dr J. Morris on this subject, I have the gravest doubts whether any of it can be assigned to British authors. See the reasons given in the second chapter of my *St Patrick : his Origins and Career* (Oxford, 1968), and also Liebeschuetz, W., 'Pelagian Evidence on the Last Period of Roman History', *Latomus* xxvi (April – June 1967), 436–47
4. See above, pp. 20–24
5. See above, p. 45
6. *Hist. adv. Paganos*, vii. 40
7. See above, pp. 51–54
8. See above, pp. 40–42
9. See above, pp. 180–91
10. See above, pp. 150–73
11. See above, pp. 100ff.
12. See above, pp. 108–9
13. See above, pp. 7, 45

Notes

14. See above, pp. 43–4
15. See above, pp. 111–6
16. See above, pp. 72–3
17. See above, pp. 201–4
18. See above, pp. 74–85
19. See above, pp. 69–70
20. See above, pp. 197–9
21. See above, pp. 193–5
22. See Bieler, L., 'Der Bibeltext des heiligen Patrick' (*Biblica* xxviii (1947) 1, 31–58, 239–63)
23. See above, pp. 125–8
24. See the discussion of this question in the fifth chapter of my *St Patrick : his Origins and Career*
25. See above, pp. 99, 100, 105–6, 110
26. See above, pp. 89–91
27. See above, pp. 68, 71–2

Index